ASPECTS OF ANCIENT INDIAN POLITY

ASPECTS OF ANCIENT INDIAN POLITY

BY
NARENDRA NATH LAW

WITH A FOREWORD BY
ARTHUR BERRIEDALE KEITH

GYAN
GYAN PUBLISHING HOUSE
NEW DELHI-110002

ASPECTS OF
ANCIENT INDIAN POLITY

ISBN : 9788121200264

BY

NARENDRA NATH LAW

Reprint in 2016 in India by
Gyan Publishing House
5 , Main Ansari Road, Daryaganj,
New Delhi - 110002
Phone : 9811692060

E-mail : books@gyanbooks.com
gyanbook@vsnl.com
Website: gyanbooks.com

FOREWORD

AMONG the gratifying consequences of the awakening of political aspirations in India must be reckoned the development of a keen interest in the history of Indian theories of polity. The discovery a few years ago of the *Arthaśāstra*, a manual of statecraft, attributed, though without adequate ground, to the wise councillor who aided Candragupta to free India from the menace of Greek domination, afforded rich material for investigation and poured a flood of light upon the obscurities of the more recent texts. To the researches which have already been conducted on this theme Mr. Narendra Nath Law has added in this work much that is novel and of importance, and has enabled us to see more clearly than before the fundamental character of Indian political thought and practice.

The subtle and profound spirit of India, which finds its fullest expression in the absolute idealism of the Vedānta of Śaṅkara and the sceptical nihilism of Nāgārjuna, is alien to the conception of man as a political organism, whose true end can be found only in and through membership of a social community. Hence India offers nothing that can be regarded as a serious theory of politics in the wider sense of that term. But there was intensive study of the practical aspect of government and of relations between states, and these topics were subjected to a minute analysis by writers on politics, who carried out their work with that love of subdivision and numerical detail which induces the authors of treatises on poetics to vie with one another in multiplying the types of hero or heroine or of figures of speech. Pedantic as is much of this work, it would be an error to ignore the acuteness of observation which it involves, or the practical, if narrow, prudence of many of the maxims laid down for the guidance of rulers. The topic has also the interest that it presents India to us from a point of view less completely Brahmanical than is usual in the literature of India.

The difficulties and perplexities of the subject are innumerable, and it will be long before certainty is obtainable on many of its aspects. Mr. Narendra Nath Law's conclusions may not always meet with our acceptance, but the clearness with which he has set out his views, the care with which he has collected the relevant evidence, and the moderation of his criticism render his work a contribution of substantial importance and lasting value.

A. BERRIEDALE KEITH.

UNIVERSITY OF EDINBURGH,
April 5, 1921.

PREFACE

THE antiquity of *Daṇḍanīti* (science of polity) among the Hindus can be traced back to the epic period like its sister subject of study, *Vārttā* (ancient Hindu economics).[1] Both the *Rāmāyaṇa* and the *Mahābhārata* mention its existence as a branch of learning, and contain political maxims and technical expressions which show a long prior study of the subject. We also find the analysis of the body politic into its component parts, the requisites of their efficiency, their inter-relation, and the lines on which they can be worked harmoniously, as well as suggestions for dealing with various political problems that at times demand solution at the hands of politicians. This may be clearly seen by a glance at II, 100 of the *Rāmāyaṇa*, and II, 5 of the *Mahābhārata*, in which is embodied, in brief, all the evidence indicated above of the long process of evolution of political ideas and institutions, and of their analysis. Expressions like 'eighteen *tīrthas*', 'six courses of action (*ṣāḍguṇyam*)', 'elements of sovereignty (*prakṛtayaḥ*)', 'statal circle (*maṇḍala*)', 'six evils (*ṣaḍ anarthāḥ*)', 'seven policies (*sapta upāyāḥ*)', and 'fourteen elements of the military strength', along with a string of technical terms such as '*daśa-pañca-catur-vargān sapta-vargaṃ ca . . . aṣṭavargaṃ trivargaṃ ca . . .*', &c., not only indicate the long period required for the said analysis and evolution, but also their use as matters of common knowledge. It is apparent from these chapters that attempts had long been made to tabulate the various requisites for an efficient conduct of the administration, in order that the sovereigns and the politicians might have them ready at hand for use. The various directions in which the mind of the Hindus operated to study the problems connected with the state can be realized by a perusal of the

[1] See my article in the *Indian Antiquary*, 1918, pp. 233 ff.

long table of contents of a treatise on polity attributed by the *Mahābhārata* (XII, 59) to Brahmā, who completed it in a hundred thousand chapters. The same epic ascribes its later abridgements into 10,000, 5,000, 3,000, and 1,000 chapters, to Śiva, Indra, Bṛhaspati, and Uśanas (or Kavi) respectively; the first two abridged versions were styled Vaiśālākṣa and Bāhudantaka, and the other two Bārhaspatya and Auśanasa (or Kāvya) after the abridgers' names. Several other names are also associated in the *Mahābhārata* (XII, 58) with the ancient treatment of polity, such as Manu, the son of Pracetas, Bharadvāja, and the sage Gauraśiras, while in the *Kauṭilīya* eighteen such names can be distinguished as those of individual authors, or of schools of political thinkers and writers (see p. 2 of this volume). This account of the existence of ancient writers on polity gains in reality by (I) the actual quotations made by the *Mahābhārata* from those sources; (II) the *Kauṭilīya* mentioning and quoting from some of the authors mentioned in the epic; (III) the *Mahābhārata* furnishing contents of a treatise on polity, and other parts of the *Mahābhārata*, as well as the *Rāmāyaṇa*, mentioning political terms and topics which tally with those contents in a sufficient measure; (IV) the terms and topics, as well as the contents, being sufficiently similar to those of the *Kauṭilīya* and extant works on polity generally as to warrant an extension of historicity to the earlier group; (V) the existence in many cases of a thread of connexion through the various changes that took place in the political ideas and institutions from the Vedic period to the post-epic as traceable with the help of the literatures of the periods, and as shown in various parts of the present volume; this serves to carry conviction that a similar connexion exists between the extant works on polity and the earlier works embodying the political thoughts and experience of earlier times, which can thus claim not to be rejected as legendary; and (VI) by the existence of the forms in which the ancient works on polity appeared to have existed, viz. verse, aphorisms, or either of these two or both mixed with prose, and which took time to come into being in chronological sequence, though, when all of them had developed, they might have existed concurrently. This process of development of the literature on polity is inferable from the data furnished by the *Mahābhārata* and the *Kauṭilīya*, which bears an analogy to the forms developed by other classes of ancient Sanskrit literature.[1]

One may be led to infer antiquity from the acquisition of a sacred character by this branch of learning (*Daṇḍanīti*) as a part of the *Itihāsa-Veda*; but in view of the tendency of the Hindu mind from ancient times to bring a branch of literature, which would otherwise be secular, into relation with the religious literature by making it an offshoot of its trunk, the *Vedas*, it would not perhaps be reasonable to allow any great length of time for its acquisition of sacredness.

It results from the above evidence that the literature on *Daṇḍanīti* had a long career before the stage at which appears the *Kauṭilīya*. It is not possible to compute the time involved in its growth, though it is certain that a few centuries must have elapsed before it could reach its high stage of development about the time of the composition of the *Kauṭilīya*. Nor would it be safe to calculate this period on the analogy of the development of the contemporary literature, if available, of the Greeks, as is sometimes done, and allot particular intervals to particular stages of evolution of the literature; for the Greek mind, and the surroundings in which it worked, could not be the same as the Hindu mind and its environment, and the amount of progress that the Greeks might have made within a definite period in a certain field of literary activities might have occupied the Hindus a considerably longer period, and vice versa. It is very probable that the attainment of a literary status by *Daṇḍanīti* must have been posterior to the allotment of the conduct of administration including the military profession to the second caste, the *Kṣatriyas*, and that it was subsequent to its conversion into a type of learning that the polity of the Hindus received a careful attention and perhaps a conscious direction.

The application of the principles of *Daṇḍanīti* within the

[1] Prof. D. R. Bhandarkar's *Carmichael Lectures* (1918), Lecture III, furnishes data upon which I have drawn for some of my arguments.

state by competent men was the obligation of the sovereign. The sovereign had, therefore, to learn it with special attention from specialists in that field. Kauṭilya includes *Daṇḍanīti* in the course of study prescribed for the prince, the subject being taught by tutors possessing knowledge of their subject in its theoretical and practical sides (*vaktṛ-prayoktṛbhyaḥ*).[1] It seems that the other two higher castes, eligible as they were for the study of all the branches of learning, studied *Daṇḍanīti* in order to have a merely general knowledge of the subject, or, according to particular needs, to have a special knowledge of some or all its aspects. The *Brāhmaṇas* learned the subject, sometimes perhaps for the sake of making their education all-inclusive, and sometimes for the purpose of teaching it to their pupils, for they were teachers not merely of theology and philosophy but also of polity, including the art of warfare and use of weapons, and of economics, as well as of the practical or fine arts and accomplishments. Only a few instances will suffice. Rāma and his cousin were taught the use of certain weapons by Viśvāmitra, the Pāṇḍavas the military art along with the use of weapons by Droṇācārya, Kṛṣṇa the various branches of learning, together with the sixty-four *kalās*, by his preceptor Sāṃdīpani. Thus the members of the first caste were often masters and teachers of the practical arts, though, of course, it must be borne in mind that the knowledge and practice of *Daṇḍanīti* were the special obligation of the *Kṣatriyas*, just as the knowledge and practice of *Vārttā* (economics) the special charge of the *Vaiśyas*.

Epigraphic confirmation of the existence of *Daṇḍanīti* as a branch of learning by professors in a college comes from a South Indian inscription[2] which records that in the Sthānagundūru *Agrahāra* 'were professors skilled in medicine, in sorcery (or magic), in logic, in the art of distorting people by incantation, in poetry, *in the use of weapons*, in sacrificing . . . and in the art of cookery to prepare the meals. While

[1] *Kauṭilīya*, i. 9.

[2] Śilā-śāsana at Taldagundy, No. 103 (L. Rice's *Mysore Inscriptions*, p. 197).

its groves put to shame the groves of Nandana, such was the glory of that great *Agrahāra* that all the surrounding country prayed to be taught in the four *Vedas*, their six *Vedāṅgas*, the three rival divisions of *Mīmāṃsā*, the *Tarka* and other connected sciences, the eighteen great *Purāṇas*, the making of numerous verses of praise, the art of architecture, the arts of music and dancing, and in the knowledge of *all the four divisions of learning* which were possessed by the *Brāhmaṇas* of the Sthānagundūru *Agrahāra*'. The four divisions of learning mentioned in the passage imply *Daṇḍanīti* as one of them, while the use of weapons has been separately mentioned as being taught in the *Agrahāra*. The inscription belongs probably to the 12th century A.D. and testifies to the fact that, up to that time at least, *Daṇḍanīti* as a branch of learning had not yet become in India unfamiliar or obsolete.

The scope of the ancient Hindu works on polity was very wide if we have to judge of it from the *Kauṭilīya* and the table of contents as furnished by the *Mahābhārata*, and it ranged from instructions on the simplest items of duty of the sovereign to those on the maintenance of desirable inter-state relations involving many knotty problems.[1]

A list of extant manuscripts on polity or its sub-topics preserved in the various libraries of the world has always been felt as a desideratum by scholars engaged in researches in this field. I have prepared and published [2] such a list, which may be consulted for the purpose. In the preparation of the list, some of the important catalogues of manuscripts have been consulted at first hand instead of through Aufrecht's *Catalogus Catalogorum*, in view of the definitive and descriptive details that such consultation can furnish. I have been guided chiefly by the express mention of the subject of each manuscript in the catalogues, as well as by the list of contents given therein. But sometimes neither the subject nor the contents are found, specially in the cases in which the *Catalogus Catalogorum* is silent in those respects, leaving the reader to

[1] See my *Inter-State Relations in Ancient India*, pt. i (Calcutta Oriental Series).

[2] See the *Modern Review*, Oct. 1917 to Jan. 1918; also March and June 1918.

infer the subject of the manuscript either from the name, which sometimes furnishes the clue, or from a first-hand consultation of those catalogues to which it refers. The latter alternative for obvious reasons is not always possible. The space devoted to polity or its sub-topics varies a good deal in the manuscripts. Some of them treat the subject from the astrological point of view. As the religious aspects of ancient Hindu polity have formed the subject-matter of a chapter in the present work, the inclusion in the list of such manuscripts as well as of a few dealing with some of the politico-religious ceremonies may be of interest to readers of the present work. It is not possible to discuss the dates of the various works, for, apart from the difficulty of the task itself, a good many of the manuscripts are out of reach and not available for copying or consultation. It cannot be denied that some of the works are recent compositions, but even these may be the lineal descendants of older ones, in which the treatment of their respective subjects was exhibited in greater freedom from influences which, multiplying by lapse of time, led to deviations from the ancient orthodox line.

In the first chapter of the present work, the list of paramount sovereigns should not be taken to imply that the sovereigns named in it were all historical personages. The list is intended only to trace back the conception of the paramountcy of sovereigns as early as the evidences permit. I have remarked at pages 12 and 13 that there was in the Vedic period hierarchies of rulers which justified the assumption by them of titles like *mahārāja*, *rājādhirāja*, &c., which should be taken to have contemplated not so much the extent of their territories as their political superiority to the subordinate states; because the area on which the Aryans spread themselves in those times was not even the whole of Northern India, and necessarily we cannot expect to find an emperor with a dominion extending from sea to sea. That a Vedic overlord had a number of rulers under his suzerainty results from the fact that in the performance of the *Aśvamedha* for the assertion of his suzerainty, he had to utilize the services of a hundred royal princes ('*rāja-putrāḥ*' which is explained as '*abhiṣikta-putrāḥ*' in the commentary), clad in armour, whose duty it was to follow the sacrificial horse, when let loose to roam through the territories of the rulers over whom his political superiority was intended to be asserted. The assent of these hundred royal princes to aid the celebrant of the horse-sacrifice implied the acceptance of his suzerainty by them and the states whence they came, if not by any others; and this alone is a reasonable ground for believing that the performer had under him rulers over whom he was the overlord. It may be objected that the services of the royal princes imply but an alliance on equal terms between the states represented by them and the sovereign performing the sacrifice; but such an objection cannot hold good in view of the fact that the suzerainty that was meant to be asserted by the sacrifice would not be suzerainty at all, if those states are purposely left out. These states could not be all equal in power and opulence, and therefore gradations among them follow as a corollary.

My treatment of the democracies in ancient India could have been expanded by the inclusion of epigraphic evidence, or materials from other sources, bearing principally on their internal organization; but, as I do not wish to deviate from the line on which the work has grown on my hands from 1914, fragments being published in a periodical, and as the object of the first chapter in which they are treated is substantially served without the additions, I have left them out for the present.

I have had occasion to express views in opposition to those of several scholars both Eastern and Western, many of whom are masters in their special field of research; but I have always given full grounds in support of my views and passed my criticisms in a manner befitting respectful differences of opinion on the points under discussion.

I am indebted to Professors A. A. Macdonell and A. Berriedale Keith for the great help derived by me from their *Vedic Index of Subjects and Names*, which has lightened the difficulty of scholars generally in getting at information on points concerning the Vedic period. Professor Berriedale Keith has laid me under a further obligation by his valuable suggestions on the whole work and by contributing to it a Foreword. I also owe it to Professor E. W. Hopkins to mention that his dissertation on the Sanskrit epic in the *J. A. O. S.*, xiii, has in many respects rendered my task easier than it would otherwise have been.

Nor must I forget the active interest taken by Dr. Radhakamal Mukherjee, M.A., Ph.D., and Mr. Nalin Chandra Paul, B.L., in this work, and by a friend of mine who refuses to accept my acknowledgement of his labours.

NARENDRA NATH LAW.

96 AMHERST STREET, CALCUTTA,
March 1921.

CONTENTS

PAGE

CHAPTER I

FORMS AND TYPES OF STATES

How far the ancient Hindus were a political people.

THE question as to how far the ancient Hindus were a political people and evolved political constitutions of their own presents an interesting line of investigation. The subject is indeed one of the many dark spaces in our early history requiring to be illuminated, one of the many forgotten chapters awaiting restoration at the hands of painstaking and sympathetic research.

Evidence on the subject: (a) administrative experience; (b) literature on politics directly or indirectly treating of same.

The fact cannot be gainsaid that the ancient Hindus knew of both small and large states, kingdoms, and empires, and acquired the necessary political experience in the administration thereof. There is besides a large literature extant treating of political topics, which has been handed down from generation to generation.[1] These professedly political works are as a rule compilations from other works, and thus serve to preserve the political experience and knowledge of the race. The *Arthaśāstra* of Kauṭilya is a moumental work of this kind which refers to previous discussions and in some points attempts a comparative study of the subject.[2] There are other works

[1] Besides the printed works on polity, such as the *Kauṭilīya-Arthaśāstra*, *Cāṇakya-sūtrāṇi*, *Śukranīti*, *Kāmandakīya-Nītisāra*, *Nītiprakāśikā* attributed to Vaiśampāyana, *Nītivākyāmṛta* of Somadeva, *Bṛhaspati-Sūtra* edited by Dr. F. W. Thomas, *Yuktikalpataru* edited by Paṇḍit Īśvara Candra Śāstrī (with their commentaries, if any, in print or manuscript), several Saṃhitās (with their commentaries, if any) treat of the subject, e.g. *Manu*, *Yājñavalkya*, &c. Over and above these, there are treatises in manuscript in several libraries in India as well as Europe dealing with the subject or its sub-topics.

The *Hindu-Rājanīti* (in Bengali) by Mr. Madhusudan Bhaṭṭācārya is a compilation of parallel passages on a number of topics of polity.

[2] The *Arthaśāstra* quotes the following individuals or schools of opinion,

which are more or less representative of their times and throw much light on the subject by their mass of information. But we should draw not merely upon these treatises, or those portions of them that deal specifically with polity, but also upon others which, though not directly treating it, throw many hints and sidelights, the combined effect of which may clear up many an obscure corner of the subject of our inquiry.

Forms of government known in ancient India. Monarchy the prevailing but not the only form. Evidence of the *Kautilīya*. Names of principal self-governing clans in ancient India.

India has seen a multitude of forms of government, and her political experience has not been derived from one form alone Monarchy was the prevailing form of government, but it was not the only form. The *Arthaśāstra* knows of a constitution in which the sovereign power is wielded by a family or clan (kula), and states, in connexion with the succession to a vacant throne, that a pure monarchy may pass into a constitution of the aforesaid kind by a combination of circumstances.[1] Kauṭilya extols this constitution for its safety and efficiency. He also mentions many self-governing clans, viz. Licchivika, Vṛjjika, Mallaka, Madraka, Kukura, Kuru, and Pancāla, as well as those of Kāmboja and Surāṣṭra.[2] Some of these clans appear in the list of the sixteen independent peoples existing at or shortly before the time when Buddhism arose, viz. Aṅgā, Magadhā Kāsī, Kosalā, VAJJĪ, MALLĀ, Cetī, Vaṃsā, KURŪ, Pañcālā

viz. Manu, Uśanas, Bṛhaspati, Bhāradvāja, Viśālākṣa, Piśuna, Kauṇapadanta, Vātavyādhi, Parāśara, Bāhudantīputra, Āmbhīyas, (see pp. 6, 13, 14, 33), Kātyāyana, Kaṇiṅka, Bhāradvāja, Dīrghacārāyaṇa, Ghoṭamukha, Kiñjalka, Piśunaputra (p. 251).

The last passage of the *Arthaśāstra* (p. 429) speaks of Kauṭilya having used many noteworthy works on polity with their commentaries :—

Dṛṣṭvā vipratipattiṃ bahudhā śāstreṣu bhāṣya-kārāṇāṃ,
Svayam eva Viṣṇu-guptaś cakāra sūtraṃ ca bhāṣyaṃ ca.

Brahmā, the originator of the science of polity, communicated his knowledge to Śiva, whose work on the subject contained 10,000 chapters and was entitled *Vaiśālākṣa*. Indra abridged it into 5,000 chapters, naming it *Bāhudantaka*. It was further compressed into 3,000 chapters by Bṛhaspati, and still further by Śukra into 1,000 chapters, their works being named *Bārhaspatya* and *Auśanasa* respectively. *MBh.*, xii. 59. 80–5.

[1] Kulasya vā bhaved rājyaṃ kulasaṅgho hi durjayaḥ,
Arājavyasanābādhaḥ śaśvad āvasati kṣitiṃ.
Arthaśāstra, I. xvii, p. 35.

[2] *Ibid.*, XI. i, p. 376. The ed. reads Vṛjika and Kāmbhoja.

Macchā, Sūrasenā, Assakā, Avantī, **GANDHĀRĀ** and Kambojā.[1] A few other clans of the time were the famous Sākiyas, Bhaggas of Suṃsumāra Hill, Bulis of Allakappa, Kālāmas of Kesaputta, Koliyas of Rāma-gāma, and Moriyans of Pipphalivana.[2]

An insight into the administrative machinery of some of these clans can be obtained from a study of the methods by which they disposed of the business of the state. The administrative together with the judicial work of the Sākiya clan, for instance, was done in a public assembly—their common Mote-Hall (*Santhāgāra*) at Kapilavastu, where both young and old met to attend to state-affairs.[3] The Mallas had a similar hall where Ānanda is said to have gone to announce Buddha's death,[4] and the Licchavis had another where Saccaka went to inform them of his desire to hold a philosophical discussion with Buddha.[5] An office-bearer, corresponding to the Greek Archon or the Roman Consul and bearing the title of Rājan, was elected to preside over the meetings and act as the administrative head.

The administration of the Sākiya clan.

Besides the Mote-Hall at the metropolis, there were several minor halls at towns and other important places, as also in every village within the dominion of each clan, where the local people did their share of administrative business.[6] The building of Mote-Halls, rest-houses, and reservoirs, the mending of roads between their own and neighbouring villages, the laying out of parks, and such other works of public utility, for instance, constantly exercised the co-operation of the villagers, including women, who were proud to take an active part in these public

[1] Dr. Rhys Davids' *Buddhist India*, p. 23.
The names common to both Kauṭilya's and other lists have been put in bolder types. The Vajjians include Videhas of Mithilā and Licchavis of Vesālī.

[2] *Ibid.*, pp. 17–22.
Rāma-gāma, i.e. Rāma-grāma, identified with Deokali—a city between Kapila and Kuśinagara. See Cunningham's *Ancient Geography of India*, pp. 420, 421. For Pipphalivana or the Pippala Forest, the site of the Charcoal Tower, see *ibid.*, p. 429.

[3] *Buddhist India*, p. 19, quoting *Ambaṭṭha Suttanta* translated in Rhys Davids' *Dialogues of the Buddha*, i. 113.

[4] *Ibid.*, p. 19, quoting *Mahā-parinibbāna Sutta*, 6. 23.

[5] *Majjhima Nikāya*, i. 228.

[6] *Buddhist India*, p. 20. Each hall was covered with a roof, but had no walls (*ibid.*).

affairs.[1] Thus the people obtained opportunities for exercising their intelligence on village and town affairs which gave them a training in the more difficult work of guiding and controlling larger interests common to many such townships and village-communities. We find an instance of such administration of larger common interests in the local self-government obtaining in the capital of Candragupta Maurya.[2]

The administration of the Vṛjjis.

The Vṛjjis or Saṃvṛjjis (i.e. United Vṛjjis) were a confederation of eight clans, of whom the most important were the Licchavis, with their capital at Vaiśālī, and the Videhas, with their chief town Mithilā. The Vṛjjis were all republicans,[3] and the Licchavis, we notice, did not elect a single chief, like the other clans already mentioned, but a triumvirate, to conduct their administration.[4] The people of Kāśī (Benares) had once their republic, which is testified to by their possession of a public hall used as a 'parliament chamber for the transaction of public business.'[5]

The evidence of Greek writers: Megasthenes;

Megasthenes records an Indian tradition that 'from the time of Dionysos to Sandrokottos, the Indians counted 153 kings and a period of 6,042 years; among these *a republic* was thrice established',[6] which, along with the following two passages from the pen of the same authority, points to democracies in ancient India:

[1] *Ibid.*, p. 49, quoting *Jātaka*, i. 99.

It is no doubt creditable that Indian ladies should discharge the responsible duties of public office. If we take note of their achievements in fields other than the political or public, we may have reason not to doubt their capabilities in the sphere of action. If we are to believe Megasthenes (see Megasthenes' *Ancient India*, McCrindle's transl., Fragm. LVI), we have to credit them with the administration of the Pāṇdyas, who, we are told, were the only race in India with women-rulers. And if the references to *Strī-rājya* in such works as the *Mahābhārata*, the *Bṛhat-Saṃhitā*, &c., have any significance, they point to political power wielded by women.

[2] See Megasthenes, *op. cit.*

[3] Beal's *Buddhist Records of the Western World*, ii. 77 n., and Dr. Rhys Davids' *Buddhist India*, pp. 25, 26; *Lalita-Vistara* (Bibl. Indica), ch. iii, p. 23. In the *Majjhima Nikāya*, i. 231, Saccaka Nigganṭha in the course of his answers to Buddha said that the power of inflicting capital punishment, or of expelling or exiling from the state, belonged not only to Pasenadi of Kosala or Ajātasattu of Magadha, but also to the *Saṅghas* and *Gaṇas*, e.g. Vajjis and Mallas.

[4] *Buddhist India*, p. 19. [5] *Ibid.*, p. 35, quoting *Jātaka*, iv. 74.

[6] *The Indika of Arrian*, transl. by McCrindle, ch. ix.

(1) 'At last, after many generations had come and gone, the sovereignty, it is said, was dissolved, and *democratic government* set up in the cities'.[1]

(2) 'Maltecorai, Singhai, Marohai, Rarungai, and Morunoi *are free, have no kings*, and occupy mountain heights where they have built many cities'.[2]

There are further evidences of non-regal states in ancient India. Arrian says that the Nysaians were free, had a president, and entrusted the government of their state to the aristocracy.[3] He also refers to the Oreitai[4] as an independent tribe with leaders, while Curtius mentions the Sabarcae as 'a powerful Indian tribe whose form of government was democratic and not regal',[5] and the Cedrosii (i. e. Gedrosioi) as a free people with a council for discussing important matters of state.[6] Diodoros describes the Sambastai as dwelling in cities with a democratic form of administration,[7] and Tauala (a name which has been restored to Patala as its correct form) as 'a city of great note with a political constitution drawn on the same lines as the Spartan; for in this community the command in war was vested in two hereditary kings of two different houses, while a council of elders ruled the whole state with paramount authority.[8] The Malloi are simply referred to by Arrian as 'a race of independent Indians',[9] but the Oxydrakai, we learn from him, were attached more than others to freedom and autonomy, which they preserved intact for a very long time before Alexander's invasion.[10] The Malloi (i. e. the Mālavas) and the Oxydrakai (the Kṣudrakas)

Arrian; Curtius Diodoros. The Malloi and Oxydrakai.

[1] Megasthenes, Fragm. I. Prof. Hopkins remarks, 'Megasthenes plainly implies that self-ruled cities in distinction from cities governed by kings were common in his day. Indeed, his words take such towns as a matter of course.' *J. A. O. S.*, xiii. 136.

[2] *Ibid.*, Fragm. LVI. The *Modern Review* (Nov. 1918, pp. 454, 455) identifies Singhai with the Sengar clan.

[3] McCrindle's *Ancient India: Its Invasion by Alexander the Great*, pp. 79, 80, 81, 338–40.

[4] *Ibid.*, pp. 167, 169.

[5] *Ibid.*, p. 252.

[6] *Ibid.*, p. 262.

[7] For the Sambastai, sometimes identified with the Sabarcae, see *ibid.*, pp. 252, n. 4, 292.

[8] McCrindle's *Ancient India*, pp. 296, 356, 357.

[9] *Ibid.*, pp. 140, 350, 351. For these tribes see Mr. V. A. Smith, *J. R. A. S.*, 1903, pp. 685–702.

[10] *Ibid.*, pp. 154, 350, 351.

figure in a few Sanskrit works, e. g. the *Kāśikā-vṛtti*[1] and the *Mahābhārata*.[2] Noteworthy also is the case of the Yaudheyas,[3] a warrior clan, known to Pāṇini, whose existence is attested as late as the time of Samudragupta, and whose coins bear symbols of the military character of the clan. There was also a race in the Punjab living under democratic institutions, viz. the Kathaioi, who formed part of the people known as the Āraṭṭas (kingless), described by Justin as robbers and denounced as such in the *Mahābhārata*, and whom Candragupta Maurya used as weapons for wresting for himself the sovereignty of the Punjab.[4]

The Yaudheyas.

The Kathaioi.

The *Mahābhārata* on the *Gaṇas* or self-governing communities; discussion of the various meanings given to the term.

The *Mahābhārata* expatiates on the policy that should be followed by the monarch in regard to the *Gaṇas*, and by the *Gaṇas* themselves for self-preservation. These *Gaṇas* appear to have been self-governing communities. Thus in the *Śānti-Parvan* (107. 6.) the word *Gaṇa* appears rather to refer to self-governing communities than to mere corporations of traders or artisans, or to the 'aristocracy in a state', as Mr. Pratāp Roy translates it, though it should be noted that the word bears other significations in other contexts. The commentary of Nīlakaṇṭha is very meagre on this chapter, but he seems to have taken the word *Gaṇa* as meaning a self-governing community. The chapter gives some details of its constitution; its members are described as the same in respect of *jāti* and *kula*, and its state affairs as conducted by a body of leaders, who are advised to keep among themselves alone the matters they discuss (see vv. 23, 24).[5] The commentators of the Vedic

[1] McCrindle's *Ancient India*, p. 350. Arrian (*ibid.*, pp. 155, 156, 167) mentions the Abastanoi, Xathroi, and Arabitai as independent tribes without any reference to their form of government. For the case of the Siboi and Agalassoi, see V. A. Smith's *Early History of India* (3rd ed.), p. 93.

[2] They formed part of the Kaurava army in the Great War (Mr. F. E. Pargiter, *J. R. A. S.*, 1908, p. 329). See also V. A. Smith, *op. cit.*, pp. 74 n. and 94.

[3] See Cunningham, *Coins of Ancient India*, pp. 75-9; Smith, *op. cit.*, p. 286.

[4] McCrindle, *op. cit.*, p. 406, Appendix, and his *Ancient India as described in Classical Literature*, p. 38 n. *Āraṭṭa* is from Sanskrit *Arāṣṭraka* (see Cunningham's *Geography of Ancient India*, p. 215).

[5] In *Manu*, iii. 154, *gaṇābhyantara*—in a list of persons who should be shunned by good *Brāhmaṇas* at sacrifices to the gods and *manes*—nc

Samhitās appear to be right in interpreting the word *Gaṇa* as 'corporation' or 'guild' in a few passages.[1]

Prof. Hopkins remarks[2] that the growth of commercial interests led ultimately to the establishment of a sort of trade-unions or guilds. They are mentioned early as of importance (see *Manu*, viii. 41), though they may belong to a late period in their full development. 'Such corporations had their own rules and laws subject to the king's inspection, the king not being allowed (theoretically) to have established, or to establish, any laws that contradicted those already approved or sanctioned by usage. The heads of these bodies are mentioned together with the priests as political factors of weight, whose views are worth grave consideration. As an informal instance of it, we find a prince (Duryodhana) defeated in battle and ashamed to return home—'for what', he exclaims, 'shall I have to say to my relatives, to the priests, and to the *heads of the corporations*.'[3] Prominence is given to the *guilds* (?) in the later books of the *Mahābhārata*. There also we find *corporations* (?) of every sort under the name *Gaṇa*; of the members of which the king is particularly recommended to be careful, since enemies are apt to make use of them by bribery. But dissension

doubt denotes, as Bühler, following Medhātithi, Govindarāja, and Nārāyaṇa, translates it, 'one who belongs to a company or corporation, i. e. of men who live by one trade.' The same sense occurs in *Yājñavalkya*, i. 161; ii. 190, 195; *Gautama*, xv. 18; and often in other works. The *Arthaśāstra* also uses the word *gaṇa* in this non-political sense, e.g. in *kāruśilpigaṇa* (II. vi, p. 60). We need only note here the various other meanings which the word may bear in other contexts, e.g. 'village-assembly' (Foy, *Die königliche Gewalt*, p. 20, n. 1), 'local committee or court' (Jolly, *Recht und Sitte*, p. 136), 'assemblage' (Dr. Fleet, *Gupta Inscriptions*, p. 291 and n. 3).

[1] *Gaṇa* (= *Vrāta*, *Śardha*) in the sense of guild appears to have had Vedic precedents, as noted by Roth in the *St. Petersburg Dictionary* in connexion with the *Pañcaviṃśa-Brāhmaṇa*, vi. 9. 25; xvii. 1. 5, 12; *Vājasaneyi-Saṃhitā*, xvi. 25; *Taittirīya-Saṃhitā*, i. 8. 10. 2. This view has been questioned by Messrs. Macdonell and Keith, who agree, however, that guilds existed in Vedic times; see Fick's *Die sociale Gliederung*, p. 182; Macdonell and Keith, *V. I.* i. 140; ii, 341, 342, 403, 404. Hopkins (*India Old and New*, pp. 169–205) has a chapter on guilds, in which, among other things, the antiquity of the institutions is traced back to about 600 B. C.

[2] *J. A. O. S.*, xiii. 81, 82.

[3] *MBh.*, iii. 249. 16 as quoted by Prof. Hopkins (*J. A. O. S.*, xiii. 82) = iii. 248. 16 (Burdwan Ed.). The text has *śreṇimukhyāḥ* = *śilpisaṅghātamukhyāḥ prakṛtayaḥ* according to Nīlakaṇṭha.

is their weak point. Through dissension and bribery they may be controlled by the king. On the other hand 'union is the safeguard of corporations'.

I should remark that the word 'corporation', as used in the above extract, is not a good rendering of *Śreṇī* or *Gaṇ* in its reference to self-ruled communities of military character. Dr. Fleet, after much discussion with Dr. Thomas over the proper rendering of *Mālava-gaṇa-sthiti*, comes to the conclusion [1] that though *Gaṇa* may have many meanings and has to be translated in each particular case according to the context, it is best rendered in the above expression by 'tribe'. Dr. Thomas objects on many grounds, one of which is that when 'coins are issued by the authority of a *Gaṇa* (which is the case with the Yaudheyas), or an era is maintained by it (which is the case with the Mālavas), plainly the absence of royalty is implied'.[2] The description of *Gaṇa* in the *Mahābhārata* (xii. 107) cited above also points to a status of independence, or at least semi-independence, which the word 'tribe' does not express. In order to bring out this essential implication of *Gaṇa*, the word 'tribe' should have some qualifying epithet, and for this reason the expression 'autonomous tribe' (used by Mr. V. A. Smith) or 'self-governing community' is preferable to 'corporation' or 'tribe'.

Oligarchies in Vedic India.

It does not appear clearly whether any oligarchies existed in the Vedic period. According to Zimmer,[3] there are traces in a passage in the Ṛg-Veda [4] that normally there was no king in some states, the members of the royal house holding equal rights. It is compared by him to the state of affairs in early Germany.[5] Messrs. Macdonell and Keith, however, are of opinion that the passage depended upon is not decisive for the sense ascribed to it, 'though of course the state of affairs is perfectly possible and is exemplified later in Buddhist[6] times'.[7] This latter view gains support from the case of Citraratha, who

[1] *J.R.A.S.*, 1915, p. 139. [2] *J.R.A.S.*, 1914, pp. 1011, 1012.
[3] *Altindisches Leben*, pp. 176, 177.
[4] *Ṛg-Veda*, x. 97. 6; *Atharva-Veda*, i. 9; iii. 4.
[5] Tacitus, *Annals*, ii. 88. [6] Cf. Rhys Davids, *Buddhist India*, p. 19.
[7] See *V.I.* ii. 216.

performed a special kind of sacrifice (*dvirātra*), which led to the result that the Caitrarathis were distinguished from other royal families by the fact that 'the chief of the clan received a markedly higher position than in most cases, in which probably the heads of the family were rather an *oligarchy* than a monarch (with) his dependants.'[1]

How far monarchy was elective in ancient India; evidence of Megasthenes and the *Rāmāyana*

Megasthenes records that the *vox populi* was recognized as an effective and potent factor which the responsible officers consulted in cases of failure of heirs in the royal house. On such occasions, 'the Indians', we are told, 'elected their sovereigns on the principle of merit'.[2] We learn from the *Rāmāyaṇa* that respect was shown to the opinion of the people in the choice of a successor to the reigning sovereign, as also on the rather rare occasions of failures of heirs in the ruling house.

Prof. Hopkins says that the assent of the people was obtained to the succession in the first place. After the king's death, the priests and people met in the royal court and decided which prince should be king. The chief priest made an address explaining the death of the king and the necessity for having a new king on the throne. The elder son (Rāma) being banished, the younger must reign to prevent the many evils of anarchy. The older councillors expressed their assent, saying, 'Even when the king was alive, we stood at your orders (*śāsane*); proceed, then; give your orders.' After this the election was practically over, and only the ceremony remained to be performed.[3]

The elective principle in Vedic times.

There are also traces of the existence of the elective principle in the Vedic times. Zimmer[4] is of opinion that the Vedic monarchy, though sometimes hereditary, as can be shown by the several cases in which the descent can be traced,[5] was yet

[1] *V. I.* i. 262, quoting *Pañcaviṃśa-Brāhmaṇa*, xx. 12. 5.
[2] Megasthenes' *Ancient India*, Fragm. L.
[3] *Rāmāyaṇa* (Gorresio), ii. 69. 1 ff., 33. See Hopkins, *J. A. O. S.*, xiii. 145, and below, Chap. IV, Regal Succession.
[4] *Altindisches Leben*, pp. 162 ff.; Weber, *Indische Studien*, xvii. 88; Bloomfield, *Hymns of the Atharva-Veda*, p. 336.
[5] e.g. Vadhryaśva, Divodāsa, Pijavana, Sudās; Purukutsa, Trasadasyu, Mitrātithi, Kuruśravaṇa, Upamaśravas, &c.; Lanman, *Sanskrit*

elective in the other instances, though it is not apparent whether the people selected from among the members of the royal house or those of all the noble clans. Geldner[1] argues, however, that the evidence for the elective monarchy is not so strong, as the passages[2] cited are regarded by him not as indicative of choice by the cantons (*Viś*) but of acceptance by the subjects. This is, of course, as Messrs. Macdonell and Keith observe, no proof that the monarchy was not sometimes elective. The practice of selecting one member of the royal family to the exclusion of another less qualified is exemplified by the legend of the Kuru brothers Devāpi and Śantanu referred to in Yāska,[3] the value of which as evidence of contemporary views is not seriously affected by the fact that the legend itself is of dubious character and validity.[4]

The power of the people was stronger in those days in proportion to the greater insecurity of the sovereign. There are several references to the latter being expelled[5] from their dominions, and to their efforts to be reinstated to their former position. The inviolability of the sovereign's authority is recognized even in the Vedic period, he himself being 'exempt from punishment' (*adaṇḍya*), but having the power to inflict on others judicial punishment (*daṇḍa-vadha*).[6] The expulsion was the last resort of the people, who could, of course, effect it more by the aid of abnormal circumstances than by dint of their unaided will. The sovereign's immunity from punishment should, therefore, be taken as the normal rule. A few instances of sovereigns deposed or expelled from the realms

[Instances of sovereigns deposed or expelled.]

Reader, p. 389. A 'kingdom of ten generations' (*Daśapuruṣamrājya*) is mentioned in the *Śatapatha-Brāhmaṇa*, xii. 9. 3. 3. Cf. v. 4. 2. 8.

[1] *Vedische Studien*, ii. 303.

[2] *Ṛg-Veda*, x, 124. 8; 173; *Atharva-Veda*, i. 9; iii. 4; iv. 22. In some passages (*A V.*, iii. 4. 1; iv. 22. 3) the use of the word Viśpati for a sovereign is taken by Zimmer (*Altindisches Leben*, pp. 164, 165) as indicative of election. The word in the *Taittirīya-Saṃhitā*, ii. 3. 1. 3, stands evidently for 'the chief representative of the *Viś*, i. e. the people or subject class'; see *V. I.*, ii. 308.

[3] *Nirukta*, ii. 10.

[4] *V. I.*, ii. 211, 269.

[5] The technical term is *aparuddha*. Cf. *A V.*, iii. 3. 4; Caland, *Altindisches Zauberritual*, pp. 37 ff.; Bloomfield's *Hymns of the A V.*, pp. 111 ff.

[6] *Śatapatha-Brāhmaṇa*, v. 4. 4. 7. Cf. *Pāraskara-Gṛhya-Sūtra*, iii. 15, where the 'staff' as the emblem of royal, temporal power, implying punishment, is said to be applied by the monarch (*rāja-preṣito daṇḍaḥ*).

may be cited here: Duṣṭaṛtu Pauṃsāyana (the first word literally means 'hard to fight'), king of the Sṛñjayas, was deposed by them from a principality that had existed for ten generations, but was restored by Pāṭava Cākra Sthapati in spite of the resistance of Balhika Prātipīya,[1] the Kuru king. Dīrghaśravas (i.e. 'far-famed') was also banished from his kingdom,[2] as also Sindhukṣit, who had to remain in exile for a long time before he could be restored.[3] The case of Vena[4] being deposed and killed in later times may also be mentioned.

The power of the people as exemplified in the ritual called *Ratnahavis.*

A trace of the deference paid to the will of the people in early times exists also perhaps in the ritual of the *Rājasūya* called the *Ratnahavis*, in which offerings were made by the king on successive days in the houses of persons termed *Ratnins*, including among others a *Kṣatriya*, village-headman, and such other individuals, who were either mere subjects, king's officials, or relatives, to whom, or at least to some of whom, the title of *Rājakartṛ* (king-maker) was applied.[5] Though in later times the ceremony may have been no more than a mere formality observed during the inauguration, yet in its inception in remoter periods it was probably associated with the deference shown to the opinion of the people, who then wielded much greater power in the state. Some of the *Ratnins* were perhaps representatives of the people or certain classes of the subjects turned into mere ceremonial figures in subsequent times by the growth of the royal power.

Monarchy the ordinary form of government in Vedic times.

The ordinary form of government in Vedic times, however, was the monarchical, as might be naturally expected from the situation of the Indian Aryans surrounded by hostile races. There are clear signs that the power of the monarch was curbed by the existence of the assembly which he had to consult, and concord between them was essential for the prosperity of the former as also of the people at large.[6]

[1] *Śatapatha-Brāhmaṇa*, xii. 9. 3. 1 ff; 8. 1. 17.
[2] *Pañcaviṃśa-Brāhmaṇa*, xv. 3. 25.
[3] *Ibid.*, xii. 12. 6.
[4] *Viṣṇu-Purāṇa*, i. 13.
[5] *Aitareya-Brāhmaṇa*, viii. 17. 5; *Atharva-Veda*, iii. 5. 7; *Śatapatha-Brāhmaṇa*, iii. 4. 1. 7; xiii. 22. 18. See Mr. K. P. Jayaswal's articles in the *Modern Review*, Jan. 1912, May and July 1913, and Chap. IX of this volume.
[6] *Atharva-Veda*, vi. 88. 3; v. 19. 15; *V. I.* ii. 431.

Gradation of kingly power.

In the titles assumed by the sovereigns, as well as the epithets by which they are mentioned, we find evidences of higher and lower positions among them. Messrs. Macdonell and Keith remark that the states were seemingly small,[1] and there are no clear signs of any really large kingdoms, despite the mention of *Mahārājas*. This may be true, but it does not negative the possibility that there were royal hierarchies among the states of the early Vedic period. The area upon which the Aryans spread themselves in those times was not even the whole of Northern India, and necessarily we cannot expect to have an emperor with a territory extending from sea to sea. Yet among the existing states one or the other rose to a supremacy over some others, which may have prompted its ruler to assume a title indicative of his superiority to the subordinate states. *Samrāj* is the epithet applied to a 'superior ruler' in the *Ṛg-Veda*[2] as also in later works, expressing a greater degree of power than that of a *Rājan* ('King').[3] *Adhirāja*,[4] frequently met with in the early Sanskrit literature, signifies an 'overlord' among kings or princes.[5]

Different titles indicating the gradation.

[1] 'Cf. Hopkins, *Transactions of the Connecticut Academy of Arts and Sciences*, xv. 32, for the *Pañcaviṃśa Brāhmaṇa*. The *Śatapatha-Brāhmaṇa* and the later parts of the *Aitareya-Brāhmaṇa*, with their traditions of *Aśvamedhas*, "horse-sacrifices", and their recollections of the glories of the Bharatas, represent a more advanced stage of social relations and city life, but even they hardly know really great kingdoms.' *V. I.*, ii. 254, n. 65.

[2] *Ṛg-Veda*, iii. 55. 7; 56. 5; iv. 21. 2; vi. 27, 8; viii. 19. 32.

[3] In the *Śatapatha-Brāhmaṇa* (v. 1. 1. 13; cf. xii. 8. 3. 4; xiv. 1. 3. 8) the *Samrāj* is higher than a king. See Weber's *Über den Vājapeya*, p. 6 (in the *Sitzungsberichte der Königlich Preussischen Akademie der Wissenschaften zu Berlin*, xxxix (1892)).

[4] *RV.*, x. 128. 9; *AV.*, vi. 98. 1; ix. 10. 24; &c.; *V. I.*, i. 19, 20.

[5] Profs. Macdonell and Keith, after giving the above meaning, express doubt whether a real 'over-king' is meant by the word, and incline to the negative view. An over-king of the early Vedic period should, however, be taken with the limitations peculiar to the age to which he belonged; and we cannot expect to find then the political conditions or the great extent of territory that made the overlords of after times what they were. It is not improbable that a powerful Vedic king might conquer others and bring them under his control. Of the battles of the time, of which we have record, we find some in which a king defeated a few others, the two parties being sometimes aided by their own allies. Sudās, for instance, helped by the Tṛtsus, defeated in a great battle the ten kings Śimyu, the Turvaśa, the Druhyu, Kavaṣa, the Pūru, the Anu, Bheda, Śambara, the two Vaikarṇas and perhaps the Yadu, who led with them as

Similarly, we have *Mahārāja*,[1] *Rājādhirāja*,[2] and *Ekarāja*.[3]

The titles in the *Aitareya-Brāhmaṇa*.

The *Aitareya-Brāhmaṇa* uses a series of terms, some of which signify overlordship, and some others distinction in the form of government. At times, a few of these may be used as mere complimentary epithets, but not always. They are *Rājya*, *Sāmrājya*, *Bhaujya*, *Svārājya*, and *Vairājya*.[4] *Ādhipatya*[5] (lit., supreme power), *Jānarājya*,[6] *Svāvaśya*[7] and *Ātiṣṭha*[8] are also found. The explanation of the words given by Sāyana,[9] the commentator, in connexion with a certain

alliesthe Matsyas, Pakthas, Bhalānas, Alinas, Viṣāṇins, Śivas, Ajas, Śigrus, and perhaps Yakṣus (*V.I.*, i. 320). There is, again, the fight in which the Sṛñjaya king Daivavāta conquered the Turvaśa king and the Vṛcīvats, and another in which the Jahnus and the Vṛcīvats contended for sovereignty (*V.I.*, ii. 319, 499). From these, I think, it is not unreasonable to infer that some at least of the terms signifying degrees of power, or superiority and inferiority of rank among kings, denote an actual counterpart created by the victories and defeats in battles which increased or decreased their powers and territories.

[1] *Aitareya-Brāhmaṇa*, vii. 34. 9; *Kauṣītaki-Brāhmaṇa*, v. 5; *Śatapatha-Brāhmaṇa*, i. 6. 4. 21; ii. 5. 4. 9, &c.

[2] *Rājādhirāja*, 'king of kings' is used as a divine epithet in the *Taittirīya-Āraṇyaka*, i. 31. 6, and as a title of paramount sovereignty in later times.

[3] In the *Ṛg-Veda* (viii. 37. 3) the term is used metaphorically. In the *Aitareya-Brāhmaṇa*, viii. 15, the word, according to Weber, *Über die Königsweihe, den Rājasūya* in the *Abhandl. d. Königlich Preussischen Akademie der Wissenschaften zu Berlin*, 1893, p. 141, n. 2, means 'a king over a *maṇḍala*'. But the expression used by the *Aitareya* itself, in a subsequent passage of viii. 15, is '*Ekarāṭ* of the earth up to the sea'. See also *AV.*, iii. 4. 1.

[4] *Aitareya-Brāhmaṇa*, viii. 12. 4, 5. Cf. *Śāṅkhāyana-Śrauta-Sūtra*, xvii. 16. 3.

[5] *Pañcaviṃśa-Brāhmaṇa*, xv. 3. 35; *Chāndogya-Upaniṣad*, v. 2. 6.

[6] See Weber's *Über den Rājasūya*, p. 31, n. 5.

[7] *Aitareya-Brāhmaṇa*, viii. 6. It means, according to Sāyaṇa, '*apāratantrya*,' i.e. lit., 'absence of dependence on others.'

Mr. K. P. Jayaswal (in the *Modern Review*, 1913, p. 538) derives the name Surat (the modern town of Western India) from Svarāṭ (republic), which, he says, the *Vṛṣṇi-Saṅgha* was, in that part of the country. But this, I think, is a mere phonetic resemblance, the word having real affinity with *Surāṣṭra*, the ancient name of the place, of which the present Surat was a town (or perhaps the capital). It is a well-known fact that a town or a capital very often takes its name after the country in which it is located.

[8] See *infra*.

[9] *Aitareya-Brāhmaṇa* with Sāyaṇa's commentary (Bibl. Indica), vol. iv, p. 188. 'Here *rājya* = *deśādhipatyam* (rule over a country); *sāmrājyam* = *dharmeṇa pālanam* (righteous government); *bhaujyam* = *bhogasamṛddhiḥ* (increase of enjoyment); *svārājyam* = *aparādhīnatyam* (absence of dependence on others); *vairājyam* = *itarebhyo bhūpatibhyo vaiśiṣṭyam*

passage in the *Aitareya-Brāhmaṇa*, is based more or less upon their literal meanings, and partakes, to some extent, of spiritual character akin to that of Śrīdharasvāmin's comment on a similar passage in the *Bhāgavata-Purāṇa*.[1] A subsequent passage of the aforesaid *Brāhmaṇa*[2] and Sāyaṇa's comments thereon give us more secular details. Indra, it is stated, was installed in the east by the divine Vasus for *sāmrājya*. Hence the several kings of the east are consecrated after the divine practice and the people call them *Samrāj*. Next, He was consecrated in the south by the divine Rudras to *bhaujya*, for which the sovereigns of the *Satvats* in the south are consecrated after the divine practice and receive the title *Bhoja*. The divine Ādityas installed Him in the west to ensure His *svārājya*. Hence the sovereigns of the *Nīcyas*, and *Apācyas*, i.e. the peoples in the south and in the west, are similarly installed and denominated *Svarāj*. Afterwards, the *Viśvedevāḥ* consecrated Him in the north to *vairājya*. That is why the sovereigns of the countries Uttara Kuru and Uttara

(enjoyment of more distinguished qualities than those possessed by other kings).' [See Weber's *Über den Rājasūya*, pp. 111, 112; Goldstücker's *Sanskrit-English Dictionary*, under '*Abhisheka*'. These terms, the commentary says, relate to this world, while the following to the other world: *pārameṣṭhyam* = *prajāpati-lokaprāptiḥ*, (i.e. attainment of the world of Prajāpati), *rājyam* (obtaining dominion there), *māhārājyam* (mighty rule), *svāvaśyam* (independence), and *ātiṣṭhatvam* (long residence)—these three also taking place in the other world. The *Gopatha-Brāhmaṇa* [pt. I. v, para. 8, pp. 77, 78 (Bibl. Indica)] says about Prajāpati that he became *rājā* by *Rājasūya*, *samrāṭ* by the *Vājapeya*, *svarāṭ* by the *Aśvamedha*, *virāṭ* by the *Puruṣa-medha*, and *sarvarāṭ* by the *Sarva-medha*.

[1] Śrīdharasvāmin's comment on x. 83, 41, attaches spiritual significance to many of the terms, as will be apparent from the following: *Sāmrājyam* = *sārvabhaumam padam* (position of an overlord); *svārājyam* = position of Indra; *bhaujyam* = enjoyment of the previous two positions; *virāṭ* = possession of qualities such as *aṇimā* (i.e. the power of becoming as small as an atom), &c.; *pārameṣṭhyam* = position of Brahma; and so forth.

He further states that the four terms *sāmrājya*, *bhaujya*, *svārājya*, and *vairājya* follow the order in which the four cardinal points are mentioned in the *Bahvṛca-brāhmaṇa*, viz. east, south, west, and north, and are applied to the presiding deities thereof—Indra, Yama, Varuṇa, and Kubera. Indra is also mentioned as *Samrāj* and Varuṇa as *Svarāj* in the *Ṛg-Veda* (see vii. 82. 2). It is difficult to state whether the titles used in connexion with the gods were subsequently applied to the sovereigns in the respective directions, or *vice versa*.

[2] The *Aitareya-Brāhmaṇa* (Bibl. Indica) with Sāyaṇa's comments, vol. iv, pp. 230 ff. Weber, *Über den Rājasūya*, pp. 115, 116, and n. 2.

Madra in the north, beyond the Himalayas, are similarly consecrated and termed *Virāj*. Next, the divine *Sādhyas* and *Āptyas* anointed Him for *rājya* in the central region, for which the kings of that region, i.e. of Kuru and Pañcāla as well as of Vaśa and Uśīnara, are similarly anointed and called Rājan.[1]

In later times, both the terms *Svarāj* and *Virāj* are found to be used as signifying monarchies of a particular grade determined by their incomes. The *Śukranīti*[2] gives the following ascending order of the monarchs based on their incomes calculated in silver *karsas*: The gradation according to the *Śukranīti*.

		Silver Karṣas.
Sāmanta	having	1 to 3 lacs.
Māṇḍalika	"	4 " 10 "
Rājan	"	11 " 20 "
Mahārāja	"	21 " 50 "
Svarāj	"	51 " 100 "
Samrāj	"	1 " 10 crores
Virāj	"	11 " 50 "
Sārvabhauma	"	51 crores or upwards.

The *Amarakoṣa*[3] gives three significations of *Saṃrāj*—(1) the performer of the *Rājasūya*, (2) the monarch exercising his control over a Maṇḍala ('circuit') consisting of twelve kings, and (3) the monarch who can have his mandates obeyed by the kings under his supremacy. The *Amarakoṣa*.

[1] Next follows Indra's consecration in the upper regions to the other-worldly positions called *pārameṣṭhya*, *māhārājya*, *ādhipatya*, *svāvaśya*, *ātiṣṭha*. See Weber's *Über den Rājasūya*, pp. 115, 116. Messrs. Macdonell and Keith look upon the above epithets of sovereigns of the several regions as embodying in all probability a sound tradition. *V. I.*, ii. 433.

[2] *Śukranīti* (Jivānanda's ed.), i. 184–7. Such a classification of monarchs is also found in other late works like the *Varadātantra* (2nd *paṭala*, quoted in the *Śabdakalpadruma*) where a *rājan* is said to have an income of a lac, *samrāj*, 10 lacs, and a *mahāsamrāj*, 100 lacs.

Lakṣādhipatyaṃ rājyaṃ syāt,
Sāmrājyaṃ daśalakṣake,
Śatalakṣe, maheśāni,
Mahāsāmrājyam ucyate.

[3] The *Śabdakalpadruma* refers to the above passage and adds 'as the opinion of others' the sense (iv) a ruler whose sway extends over the earth from sea to sea.

Epithets for paramount sovereignty.

We meet with other epithets such as *Cakravartin*, *Parameśvara*, *Paramabhaṭṭāraka*, *Mahārājādhirāja*, *Sārvabhauma*, *Akhaṇḍabhūmipa*, *Rājarāja*, *Viśvarāja*, *Caturanteśa*, &c.[1] Monier Williams explains *cakravartin* as 'a ruler, the wheels (*cakra*) of whose chariot roll everywhere without obstruction; emperor; sovereign of the world; ruler of a *cakra*, i.e. country extending from sea to sea'.[2] It is also explained another way: a discus (*cakra*)—the sign of the god Viṣṇu—is to be found among the marks on the hands of all *Cakravartins*; and such a ruler is one whose prowess cannot be withstood even by the gods'.[3] Some of the other epithets such as *Paramabhaṭṭāraka*,[4] *Parameśvara*,[5] *Mahārājādhirāja* are found in close connexion with one another in the inscriptions, and are very elastic in their application,[6] the other titles in the above list being but synonyms of these. A distinction is, however, observed between the use of this set of titles and another comprising such terms as *Mahārāja*, *Bhattāraka*, &c., found in connexion with the names of tributary kings.[7]

[1] In the Buddhist literature, *cakkavattī* is sometimes used in the sense of a universal monarch. See R. C. Childers's *Pali Dictionary*, quoting *Abhidhānappadīpikā*, 335, and Turnour's *Mahāwanso*, 27. See also *Dīgha Nikāya* (Mahā-parinibbāna Sutta), vol. ii (P.T.S.), pp. 172 ff.; *Mahābodhivaṃsa* (P. T. S.), pp. 66 ff.; and *Lalita-Vistara* (Bibl. Indica), pp. 15 ff.

[2] Monier Williams' *Sanskrit-English Dictionary*.

[3] H. H. Wilson's Translation of the *Viṣṇu-Purāṇa*, i. p. 183. Dr. Fleet adds (*Gupta Inscriptions*, p. 183, n. 4) that the word *Cakravartin* denotes a universal ruler and is one of the technical terms of 'paramount sovereignty', though it is not so frequently used in the inscriptions as the others are. The expression 'paramount sovereign' is used by him in the sense of 'a sovereign supreme in his own dominion, but not necessarily reigning over the whole of India' (*ibid.*, Index, p. 332), from which it seems that it signifies nothing more than an independent sovereign as opposed to one whose control over his dominion is under a limitation, e. g. a feudatory king. Hence all the titles found in the *Gupta Inscriptions* and described as implying paramount sovereignty may apply to any independent ruler, ranging from a sovereign of the position of Samudragupta, whose power and territory were imperial, to one of a much lower rank, e.g. Sarvavarman, the Maukhari (Fleet, *op. cit.*, p. 221), who is called *Mahārājādhirāja*.

[4] i. e. 'most worshipful one.'

[5] i. e. 'supreme lord.'

[6] See note in connexion with *Cakravartin*.

[7] See Fleet, *op. cit.* Like the above, we meet with other titles applied to the wives of the sovereigns, and indicative of the ranks they enjoyed by virtue of those of their husbands, e. g. *Paramabhaṭṭārikā*, *Paramadevī*, *Bhaṭṭārikā*, &c. *Mahādevī* applies to the wife of a *Mahārājādhirāja*, as in

Names of paramount sovereigns in the *Aitareya-Brāhmaṇa.*

The supreme rulers enumerated in the *Aitareya-Brāhmaṇa* [1] are:—

SUPREME RULER.	LINEAGE	CONSECRATING PRIEST
Janamejaya	son of Parikṣit	Tura Kāvaṣeya
Śāryāta	of the race of Manu	Cyavana Bhārgava
Śātānika	of the race of Satrājit	Somaśuṣman Vājaratnāyana
Āmbāṣṭhya		Parvata and Nārada
Yudhāṃśrauṣṭi	of the race of Ugrasena	Parvata and Nārada
Viśvakarman	of the race of Bhuvana	Kaśyapa
Sudās	son of Pijavana	Vasiṣṭha
Marutta	of the race of Avikṣit	Saṃvarta, of the race of Aṅgiras
Aṅga	of the race of Virocana	Udamaya, of the race of Atri
Bharata	son of Duḥṣanta	Dīrghatamas, son of Mamatā
Durmukha, king of Pañcāla		Bṛhaduktha
Atyarāti	son of Janantapa	a descendant of Satyahavya, sprung from the race of Vasiṣṭha

The significance of the *Rājasūya.*

It is stated in the *Aitareya-Brāhmaṇa* that all the kings in the above list 'subdued the earth' by virtue of the *Rājasūya* (royal sacrifice) which they had performed. The performance of this sacrifice cannot, however, be *always* taken as a mark of paramount sovereignty, for it was a ceremony for the inauguration of a king and 'a state ceremonial to which any petty ruler might fairly think himself entitled'.[2] Dr. Mitra, however, states, 'From its very nature, a ceremony like the *Rājasūya* could not be common anywhere or at any time, much less during the Hindu period when India was never held by a single monarch,' basing his statement upon a passage from the *Taittirīya-Brāhmaṇa*—'*rājā svārājyakāmo rājasūyena yajeta*' which he interprets as 'none but a king who wishes to

the case of Kumāradevī (Fleet, *op. cit.*, p. 221), but the simple *Devī* serves the same purpose at a later period (*ibid.*, p. 232).

[1] *Aitareya-Brāhmaṇa*, viii. 21–3, where the great unction (*mahābhiṣeka*) is mentioned. Cf. Weber, *Episches im Vedischen Ritual*, p. 8; *Über den Rājasūya*, pp. 117, 118; and Colebrooke, *Miscellaneous Essays*, i. 39–43.

[2] See Eggeling, *S.B.E.*, xliv, p. xv.

be a universal monarch exercising supremacy over a large number of princes can perform the sacrifice.'[1] These differences may perhaps be reconciled by keeping in view that in later times the sacrifice lost its simplicity and changed into a complex state-function performable by suzerains.[2]

The ceremony of the conquest of the four quarters forming part of the *Rājasūya* was for conferring upon the king a prospective blessing, and did not imply, at least in the earlier periods, a condition precedent to the ceremonial.[3] The *Vājapeya*, a Soma sacrifice, was at one time of lesser importance than the *Rājasūya*, followed in the case of a king by the latter sacrifice, and in the case of a Brāhmaṇa by the *Bṛhaspatisava* (i.e. festival for his appointment as a royal *Purohita*).[4]

The *Vājapeya*;

But the *Śatapatha-Brāhmaṇa*[5] exalts the *Vājapeya* over the *Rājasūya*, maintaining that the latter confers on the sacrificer mere royal dignity, while the former confers overlordship.

The *Aśvamedha*.

The performance of the *Aśvamedha* (or horse-sacrifice) involved 'an assertion of power and a display of political authority such as only a monarch of undisputed supremacy could have ventured upon without humiliation'.[6] In its earliest

[1] See R. L. Mitra's *Indo-Aryans*, ii. 2, 3; cf. Hopkins, *J.A.O.S.*, xiii. 145, 146. The passage does not, so far as I see, occur in the text of the *Taittirīya-Brāhmaṇa*, but in Sāyaṇa's commentary on the *Taittirīya-Saṃhitā*, i. 8. 1. Dr. Mitra states that the rituals of the *Aitareya-Brāhmaṇa* recommend three kinds of bathing: 1st, called *Abhiṣeka* for kings; 2nd, *Punarabhiṣeka* for superior kings; and 3rd, *Mahābhiṣeka* for emperors (*Indo-Aryans*, ii. 46, 47). The *Aitareya-Brāhmaṇa*, however, details only *Punarabhiṣeka* and *Mahābhiṣeka*, which, I think, operate in unison. See *Aitareya-Brāhmaṇa*, viii. 5–11, 15–23, on this point.

[2] Cf. V. S. Dalal's *History of India*, i. 131, 153.

[3] There is a sacrifice named *Pṛthisava* celebrated for the attainment of supremacy. It comprehends some of the rituals of the *Rājasūya*, but lasts only about a day. [*Taittirīya-Brāhmaṇa*, ii. 7. 5.]

[4] *V.I.*, ii. 256. See also Eggeling, *S.B.E.*, xli, pp. xxiv, xxv. See ch. ix, pp. 325 ff.

[5] *Śatapatha-Brāhmana*, v. 1. 1. 1 ff.; 2. 1. 19; cf. *Kātyāyana-Śrauta-Sūtra*, xv. 1. 1. 1–2. Weber, *Über den Vājapeya*, interprets the situation differently from Eggeling; *V.I.*, ii. 256, and Eggeling, *S.B.E.*, xli, p. xxiv.

[6] Eggeling, *S.B.E.*, xliv, p. xv. Cf. *Taittirīya-Brāhmaṇa*, iii. 8. 9. 4, and *Āpastamba-Śrauta-Sūtra*, xx. 1. 1: 'a king ruling the whole land (*sārvabhauma*) may perform the *Aśvamedha*; also one not ruling the whole land.'

phase, however, it was very simple. The horse was let loose after some preliminary rite to wander for some time, and, on return, was anointed and slaughtered.[1] Its complex formalities in its fully developed form were later accretions.

Prof. Eggeling remarks that as a rule the closely watched animal would not probably range very far from the place where sacrifice would be performed, and, though the officers in charge were not allowed at any time to force it to retrace its steps, they could have had little difficulty in keeping it within a certain range of grazing. Not to take up the challenge implied in the progress of the horse was regarded as a mark of cowardice. In any case, a strong ruler who had already made his power felt amongst his neighbours would run little risk of having his horse kidnapped, even if it had strayed beyond his dominions, while a weak prince might find it very difficult to keep it secure even within his own territory.[2]

The list of names of *Aśvamedha* sacrificers in the *Śatapatha-Brāhmaṇa*.

The list of performers of the horse-sacrifice given by the *Śatapatha-Brāhmana*[3] contains the following names:

1. Janamejaya Pārikṣita, having as his priest Indrota Daivāpa Śaunaka;
2. Bhīmasena, 3. Ugrasena, 4. Śrutasena } the Pārikṣitas;
5. Para Āṭṇāra, the Kauśalya king;
6. Purukutsa, the Aikṣvāka king;
7. Marutta Āvikṣita, the Āyogava king;
8. Kraivya, the king of the Pañcālas;
9. Dhvasan Daitavana, the king of the Matsyas;
10. Bharata Dauḥṣanti;
11. Ṛṣabha Yājñatura;
12. Sātrāsāha, the king of the Pañcālas;
13. Śatānika Sātrājita.[4]

[1] See Eggeling, *op. cit.*, and V. S. Dalal's *History of India*, pp. 132, 133. For details, see Chap. IX.

[2] *Ibid.*, pp. xxviii, xxix, xxx.

[3] *Śatapatha-Brāhmaṇa*, xiii. 5. 4. 1–19.

[4] The list in the *Śāṅkhāyana-Śrauta-Sūtra* (xvi. 9.) has Janamejaya, Ugrasena, Bhīmasena, Śrutasena, Ṛṣabha Yājñatura, Vaideha Alhāra, and Marutta Āvikṣita.

Names of paramount sovereigns in the *Purāṇas.*

I next proceed to enumerate from the *Purāṇas* and other Sanskrit works a few names associated either with extensive conquests or with the performance of sacrifices indicative of supreme political position.

We find Pṛthu in the *Agni-Purāṇa*[1] as also in the *Bhāgavata*,[2] *Brahma*,[3] *Brahmāṇḍa*,[4] and *Śiva*;[5] Sagara in the *Vāyu*,[6] *Viṣṇu*,[7] *Bhāgavata*,[8] *Brahma*,[9] and *Padma*;[10] Marutta in the *Mārkaṇḍeya*,[11] and *Padma*;[12] Bharata, son of Duṣmanta, in the *Vāyu*,[13] *Viṣṇu*,[14] *Brahma*,[15] and *Agni*;[16] Duṣmanta in the *Agni*;[17] Māndhātṛ in the *Bhāgavata*,[18] *Agni*,[19] and *Brahma*,[20] with his father Yuvanāśva in the *Agni*;[21] Mucukunda, son of Māndhātṛ in the *Agni*[22] and *Bhāgavata*;[23] Yayāti in the *Brahma*,[24] *Liṅga*,[25] and *Padma*;[26] Purūravas in the *Matsya*,[27] *Agni*,[28] *Mārkaṇḍeya*,[29] and *Brahma*;[30] Hariścandra in the *Brahma*[31] and *Śiva*,[32] while his great grandson Vijaya in the former *Purāṇa*;[33] Kārtavīrya in the *Vāyu*,[34] *Skanda*,[35] *Mārkaṇḍeya*,[36] *Liṅga*,[37] and *Brahma*;[38] Citraratha in the *Śiva*,[39] Candra in the *Viṣṇu*,[40] Vasumanas in the *Kūrma*,[41] Manu in the *Padma*,[42] Bhīma (a grandson

[1] Vālakhilyādimunayo Vyāsavālmīki-mukhyakāḥ,
Pṛthur Dilīpo Bharato Duṣmantaḥ Śatrujid Valī.
Mallaḥ Kakutsthaś cānenā Yuvanāśvo Jayadrathaḥ,
Māndhātā Mucukundaś ca pāntu tvāñ ca Purūravāḥ.
Agni-Purāṇa, ccxix. 50, 51.

These two couplets contain the following names: Pṛthu, Dilīpa, Bharata, Duṣmanta, Śatrujit, Vali, Malla, Kakutstha, Anenas, Yuvanāśva, Jayadratha, Māndhātṛ, Mucukunda, and Purūravas. These names form part of the *mantras* recited at the coronation described in the *Agni-Purāṇa*. The names are evidently those of renowned emperors invoked to bless the king who is being inaugurated.

[2] iv. 21. 9, 10. [3] ii. 24. [4] lxix. 3.

[5] *Dharma-saṃhitā*, xxiv. 65, 66. [6] lxxxviii. 144.

[7] Akhilabhūmaṇḍalapatir ativīryaparākramo 'nekayajñakṛd arātipakṣakṣayakartā tavodare *cakravartī* tiṣṭhati. *Viṣṇu-Purāṇa*, iv. 3.

[8] ix. 8. 4. [9] viii. 32. [10] *Pātāla-khaṇḍa*, iv. 116. [11] xxxii. 4.

[12] *loc. cit.* [13] xcix. 133. [14] iv. 19. 2. [15] xiii. 57.

[16] ccxix. 50. [17] *Ibid.* [18] ix. 6. 34. [19] ccxix. 51. [20] vii. 92.

[21] *loc. cit.* [22] *loc. cit.*

[23] x. 51. 51. 1st couplet. *Ślokas* 52 and 58 call him *svarāj* and *sārvabhauma*.

[24] xii. 18. [25] *Pūrva-khaṇḍa*, lxvi. 68. [26] *Pātāla-khaṇḍa*, iv. 116.

[27] xxiv. 10, 11. [28] ccxix. 51. [29] cxi. 13. [30] x. 9, 10. [31] viii. 25.

[32] *Dharma-saṃhitā*, lxi. 21 (identical with the preceding reference).

[33] viii. 27. [34] xciv. 9. [35] *Prabhāsa-khaṇḍa*, xx. 12. [36] xviii. 9.

[37] *Pūrva-khaṇḍa*, lxviii. 9. [38] xiii. 160, 166, 175.

[39] *Dharma-saṃhitā*, *Uttarabhāga*, xxiv. 35. [40] iv. 6. 6.

[41] xx. 31. [42] *Pātāla-khaṇḍa*, iv. 116.

of Purūravas) and Śamīka, a Bhoja sovereign (son of Śyāma), in the *Brahma*,[1] and Uśanas in the *Vāyu*[2] and *Liṅga*;[3] Malla, Kakutstha, Anenas, Jayadratha, and others have already been referred to in the quotation from the *Agni-Purāṇa* in connexion with Pṛthu. The *Matsya-Purāṇa*[4] mentions some *asuras* such as Hiraṇyakaśipu, Vali, &c., as overlords, while the *Devī-Purāṇa*[5] describes the *daitya* named Ghora as an Ekarāṭ. Śaśavindu, son of Citraratha, became a *Cakravartin* according to the *Liṅga-Purāṇa*.[6] Yudhiṣṭhira figures in the *Skanda-Purāṇa*[7] as the performer of a *Rājasūya* and five *Aśvamedha* sacrifices, and as the conqueror of a good many independent princes, while Dilīpa is mentioned in the *Agni-*[8] and *Padma-Purāṇas*,[9] as also in the *Mahābhārata*,[10] which enumerates a good many great kings of yore:—

Names of paramount sovereigns in the *Mahābhārata*.

1. Marutta, son of Avikṣit.
2. Suhotra, son of Atithi.
3. Bṛhadratha, the king of the Aṅgas.
4. Śivi, son of Uśīnara, who brought the whole earth under subjection.
5. Bharata, son of Duṣmanta.
6. Rāma, son of Daśaratha.
7. Bhagīratha, son of Sagara.
8. Dilīpa.
9. Māndhātṛ, son of Yuvanāśva, who subdued the whole earth extending from the place of sunrise to that of sunset.
10. Yayāti, son of Nahuṣa.
11. Ambarīṣa, son of Nābhāga, under whom were hundreds of tributary kings.
12. Śaśabindu, son of Citraratha.
13. Gaya, son of Amūrtarayas.
14. Rantideva, son of Saṃkriti.
15. Sagara of the Ikṣvāku dynasty, during whose reign 'there was but *his* umbrella opened on the whole earth'.
16. Pṛthu, son of Veṇa.

[1] x. 13; xiv. 33. [2] xcv. 23. [3] *Pūrva-khaṇḍa*, lxviii. 26.
[4] xlvii. 55–7. See also *Skanda-Purāṇa*, *Prabhāsa-khaṇḍa*, xx. 1, 2.
[5] ii. 39 ff. [6] *Pūrva-khaṇḍa*, lxviii. 25.
[7] *Nāgara-kha ḍa*, cxl. 3, 4; xxi. 51.
[8] ccxix. 50. [9] *Pātāla-khaṇḍa*, iv. 114. [10] xii. 29.

Names of paramount sovereigns in the *Kauṭilīya.*

The *Kauṭilīya*[1] mentions a few emperors who though universal lords (*cāturanta*) lost their high positions through one or other of the vices. The list contains the following names: Dāṇḍakya Bhoja, Janamejaya, Aila, Rāvaṇa, Ḍambhodbhava, Vātāpi, Vaideha Karāla, Tālajaṅgha, Ajavindu Sauvīra, Duryodhana, Haihaya Arjuna. Vṛṣṇi-Saṅgha (the autonomous community of the Vṛṣṇis) is also mentioned. Jāmadagnya, Ambarīṣa, and Nābhāga long 'ruled the earth' through righteousness.

Of these, the first six and the last two as well as the Vṛṣṇi-Saṅgha are found in the *Kāmandakīya*[2] and *Śukranīti.*[3]

Example of division of sovereignty between the king and the people in Southern India.

According to Mr. Kanakasabhai, India has seen not merely pure democracies or pure monarchies, but also constitutions in which there were hereditary monarchs between whom and the subjects there were distinct organs to restrict the powers of the former and act as buffers. In this arrangement there was an organized institution of the state to voice forth the people's views. We find examples of such an organization in each of the three kingdoms of Cera, Cola, and Pāṇḍya of the extreme south about eighteen centuries ago. There the hereditary monarch, along with the 'Five Great Assemblies'[4] consisting of the representatives of the people, priests, physicians, astrologers, and ministers respectively, wielded the sovereign-power, and not the monarch alone. The first council safeguarded the rights and privileges of the people, the second directed all religious ceremonies, and the third all matters affecting the health of the king and the public. The fourth, like the Roman augurs, fixed auspicious times for public ceremonies and predicted important events, while the fifth

[1] *Kauṭilīya,* I. vi, p. 11. See also IX. i, p. 338, for the extent of *Cakravarti-kṣetra.*

[2] *Kāmandakīya,* 54, 56, 57, 58.

[3] It has the same verses as the *Kāmandakīya.* See in this connexion Prof. R. K. Mukerji's work, *The Fundamental Unity of India* (*from Hindu Sources*), which utilizes the lists of emperors from its special point of view.

[4] *The Tamils 1800 Years Ago,* by V. Kanakasabhai, pp. 109, 110, quoting *Chilapp-athikaram,* iii. 126; v. 157; and xxvi. 38; and *Maṇimekhalai,* i. 17.

attended to the administration of justice and the collection and expenditure of revenue.[1] This system of government, there is reason to believe, as Mr. Kanakasabhai says, was not peculiar to the south, but had its original in the Magadhan Empire of the North, from which the founders of the three kingdoms had formerly migrated.

[1] Each council had a separate place in the metropolis for the transaction of its business and for holding its meetings (Kanakasabhai, p. 110).

CHAPTER II

THE STATE-COUNCIL

Terms to denote the council in Sanskrit literature.

THE Council, as a part of the administrative machinery, had its origin in very early times. The terms indicative of the existence of the institution are abundant in early Sanskrit literature. Among them may be mentioned *Sabhā*, *Samiti*, *Saṃgati*, *Vidatha*, *Pariṣad*, as also the compounds like *sabhāpati*, *sabhāpāla*, *sabhācara*, *sabhāsad*, &c. The references to the existence of this institution among the gods also point to its use by men.[1]

Their exact meanings in Vedic literature.

In Vedic literature, *Sabhā* stands for an assembly of the Vedic Indians as well as for the hall where the assembly met.[2] The *Samiti* also signifies an assembly, which according to Hillebrandt is much the same as the *Sabhā*,[3] with this distinction, that the latter points primarily to the place of assembly. *Saṃgati* seems to have the same sense as the *Samiti*.[4] *Vidatha* is a word of obscure sense, which according to Roth primarily means 'order',[5] then the 'body' that issues the order, and next the 'assembly' for secular[6] or religious ends[7] or for war.[8]

[1] *Ṛg-Veda*, x. 11. 8, mentions daivī samitiḥ; *Jaiminīya-Upaniṣad-Brāhmaṇa*, ii. 11. 13, 14 refers to the *Sabhā* of the gods.

[2] *Ṛg-Veda*, vi. 28. 6; see *V. I.* ii. 426, 427.

[3] Hillebrandt, *Vedische Mythologie*, ii. 123–5.

[4] *Ṛg-Veda*, x. 141. 4.

[5] *Ṛg-Veda*, i. 31. 6; 117. 25, etc.

[6] *Atharva-Veda*, ii. i. 4; 27. 12, 17, &c. Whitney renders the word as 'council' in the *Atharva-Veda*, i. 13. 4.

[7] *Ṛg-Veda*, i. 60. 1; ii. 4. 8, &c.

[8] *Ṛg-Veda*, i. 166, 2; 167. 6, &c. Ludwig takes the word *Vidatha* to mean primarily an assembly, specially, of the *Maghavans* (rich patrons) and *Brāhmaṇas* (see Ludwig's Translation of the *Ṛg-Veda*, iii. 259 and ff.). Geldner (e.g. in *Vedische Studien*, i. 47) and Bloomfield (*J. A. O. S.*, xix, 12 ff.) do not support Roth and Ludwig.

Pariṣad has among other senses that of the 'council of ministers of a prince'[1] in later Vedic literature.

The compound *sabhā-pāla*[2] denotes the keeper of an assembly hall, and *sabhā-pati*[3] the lord of the assembly. The *sabhā-cara*[4] and *sabhā-sad*[5] had perhaps more to do with the assembly in its legal capacity, though their connexion with it as a general deliberative body cannot be altogether denied.

Composition of the *Samiti* and *Sabhā*.

As to the composition of the *Samiti*, Ludwig holds that it included all the people, primarily the *viśaḥ* or subjects, but also the *Brāhmaṇas* and *Maghavans* (rich patrons) if they desired, though the *Sabhā* was their special assembly.[6] This view does not seem to be correct, nor is that of Zimmer,[7] who takes *Sabhā* to be a village assembly presided over by the Grāmaṇī (the village headman). Hillebrandt seems to be right in holding that the *Sabhā* and the *Samiti* cannot be distinguished and that they were both attended by the king.[8] The *Sabhā* does not seem to have counted among its members any ladies.[9] The reference to well-born (*su-jāta*) men in session in the assembly does not, according to Hillebrandt, imply one class of Aryan members as opposed to another, but the Aryan members as opposed to Dāsas or Śūdras.[10]

[1] Cf. Jolly, *Recht und Sitte*, pp. 136, 137; Foy, *Die königliche Gewalt*, pp. 16–19, 33–7, 66; Bühler, *Zeitschrift der Deutschen Morgenländischen Gesellschaft*, xlviii. 55, 56, where Bühler says that M. Senart's translation of the phrase *Parisā* or *Palisā* by 'assembly of clergy' in Asoka's Rock Edict VI is too narrow. The word stands also for royal court or *darbār*, e.g. in *Jātaka*, iii. 240, l. 7, and v. 238, l. 6, rendered by 'assembly' in Cowell's translation. See also Hillebrandt's *Vedische Mythologie*, ii. 124.

[2] *Taittirīya-Brāhmaṇa* (iii. 7. 4. 6).

[3] (In the *Śatarudrīya* in) *Vājasaneyi-Saṃhitā*, xvi. 24; *Taittirīya-Saṃhitā*, iv. 5. 3. 2; *Kāṭhaka-Saṃhitā*, xvii. 13, &c.

[4] *Vājasaneyi-Saṃhitā*, xxx. 6; *Taittirīya-Brāhmaṇa*, iii. 4. 2. 1, with Sāyaṇa's note. Cf. Weber, *Indische Streifen*, 1, 77, n. 1.

[5] *Atharva-Veda*, iii. 29. 1; vii. 12. 2; &c.

[6] Translation of the *Ṛg-Veda*, iii. 253–6.

[7] *Altindisches Leben*, pp. 172 et seq.; see *V. I.* i. 427.

[8] *Vedische Mythologie*, ii. 123–5; for a criticism of Bloomfield's (*J. A. O. S.*, xix. 13) view that *Sabhā* refers to the 'society room' in a dwelling-house, see *V. I.*, ii. 427.

[9] *Maitrāyaṇī Saṃhitā*, iv. 7. 4, 'nirindriyā strī, pumān indriyavāṃs, tasmāt pumāṃsah sabhāṃ yānti na striyah.' (Woman is weak, man is strong; hence men go to the assembly, not women.)

[10] *Ṛg-Veda*, vii. 1. 4.

Their functions in Vedic times.

The assembly or a chosen body of its members performed judicial works. We gather this indirectly from the fact of the *sabhā-cara* being dedicated to Justice (Dharma) at the Puruṣamedha (human sacrifice) in the *Yajur-Veda*,[1] from the use of the term *Sabhā* to denote a law-court, and also from the word *sabhā-sad*, which denotes a member of the assembly which met for justice as well as for general discussion on public matters. The assembly-hall was also used for other purposes, such as dicing,[2] social intercourse, and general conversation about material interests, such as cows, &c.[3]

According to Messrs. Macdonell and Keith, 'it is reasonable to assume that the business of the council was general deliberation on policy of all kinds, legislation so far as the Vedic Indian cared to legislate, and judicial work'.[4] There is, owing to the nature of the texts, little or no evidence directly bearing on the programme of business in Vedic times, for which we have to fall back upon indirect evidence from which the above inference has been drawn. Zimmer holds that it was a function of the assembly to elect the king.[5] Geldner[6] opposed him on the ground that the passages cited do not expressly indicate selection by the people (*viśah*) but acceptance by them. This point will be adverted to hereafter.

Their functions in the epics.

Coming to the epic period[7] as reflected in the *Rāmāyaṇa* and the *Mahābhārata*, we find *Sabhā* to be an assembly of any sort. It may be the law-court, the royal court, or the convivial assembly, as also a political assembly.

The *Sabhā* as a judicial assembly appears, for instance, in this passage of the *Mahābhārata*—'na sā *sabhā* yatra na santi vṛddhā, na te vṛddhā ye na vadanti dharmam',[8] i. e. 'that is no

[1] *Vājasaneyi-Saṃhitā*, xxx. 6.

[2] The assembly-hall was used for dicing when the session for public business was over. Cf. *Ṛg-Veda*, x. 34. 6; *Atharva-Veda*, v. 31 6; xii. 3. 46.

[3] *Ṛg-Veda*, vi. 28. 6; viii. 4. 9; *Atharva-Veda*, vii. 12. 2, addresses the assembly as 'nariṣṭā', i. e. merriment. *Ibid.*, vii. 12. 3, refers to serious speech in the *Sabhā*. For serious public business leavened with amusement, cf. Tacitus, *Germania*, 22.

[4] *V. I.*, ii. 431.

[5] *Altindisches Leben*, p. 175.

[6] *Vedische Studien*, ii. 203.

[7] In tracing the history of 'council' in the epic period, I have mainly followed Prof. Hopkins' article in the *J. A. O. S.*, xiii. 148-62.

[8] *MBh.*, v. 35. 58.

assembly where there are no elders; those are not elders who do not declare the law'. As a term for a convivial assembly, it is found, to take a single example, in the title of the second book of the *Mahābhārata*,[1] and as such it is akin to *saṃsad*. The compound word *sabhā-sad*, 'sitter at an assembly', means in the epic a courtier of the king's court,[2] and the *sabhāstāra* signifies only one who is at the royal court or a lower officer in the position of dice-master. Yudhiṣṭhira, during the period of his stay at Virāṭa's court, becomes a *sabhāstāra* and is very ignominiously treated. In the *Rāmāyaṇa*, the *sabhā-sads* are mere courtiers,[3] the important state duties resting on the king and his ministers, who take part in the king's council. The term *Sabhā*, therefore, in these compounds refers to the royal court.

The relations between king and council are not constitutionally fixed.

The relations that obtained between the king and the council are an interesting study. Different kings differently regard their council. Sometimes the *Kṣatriya* element is predominant, the majority of the council being recruited from the royal relations. Bhiṣma, Vidura, and Droṇa are sages and ministers, but the two first are relatives of the king and the last a fighting *Brāhmaṇa*. Kaṇika and Jābāli are also seldom consulted, and the former is not necessarily a *Brāhmaṇa*. Yudhiṣṭhira has as little to do with ministerial or Brāhmaṇic advice as his uncle Dhṛtarāṣṭra. When resolved to stake his kingdom at the gambling, he does not seek advice from anybody. Dhaumya is never sought for advice in political matters, though he is the chief priest, and never fills an officer's place of any sort until he is left in charge of the capital with Yuyutsu in the fifteenth book (*Āśramavāsika-parvan*) of the *Mahābhārata*. Duryodhana shows also similar waywardness, and consults his advisers when it suits his whim or interests. He calls the priests to advise as to the best means of raising a required sum of money, but not otherwise. Resolving on war, kings and allies both of Kurus and Pāṇḍus deliberate among themselves without consulting the priests, though they are present at the meeting. Duryodhana attends the meeting against his will, and though

[1] Cf. *Ṛg-Veda*, x. 34. 6, describing a like scene of gambling.
[2] ii. 78. 3.
[3] ii. 4. 24 (Gorresio's edition) = ii. 5. 24 (Bombay ed.).

the advice of the council is to avoid war, he remains as determined as ever, the decision of the council producing no effect upon his mind.[1]

In some parts of the *Mahābhārata*, the *Brāhmaṇa* element of the council attains predominance.

The didactic parts of the *Mahābhārata*, which are by several authorities looked upon as later than the main portion of the epic as contained in the preceding chapters, inculcate the necessity of mutual support between the temporal power of the *Kṣatriyas* and the spiritual power of the *Brāhmaṇas* for the welfare of the state.[2] The king's power is derived from wisdom, of which the *Brāhmaṇa* is the repository. Henceforth, the monarch's dependence upon the advice of the *Brāhmaṇas* becomes higher and higher.[3] The didactic portion of the *Mahābhārata* tries to make the tutor and the family priest (who are often identical) the controllers of the king's mind.[4] The king is enjoined to abide by the judgement of the family priest, who is as much conversant with the principles of polity (*Daṇḍanīti*) as with the sacred literature, and whose position as such might have brought him much worldly power. Everything of course could go on smoothly if Brāhmaṇas would always be

[1] *J. A. O. S.*, xiii. 150, referring to *Mbh.*, v. 1, 148–50.

[2] Cf. *Manu*, ix. 323 (S.B.E.)—'*Kṣatriyas* prosper not without *Brāhmaṇas*, *Brāhmaṇas* prosper not without *Kṣatriyas*; *Brāhmaṇas* and *Kṣatriyas*, being closely united, prosper in this world and in the next.'

[3] Prof. Hopkins is of opinion that the deification of the king commences from this time as his reward for exalting the priest. 'For the priest did not scruple to defy the king so long as he could himself maintain the claim of being "the god of the gods"'—*MBh.*, xiii. 152. 16'; see *J. A. O. S.*, xiii. 152, 153. The main contention of this portion of the article may be right, but injustice has been done to the unfortunate priest by the misinterpretation of this passage: he interprets i. 140. 54,

> Guror apy avaliptasya kāryākāryam ajānatah,
> Utpathapratipannasya nyāyaṃ bhavati śāsanam,

into 'The order given even by a sinful priest is good' (*J. A. O. S.*, xiii. 153). The real meaning is just the opposite, viz. 'even a preceptor, if he be vain, ignorant of what should be done and what left undone, and vicious in his ways, should be chastised.'

[4] The *Purohita* did not as a rule sit in the council properly so-called, but perhaps tried to control the king's mind and indirectly the decisions of the council by his advice to the king. 'The person usually mentioned is the *Purohita* (family priest), who may or may not have been his tutor (*guru*) but who is *ex officio* his *guru* or venerable adviser, when an appointed or inherited minister.' (*J. A. O. S.*, xiii. 155 n.) Prof. Hopkins seems to use the word *guru* in its general sense in the second case, viz. any respected person, and not in its technical meaning (*vide* ch. 'The Royal Priest').

as self-controlled and as indifferent to power as they are enjoined to be. But in the world of reality there are deviations from the ideal, giving rise to aberrations like the one depicted in this episode: 'There was once a king of the Magadhas, in the city of Rājagṛha, who was wholly dependent on his ministers. A minister of his called Mahākarṇin became the sole lord of the realm (*ekeśvara*). Inflated by his power, this man tried to usurp the throne, but failed solely because of Fate.'[1] Likewise, on the other hand, we should not suppose that the kings were in all cases equally docile in their attitude towards the *Brāhmaṇas*. Their military impatience did sometimes crop up, as evidenced in passages like this: 'the place for priests is in the hall of debate; good are they as inspectors; they can oversee elephants, horses and war-cars; they are learned in detecting the faults of food—but let not the (priestly) teachers be asked for advice when emergencies arise.'[2]

Evidences of perfect secrecy in council first appear in the epics.[3] As a corollary to this, follow the restrictions on the Secrecy in council.

[1] *MBh.*, i. 204. 16 ff.; *J. A. O. S.*, xiii. 160.

[2] *Ibid.*, iv. 47. 25 ff. In this connexion, chapter iii in Muir's *Sanskrit Texts*, part I, on the early contests between the *Brāhmaṇas* and *Kṣatriyas*, should be consulted. It gives Manu's list of 'refractory' monarchs, viz. Veṇa, Nahuṣa, Sudās the son of Pijavana, Sumukha, and Nemi (see *Manu*, vii. 41). Muir also cites Purūravas, Viśvāmitra, Paraśurāma.

The conclusions of Prof. Hopkins on the growth of political power of the *Brāhmaṇas* (*J. A. O. S.*, xiii. 161, 162) appear to me to be rather one-sided and based on insufficient data. Though the *Brāhmaṇas* appear to be responsible for the change of the open council into a secret conclave, their influence should not be taken as the only factor in the field. The state of the country, divided, as it often was, into a number of principalities, made it expedient for the monarch to have secrecy. Of course, this could have been secured by keeping secret only those matters for which secrecy was essential, thus permitting representatives of other classes to deliberate on those important matters of state regarding which publicity was not detrimental. But the course of evolution took a different direction, bringing political matters within the knowledge only of a select few in the confidence of the monarch.

[3] Prof. Hopkins says, 'Absolute secrecy in council is a *late practice* (?), but as a rule is strongly urged. The king should go to the house-top or a hill-top when he consults with his ministers. . . . Some forms of the rule specify "a secret chamber" as the place for council' (*J. A. O. S.*, xiii. 151 n.).

A few passages in the epics bearing on secrecy are *MBh.*, ii. 5. 30 [= *Rāmā.* ii. 100. 18]; v. 38. 15, 16, 20; xii. 80. 24, 49 ff. The statements in the *Purāṇas* regarding place of council, &c., also bear on secrecy of council, but they are quoted elsewhere in connexion with the aforesaid points.

number of councillors, the selection of a secret place for council, the avoidance of undesirable persons and things in and near council, and the check on councillors for divulgence of secrets.

Besides the *Mahābhārata*, there are descriptions of the council in the *Arthaśāstra*, *Smṛtis*, and *Purāṇas*, as also in several other Sanskrit works which agree with one another in main particulars.

The number of councillors is determined mainly by considerations of secrecy and dispatch of business; the number according to Kauṭilya and other writers.

Among the considerations that determine the number of councillors, the maintenance of secrecy and speedy dispatch of business are the most important. Kautilya quotes the views of several politicians on this point. The extreme view is held by Bhāradvāja, who reduces the number of the council to the king alone, the reason being that councillors have their own councillors who in their turn have others for their consultation.[1] Viśālāksa opposes the view on the ground that deliberation by oneself can never be fruitful. Persons of mature wisdom should be on the council; no opinion should be slighted. The wise make use of the sensible utterances of even a boy. Pārāśara regards this as not conducive to secrecy. Kauṭilya does not quote Pārāśara's opinion on the number of councillors, but gives us his own view, which recommends consultation with three or four councillors (*mantriṇaḥ*)[2] but not more as the general rule. He does not prohibit altogether consultation with a single or two councillors, or even deliberation without their aid in exceptional cases depending upon the time, place, and nature of the business on hand.

The number according to the epics.

As to the number of councillors, we find the same injunction

There is a passage in the *Mārkaṇḍeya-Purāṇa* (xxvii. 5) which as a general injunction should be placed here—Ātmā ripubhyaḥ saṃrakṣyo bahirmantravinirgamāt. Cf. *Manu*, vii. 148; *Yājñavalkya*, i. 344; *Kāmandakīya-Nītisāra*, xi. 53, &c.; and *Kālikā-Purāṇa*, lxxxiv. 107, 108; see also *Raghuvaṃśa*, xvii. 50.

[1] *Arthaśāstra*, I. xv, p. 27.

[2] The reasons for which he recommends three or four ministers are that consultation with a single councillor leads to no definite conclusion on difficult problems. Moreover, the councillor may act waywardly. In consultation with two councillors, the king may be overpowered by their combination or ruined by their enmity. With three or four councillors, he does not meet with serious harm, but arrives at satisfactory results. If the number of councillors be larger, conclusions are arrived at with difficulty and secrecy is hard to maintain. See *ibid.*, p. 28.

in the *Purāṇas* as in the didactic portions of the *Rāmāyaṇa*[1] and *Mahābhārata*.[2] The *Matsya-Purāṇa*[3] advises the king never to make a decision alone nor to consult many in regard to a matter of state. The same is the injunction of the *Agni-Purāṇa*[4] which is followed up by the later *Kālikā*[5]—and *Bṛhaddharma*[6]—*Purāṇas*. According to the *Purāṇas*.

The directions as to the places suitable for holding the council evidently contemplate two states of things, viz. when the monarch is in his palace as ordinarily, and when he is elsewhere at other times, as, for instance, during war. Place of holding council meetings.

In the *Mahābhārata*, a secret place in the royal palace (*prāsādaṃ vā raho gataḥ*) is recommended in the former case, and *giripṛṣtha* (hill-top), an open space cleared of *kuśa* and *kāśa* grass (*śūnyaṃ sthalaṃ prakāśaṃ kuśakāśalīnam*), a place in a forest devoid of weeds (*araṇye niḥśalāke*), and a boat (*nau*) are recommended in the latter case.[7] Kauṭilya enjoins a similarly secret place with an eye to absolute seclusion. It should be a secluded spot, not visible even to birds, and also such as permits no sound to escape outside.[8] The injunctions in *Manu*[9] bear almost a *verbatim* resemblance to the two verses from the *Mahābhārata*, v. 38. 17, 18. The *Kālikā-Purāṇa* seems to be the only *Purāṇa* that speaks of the place for council.[10] The *Kāmandakīya*[11] is very explicit on this point. It says that council should be held by the king unwatched by others in the royal palace at a spot having no pillars, windows, Precautions for secrecy.

[1] ii. 100. 18 (a small number only to be consulted).

[2] ii. 5. 30 (MBh. *loc. cit.*); xii. 83. 47 (at least three councillors to be consulted).

[3] ccxx. 37. [4] ccxxv. 18–20. [5] lxxxiv. 104, 105.

[6] *Uttara-khaṇḍa*, iii. 3. [7] v. 38. 17, 18; xii. 83. 57.

[8] Taduddeśaḥ saṃvṛtaḥ kathānām anisrāvī pakṣibhir apy anālokyas syāt. —*Arthaśāstra*, I. xv, p. 26. Mr. R. Śyāma Śāstrī appears to be incorrect in his translation of *uddeśaḥ* into 'subject-matter of a council'. It should be evidently '*spot* for a council'.

[9] *Manu*, vii. 147:

> Giripṛṣṭhaṃ samāruhya prāsādaṃ vā raho gataḥ,
> Araṇye niḥśalāke vā mantrayed avibhāṣitaḥ.

In the translation of this couplet, Bühler has 'solitary' for 'niḥśalāke', pursuant to the commentaries of Nārāyaṇa, Kullūkabhaṭṭa, and Rāghavānanda. Medhātithi, Govindarāja, and Nandanācārya interpret it as 'free from grass and so forth'.

[10] lxxxiv. 105, 106. [11] ii. 66.

clefts, or any thing that might harbour an eavesdropper, or in a forest.

The vicinity of the council is to be kept clear of dwarfs, idiots, eunuchs, women, the crooked, lame, blind, and emaciated, as also animals. Kauṭilya likewise taboos the animals, on the ground that the parrot (*śuka*), Mainā (*śāri*, i.e. either the Gracula Religiosa, or Turdus Salica), dog, and other animals are known to have divulged council-secrets.[1] The *Mānava*[2] injunction, as also that of the *Kālikā-Purāṇa*,[3] is almost to the same effect.

According to Kauṭilya, cabinet secrets can leak out through the *pramāda* (carelessness), *mada* (intoxication), *suptapralāpa* (talk during sleep), and kāmādi (sensuality, &c.) of councillors.[4] Passages in the *Mahābhārata*,[5] *Agni-Purāṇa*[6] and *Kāmandakīya*[7] repeat similar causes of violation of cabinet-secrecy.

The business of the council according to Kauṭilya.

It is stated by Messrs. Macdonell and Keith that it is reasonable to assume that the business of the council in Vedic times was general deliberation on policy of all kinds and legislation so far as the Vedic Indian cared to legislate, of which, however, little or no evidence is directly available, perhaps as a result of the nature of the texts.[8]

More light is thrown by later literature upon the programme of work of the council in subsequent times. The details of work given by Viśālākṣa as quoted in the *Kauṭilīya* are:

(1) *anupalabdhasya jñāna*, 'knowledge of the unperceived;'

(2) *upalabdhasya niścayabalādhāna*, 'making certain of the perceived;'

(3) *arthadvaidhasya saṃśayacchedana*, 'removal of doubts regarding a subject susceptible of differences of opinion;' and

(4) *ekadeśadṛṣṭasya śeṣopalabdhi*, 'cognisance of the whole of a subject, a part of which is perceived.'[9]

[1] *Arthaśāstra*, I. xv, p. 26. It refers to the avoidance of the disguised and despicable by the words *pracchanna* and *avamata* in line 1, p. 27.

[2] vii. 149, 150.

[3] lxxiv. 106, 107.

[4] *Arthśāstra*, *loc. cit.*, pp. 26, 27.

[5] v. 39. 38, 39.

[6] ccxli. 6. The divulgence of political secrets is made the subject of capital punishment in the *Kauṭilīya*, *loc. cit.*, p. 26.

[7] *Kāmandakīya*, xi. 65.

[8] *Vedic Index*, ii. 431.

[9] *Arthaśāstra*, *loc. cit.*, p. 27.

According to Kauṭilya himself, the agenda comprises deliberation as to the following five items:—

(1) means of commencing operations (*karmaṇām ārambhopāya*);

(2) providing men and materials (*puruṣadravyasampad*);

(3) distribution of place and time (*deśakālavibhāga*);

(4) counteraction of disaster (*vinipātapratīkāra*); and

(5) successful accomplishment (*kārya siddhi*).[1]

These five aspects are to be duly considered in regard to every item of work put before the council for consideration, the councillors being questioned both individually and collectively,[2] and their opinions being always accompanied by reasons.[3]

The business according to the *Agni-Purāṇa* and *Kāmandakīya*.

The continuance in later times of the traditional list of duties of the council is evidenced by passages in the *Agni-Purāṇa* and *Kāmandakīya*.[4]

Kāmandaka adds two points, one of which is perhaps implied in the *Kauṭilīya* passages, while the other is not mentioned at all. The first is that an item of the council-agenda should be discussed again and again before its final disposal.[5] The second is that the matter already resolved upon in the council should again be deliberated upon by the monarch himself in order that all flaws may be removed therefrom.[6] Should a flaw be found, reference is perhaps again made to the council.

Yājñavalkya's injunction.

Yājñavalkya interposes an additional stage in the procedure; after the passage of a measure through the council, it is to be referred by the monarch to his domestic priest for his opinion.[7] Most probably, the priest

[1] *Arthaśāstra*, *loc. cit.*, p. 28

[2] *Ibid.*, p. 28—tān ekaikaśaḥ pṛcchet samastāṃś ca. The commentator of the *Kāmandakīya* quotes this very passage from Kauṭilya in support of xi. 69, praviśet svahitānveṣī matam eṣām pṛthak pṛthak.

[3] Mr. R. Śyāma Śāstrī has translated the word matipravivekān (*ibid.*, p. 28) differently. I think it should be translated 'individual opinions', praviveka meaning 'separateness'.

[4] ccxli. 3, 4. These two couplets sum up the details of work mentioned by Viśālākṣa and Kauṭilya together. The same two verses, with one or two unimportant variations, occur in the *Kāmandakīya*, xi. 50, 56.

[5] The text in Mr. Jīvānanda's edition of the *Kāmandakīya*, xi. 64, begins with 'nāvarttayet, &c.', which has been rejected by the commentator of the Bibl. Indica edition, wherein another passage to the above effect has been accepted.

[6] *Kāmandakīya*, xi. 60.

[7] i. 312.

judged of it from the astrological point of view, suggesting changes if necessary. After the priest's approval, he subjects it to further personal deliberation as already stated.[1]

When a resolution is approved, it is recommended that it be acted upon at the earliest opportunity. The *Rāmāyaṇa*,[2] *Mahābhārata*,[3] *Kauṭilīya*,[4] and *Kāmandakīya*[5] are at one on this point. The last treatise enjoins a fresh discussion on the resolution, if it is not carried out at the opportune time.[6]

Some time, however, generally elapses between the formation of a resolution and its performance. During this period the secrecy of the resolution follows as a corollary to the secrecy maintained in its previous stages. Its divulgence may take place through what Kauṭilya calls *ākāra* (lit. appearance, explained by Kauṭilya as the interpretation of the physical expression), and *iṅgita* (i.e. behaviour disturbed by strong emotion), of the envoy, minister, and king himself.[7]

Need for secrecy before action is taken.

This instruction for the suppression of external expressions should not be mistaken *as a caution* against divulgence of secrets among the councillors themselves *when the council is in session*. There is no passage to that effect in the *Kauṭilīya*, but there are passages regarding the maintenance of order, &c., in the council in other works such as the *Mahābhārata*.[8] The periods for holding the council have been touched upon in connexion with the king's daily routine of work. There is

[1] *Kāmandakīya* (xi. 70) recommends the acceptance, among all the suggestions, of that of a numerously supported, intelligent, well-wishing councillor, whose counsel is in accordance with the *Śāstras*.

[2] ii. 100. 19.

[3] ii. 5. 31, a verse almost identical with that of the *Rāmāyaṇa*.

[4] *Ibid.*, *loc. cit.*, p. 28—Avāptārthaḥ kālaṃ nātikrāmayet.

[5] xi. 72, 73.

[6] *Ibid.*, xi. 71.

[7] *Arthaśāstra*, *loc. cit.*, p. 26—mantrabhedo hi dūtāmātyasvāminām iṅgitākārābhyām. Iṅgitam anyathāvṛttiḥ. Ākṛtigrahaṇam ākaraḥ. Iṅgita = anyathāvṛttiḥ, which means, according to Monier Williams' *Dictionary*, 'behaviour disturbed by strong emotion.' Mr. R. Śyāma Śāstrī's translation of these passages is confused.

[8] xii. 83. 57:

> . . . Vāgādi-doṣān parihṛtya sarvān
> Sammantrayet kāryam ahīnakālam,

and the comments of Nīlakaṇṭha in this connexion, viz. vāgdoṣa = loud speaking, &c., aṅgadoṣa = distortion of eyes, mouth, &c.; with these one should not insult or scold another.

no limit to the time for which a session may last except the existence of the next time-division allotted to some other works. If, however, there are at the king's council members who are partisans of those whom he desires to injure, a prolonged session is prohibited by Kauṭilya.[1]

The counc and *Mantri-pariṣa* are not identical bodies, as usually assumed

In this connexion, we should note the difference between the council and the *Mantri-pariṣad*, as it is generally overlooked.[2] Kauṭilya,[3] in the chapter on council, first discusses the proper number of councillors to be allowed at each sitting. Next, he discusses the number of ministers that should form the *Mantri-pariṣad*. He quotes the opinions of a few political schools recommending different numbers, that of Manu going in for *twelve*, and those of Bṛhaspati and Uśanas for *sixteen* and *twenty* respectively. Kauṭilya himself is for the number to be commensurate with the strength of the State (to retain their services and provide work enough for them all).[4]

The *Pariṣad* most probably did not comprise the whole number of councillors in the royal *entourage* including the principal ministers. The commentary in the Bibliotheca Indica edition of the *Kāmandakīya* states that the *Pariṣad* was in addition to the three or four principal councillors.

The functions of the *Mantri-pariṣad* according to Kauṭilya.

The duties of the members of the *Mantri-pariṣad* are outlined by Kauṭilya: they comprised matters regarding both the monarch and his enemies—the commencement of work not begun (*akṛtārambha*), completion of works begun (*ārabdhā-nuṣṭhāna*), improvement of accomplished works (*anuṣṭhita-viśeṣa*), and proper execution of the orders passed (*niyoga-sampad*).[5]

[1] *Arthaśāstra, loc. cit.*, p. 29—na dīrghakālaṃ mantrayeta ca teṣāṃ pakṣair yeṣām apakuryāt.

[2] It has been overlooked for instance by Mr. M. N. Dutt, who in his translation of the *Kāmandakīya* (xi. 75, p. 180, corresponding to xi. 68 in the Bibl. Indica text), refers to the admission of as many councillors as are available into the *cabinet*. Apart from the mistake that creeps into the rendering for other reasons, the choice of the word 'cabinet' for *pariṣad* has caused an error.

[3] *Arthaśāstra, loc. cit.*

[4] *Ibid.*, p. 29. The substance of these passages has been versified by Kāmandaka in the *Kāmandakīya*, xi. 67, 68.

[5] *Ibid.*, p. 29. The commentary on the *Kāmandakīya* (Bibl. Indica)

It appears that the members of the *Mantri-pariṣad* did not ordinarily take part in the council, but only looked after their respective charges, thus assisting the supreme councillors. The king consulted only the latter as a matter of course, calling the former as well only in connexion with urgent works.[1] When the chief councillors and the members of the *Pariṣad* coalesced to form the council, the sovereign followed either the advice of the majority, or the one appealing to him as most conducive to success.[2]

The use of the term *Pariṣad* in the *Smṛtis.*

The word *Pariṣad* is generally used in the *Smṛtis*,[3] as also in later Sanskrit literature, to signify a judicial assembly. The epics sometimes use it as a synonym of *Sabhā* (i.e. the royal court), in which the subjects may be present together with the councillors.[4]

The *Pariṣad* in the *Mahābhārata.*

There is a long passage in the *Mahābhārata* which may be easily interpreted if read in the light thrown by some of the aforesaid works on the nature of the council and its relation to the *Pariṣad.* It states that four *Brāhmaṇas*, eight *Ksatriyas.* twenty-one *Vaiśyas*, three *Śūdras*, and one *Sūta*, each with qualifications specified, should be appointed ministers by a king. Of these thirty-seven ministers, nine only should be eligible to hold counsel with the king; and it was from among these nine that the number of councillors required for a single cabinet-sitting was recruited. Such being the case, the nine

quotes a *śloka* which does not appear in the text and which speaks of works being entrusted to five, seven, or more councillors. The *śloka* is as follows :—

Ekatra pañca saptāpi vaiṣamya-kriyayā yutāḥ,
Mantriṇo bhūbhujā kāryā iti kecid vadanti vai.

The comment on 'ekatra' says that it means a particular work consisting either in controlling a province, making peace, or declaring war with another sovereign, exploiting mines, collecting revenue, or protecting subjects' properties. The comment next speaks of the appointment of councillors to different works, or different portions of the same piece of work, requiring varying abilities for their performance, and adds that '*api*' in 'pañca saptāpi' denotes the appointment of more councillors if necessary.

[1] *Arthaśāstra, loc. cit.*, p. 29—Ātyayike kārye mantriṇo mantripariṣadaṃ cāhūya brūyāt.

[2] *Ibid.*—Tatra yad bhūyiṣṭhāḥ kārya-siddhikaraṃ vā brūyus tat kuryāt.

[3] Cf. *Vasiṣṭha*, iii. 20; *Manu*, xii. 111; *Baudhāyana*, I. 1. 1. 8; *Parāśara*, viii. 34.

[4] Cf. *Rāmāyaṇa* (Gorresio), ii. 114. 1; also *MBh.*, xvi. 3. 17.

ministers should be called principal ministers (*mantriṇaḥ* as Kauṭilya calls them) and the rest *mantri-pariṣad*. Nīlakaṇṭha appears to be under a misconception in his comments on this point. He limits the principal councillors to be the four Brāhmaṇas, three Śūdras, and one Sūta—an arrangement that is unwarranted by the text as well as by the works on polity.[1]

Résumé.

From the above account, it appears that the council of the Vedic period was more or less of a democratic character. It was long in abeyance in the epic period, but towards its close it emerges in a modified form as a potent institution regarded as essential to the conduct of government. Changed though it was in its character, it asserted itself as an important adjunct of statecraft, counsel, according to Kauṭilya, being essential to the commencement of every political action.[2] It became secret and exclusive, and developed another body, the *Pariṣad*, to which it stood in a close relation. The changes introduced adapted it to the new standpoint from which the Hindu statesman of the time continued to govern the state and which is noted in Sanskrit works beginning with the epics.

> Nāsya cchidraṃ paraḥ paśyec chidreṣu paraṁ anviyāt,
> Gūhet kūrma ivāṅgāni rakṣed vivaram ātmanaḥ.[3]

[i.e. his (the king's) enemy must not know his weaknesses, but he must find out those of his enemy; as the tortoise hides its limbs, so let him secure the members (of his government against treachery), let him protect his own weak points.]

[1] See *MBh.*, xii. 85. 6-11, and Nīlakaṇṭha's comments thereon. In addition to what I think to be a misconception of the commentator, there is what appears to me to be an exegetical error in connexion with *śloka* 9, in which he interprets *pañcāśad-varṣa-vayasam* (fifty years old) to be a qualifiying epithet for all the thirty-seven ministers, leaving the succeeding ones to be qualificatory of the last-mentioned Sūta alone. All the adjectives, to be logical, should, however, be taken either as qualifying *all the ministers*, or the *Sūta alone*.

[2] Cf. *Kauṭilīya*, *loc. cit.*, p. 26—Mantra-pūrvās sarvārambhāḥ. The *Kāmandakīya* (xi. 75) speaks of the evil arising from the monarch's disregard of the advice of his council.

[3] *MBh.*, xiii. 83. 49. Cf. *Kauṭilīya*, p. 29—

> Nāsya guhyaṃ pare vidyuś chidraṃ vidyāt parasya ca,
> Gūhet kūrma ivāṅgāni yat syād vivṛtam ātmanaḥ.

Cf. *Manu*, vii. 105, with Bühler's translation (followed above), and also *Raghuvaṃśa*, xvii. 61.

CHAPTER III

THE ROYAL PRIEST

VEDIC PERIOD.

THE royal priest (*purohita* = lit. placed in front, appointed) is an important personage from the very earliest times of which we have record. *Name of the priest's office.* His office is called *purohiti*[1] or *purodhā*,[2] and his formal installation to this office was celebrated by the performance of a sacrifice named *Bṛhaspati-sava* mentioned in some of the *Brāhmaṇas*.[3] *Ceremony for appointment.* His post should be distinguished from those of the 'sacrificial priests' (*ṛtvijaḥ*) whose duties were solely with the performances of the sacrifices. *'Sacrificial priest' distinguished.* *Duties.* The *Purohita* also took part in the sacrifices as *Hotṛ*, the singer of the most important of the songs, and as general supervisor of the whole conduct of the rituals, of which particular portions were entrusted to particular *ṛtviks* with special names; and when, later on, there was a decline in importance of the hymns recited by *Hotṛ*, and the greatest weight was attached to the general supervision and repairing of flaws in sacrifices by the priest's direct exercise of supposed supernatural powers, the *Purohita* acted in the new capacity of *Brahman* instead of as *Hotṛ*.[4] In addition to this sacrificial duty, he was the adviser of the sovereign in all religious matters.[5]

Purohita's peculiar duties It was spiritual and religious duties that gave him influence over the monarch, not only in domestic and religious, but also

[1] *RV.* vii. 60. 12; 83. 4.

[2] Mentioned in the *Atharva-Veda* (v. 24. 1) and later.

[3] *Taittirīya-Brāhmaṇa*, ii. 7. 1. 2; *Pañcaviṁśa-Brāhmaṇa*, xvii. 11. 4; xxv. 1. 1. 7. Cf. *Kāṭhaka-Saṁhitā*, xxxvii. 7.

[4] There is a difference of opinion between Oldenberg (*Religion des Veda*, pp. 380 ff.), and Geldner (*Vedische Studien*, ii. pp. 143 ff.), as to whether the *Purohita* acted as *Brahman* priest (general supervisor of the sacrificial rituals) from the time of the *Ṛg-Veda*. The former is correct, according to the *V. I.*, i. 113, 114, and has been followed here. (See also *V. I.*, ii. 78).

[5] *V. I.*, i. 113.

in all important secular matters, including public and political questions.[1] It was through these duties that the tie between him and the sovereign was knit tight. Upon him depended, at a certain time of the Vedic period and later on, the propitiation of the gods on the king's behalf, for the gods would not accept the offerings otherwise than from his hands.[2] The sacrifice for the monarch was intended to bring about not merely his personal welfare but also indirectly that of his people, without whose prosperity no king can be prosperous. Hence the 'prayer for welfare'[3] in sacrifices, though expressly mentioning the priest and the king, refers indirectly to the people also in connexion with the prosperity of both cattle and agriculture. The *Purohita* procured the fall of rain for the crops,[4] guarded the kingdom like a flaming fire, for which he was called *rāṣṭragopa* ('the protector of the realm'), ensured the king's power over his subjects[5] and his safety and victory in battle.[6] Divodāsa in trouble was rescued by Bharadvāja.[7] The *Purohita* accompanied the king to battle at times and, like the clergy of mediaeval Europe, was not perhaps unprepared to fight,[8] e.g. Viśvāmitra[9] seems to have

giving him influence, political and otherwise.

[1] *V.I.*, ii. 90, 214.

[2] *Aitareya-Brāhmaṇa*, viii. 24. Zimmer (*Altindisches Leben*, pp. 195, 196) thinks that, at this stage even, the king could act as his own *Purohita*, citing King Viśvantara, who, according to him, sacrificed without the help of the Śyāparṇas (*Aitareya-Brāhmaṇa*, vii. 27; Muir, *Sanskrit Texts*, v. 436–40), and Devāpi, who acted as *Purohita* for his brother on a particular occasion (*RV.* x. 98. 11). The *V.I.*, ii. 6. 7, opposes this view on the grounds that the text quoted does not say that Viśvantara sacrificed without priests, and that Devāpi is not regarded as king nor as a *Kṣatriya* and brother of Śantanu in the *Ṛg-Veda*. It is Yāska only who in his *Nirukta* (ii. 10) expresses this opinion, which there is no reason to suppose correct.

[3] *Vājasaneyi-Saṃhitā*, xxii. 22; *Taittirīya-Saṃhitā*, vii. 5. 18; *Maitrāyaṇī-Saṃhitā*, iii. 12. 6; *Kāṭhaka-Saṃhitā*, v. 5. 14, &c.

[4] *RV.*, x. 98.

[5] *Aitareya-Brāhmaṇa*, viii. 24, 25.

[6] *AV.*, iii. 18; *RV.*, vii. 18. 13, from which Geldner (*Vedische Studien*, ii. 135, n. 3) holds in opposition to Hopkins (*J.A.O.S.*, xv, 263 n.) that the priest (Viśvāmitra) prayed in the 'house of assembly' (*Sabhā*) for the victory of his *yajamāna* against Sudās while the former was on the battle-field. Cf. *Āśvalāyana-Gṛhya-Sūtra*, iii. 12 (specially last two paragraphs), 19, 20.

[7] *Pañcaviṃśa-Brāhmaṇa*, xv. 3, 7.

[8] See *RV.*, iii. 53. 12, 13; i. 129. 4; 152. 7; 157. 2; vii. 83. 4; x. 38; 103, &c.; Ludwig, *Transl. of the Ṛg-Veda*, iii. 220–6; Geldner, *Vedische Studien*, ii. 135 n. 3.

[9] Hopkins, *J.A.O.S.*, xv. 260 ff. (*V.I.*, ii. 275).

joined Sudās's enemies and taken part in the attack of the ten kings against him, while Vasiṣṭha assisted him.[1] An indication of this close relation may also be found in the reproach of King Tryaruṇa Traidhātva Aikṣvāka to his domestic priest Vṛśa Jāna when both were out in a chariot, and, owing to excessive speed in driving, ran over a *Brāhmaṇa* boy to death. As Vṛśa held the reins, they accused each other. The Ikṣvākus being consulted threw the responsibility on the priest, who revived the boy.[2] The good will of the priest and his mediation with the higher powers were looked upon as essential by the king and the people for the prosperity of the kingdom. The connexion between the *Brāhmaṇas* and the *Kṣatriyas* was recognized generally as indispensable to the welfare of both, and the close relation between the monarch and his *Purohita* was but an offshoot of that connexion, where amity was more needed than anywhere else.[3]

Disputes between the king and his *Purohita*.

In spite of this close connexion, they at times fell out with each other. Viśvantara Sauṣadmana ('descendant of Suṣadman') set aside his priests, the Śyāparṇas, and performed a sacrifice presumably with the aid of other priests, but Rāma Mārgaveya, their leader, succeeded in bringing about their reinstatement.[4] The disputes between Janamejaya and his priests, the Kaśyapas,[5] between Asamāti and the Gaupāyanas,[6] and between Kutsa Aurava and his priest Upagu Sauśravasa, killed for paying homage to Indra, to whom the former was hostile,[7] may also be instanced. But such quarrels were not

[1] *RV.*, vii. 18. The Bhṛgus appear with the Druhyus perhaps as their priests in the above battle, but this is not certain. See *RV.*, viii. 3, 9; 6. 18; 102. 4; vii. 18. 6; ix. 101. 13. (Hopkins, *J. A. O. S.*, xv. 262 n.)

[2] *Pañcaviṃśa-Brāhmaṇa*, xiii. 3. 12. In the Tāṇḍaka recension cited in Sāyaṇa on *RV.*, v. 2, Trasadasyu is given as the king's name. The story with some variations also occurs in other works, e. g. the *Bṛhaddevatā*, and *Jaiminīya-Brāhmana*.

[3] Cf. Hopkins, *J. A. O. S.*, xiii. 76; *V. I.*, i. 204.

[4] *Aitareya-Brāhmaṇa*, vii. 27. 3, 4; 34. 7, 8. Cf. Muir, *Sanskrit Texts*, i. 431–40; Eggeling, *S. B. E.*, xliii. 344 n.

[5] *Aitareya-Brāhmaṇa*, vii. 27, 35.

[6] *Jaiminīya-Brāhmaṇa*, iii. 167 (*J. A. O. S.*, xviii. 41 ff.); Śāṭyāyanaka, cited in Sāyaṇa on *RV.*, x. 57. 1; 60. 7; *Bṛhaddevatā*, vii. 83 ff. with Macdonell's notes; *Pañcaviṃśa-Brāhmaṇa*, xiii. 12. 5.

[7] *Pañcaviṃśa-Brāhmana*, xiv. 6, 8.

looked upon as conducive to the common weal, especially for the belief that the *Brāhmaṇa*, not to speak of the *Purohita*, could ruin the *Kṣatriya* by embroiling him with the people,[1] or with other *Kṣatriyas* by means of sacrifices.[2]

Political control over the priest maintained on the whole.

On the whole, however, the king and his priest went on amicably, the latter willingly submitting to the limits to his powers, which enabled the former to maintain a general political control over the priest and persons of his caste.[3]

The origin of power of the *Purohita* and priesthood.

The power of the *Purohita* and the *Brāhmaṇas* generally owed its existence to a considerable extent to the sacrifices and the special lore required therefor. When the sacrifices increased in number and therewith the amount of sacred lore needed for conducting them with strict faithfulness to all their details, there grew up a hereditary class devoted to the work. The creation of the office of the *Purohita* followed as a corollary. This office should not be regarded as the origin of the power of priesthood. The origin lay in the sacrifices. The establishment of the *Purohita*-ship no doubt served to ensure and stereotype the power and become the nucleus of further powers.[4]

Originally, the prince could be his own *Purohita*. The time when the office of *Purohita* arose.

Previous to the origin of caste and even in the period when their functions were not yet stereotyped, the king could sacrifice for himself and his subjects unaided. Devāpi, a prince, is described in the *Nirukta*[5] acting as a *Purohita* on a particular occasion. This would imply that, at the time the remark was made, no hesitation was felt in assigning to the prince the duties of a *Brāhmaṇa*—an indication of the

[1] *Taittirīya-Saṃhitā*, ii. 2. 11. 2; *Maitrāyaṇī-Saṃhitā*, i. 6. 5; ii. 1. 9; iii. 3, 10; *Kāṭhaka-Saṃhitā*, xxix. 5, &c.

[2] *Maitrāyaṇī-Saṃhitā*, iii. 3, 10, &c.

[3] A passage of the *Aitareya-Brāhmaṇa* (vii. 29) bearing on the relations and functions of the castes says that a *Brāhmaṇa* is a receiver of gifts (*ā-dāyī*), a drinker of Soma (*ā-pāyī*), . . . and *yathākāma-prayāpyaḥ*, i.e. liable to removal at will. Muir (*Sanskrit Texts*, i. 436), Haug (transl. of the *Aitareya-Brāhmaṇa*), and Weber (*Indische Studien*, x. 14) take the word as active in sense and interpret it as 'moving at will'. But a passive causative sense being required, the probable reference, according to the *V. I.* (ii. 255), is to the political control of the sovereign over the priest, whom he can move on from place to place.

[4] See Oldenberg's *Religion des Veda*, pp. 382, 383.

[5] Here Yāska (*Nirukta*, ii. 10) puts his own explanation on *RV.*, x. 98.

state of things up to the time of the *Nirukta*.[1] Viśvāmitra, according to some of the *Brāhmaṇas*,[2] was a priest and a prince. Śunaḥśepa is mentioned in the *Aitareya-Brāhmaṇa*[3] as acquiring the learning of the Gāthins and the sovereignty of the Jahnus. Prince Dhṛtarāṣṭra[4] Vaicitravīrya ('descendant of Vicitravīrya') appears in the *Kāṭhaka-Saṃhitā*[5] as engaged in a dispute on a ritual-matter with Vaka Dālbhya. In the *Ṛg-Veda*, the use of the term '*varṇa*' (lit. colour contrasting the *dāsa* with the *ārya*, and indicative only of classes and not of castes) is not conclusive for the question,[6] the *puruṣasūkta*,[7] 'hymn of man,' of the same work clearly contemplating the division of men into four orders—*Brāhmaṇa*, *Rājanya*, *Vaiśya*, and *Śūdra*. The hymn is, however, admittedly late, and its evidence cannot apply to the bulk of the hymns composed at earlier dates.[8] On some of these and other grounds, Zimmer has very forcibly maintained the view that it was produced in a society that knew no caste-system,[9] and pointed out that the *Pañcaviṃśa-Brāhmaṇa*[10] shows the Vedic Indians on the Indus as being without the system, the Veda being the product of Aryan tribes who, after removing farther east from the Indus region and the Punjab, developed the organization. According to this opinion, therefore, the office of *Purohita* could have arisen some time after the settlement of the Aryans on the Indian soil. This view of the development of caste has been generally accepted, and may be regarded as the recognized version.

[1] For the comparative lack of fixity of caste in the Vedic period, see *V. I.*, ii. 249, 251, 260, 263, 334, 390.

[2] *Pañcaviṃśa-Brāhmaṇa*, xxi. 12; *Aitareya-Brāhmaṇa*, vii. 17. 6, 7.

[3] *Aitareya-Brāhmaṇa*, vii. 18. 9; also *V. I.*, ii. 224, 312, and i. 280, 281.

[4] Probably Dhṛtarāṣṭra of the *Śatapatha-Brāhmaṇa* (xiii. 5. 4. 22), king of Kāśī.

[5] *Kāṭhaka-Saṃhitā*. i. 2. 13; 12. 1.

[6] *V. I.*, ii. 247.

[7] *RV.*, x. 90. 12.

[8] Max Müller, *Sanskrit Literature*, pp. 570 ff.; Muir, *Sanskrit Texts*, i. 7–15; Weber, *Indische Studien*, ix. 3 ff.; Colebrooke, *Essays*, i. 309; Arnold, *Vedic Metre*, p. 167.

[9] Zimmer, *Altindisches Leben*, pp. 185, 203.

[10] *Pañcaviṃśa-Brāhmaṇa*, xvii. 1. See also Muir's *Sanskrit Texts*, i. 239 ff., specially 258. (*V. I.*, ii. 248, 249.)

Some scholars, however, such as Haug,[1] Kern,[2] Ludwig,[3] and more recently Oldenberg[4] and Geldner,[5] incline to the opposite opinion. If we base our conclusion upon the data supplied by these scholars, the rise of the *Purohita*-ship has to be put much earlier.

Professors Macdonell and Keith take the *via media*, holding that the caste-system has progressively developed, and while on the one hand it is not justifiable to see in the *Ṛg-Veda* the full-fledged caste-system of the *Yajur-Veda*, so, on the other, it is not right to doubt that it was, at that time, already well on its way to general acceptance.[6]

The creation of the office of *Purohita*, therefore, should lie between the chronological limits of the two extreme views. In any case, it does not appear possible at present to locate the period with greater precision owing to the nature of the data from which the inference has to be drawn. This, however, is certain, that the office came into being very early, and that it was synchronous with the first emergence of the rigidity of caste.

A king had only one *Purohita* at a time.

The *Purohitas* in the *Ṛg-Veda* are Vasiṣṭha and Viśvāmitra already mentioned, Kavaṣa of King Kuruśravaṇa,[7] and, according to Yāska, Devāpi of Śantanu for the nonce.[8] A king had only one *Purohita* at a time.[9] In later Vedic literature we meet with many names of royal priests.

[1] *Brahma und die Brahmanen* (1871).

[2] *Indische Theorien over de Standenverdeeling* (1871). Cf. for this and the previous work, Muir's *Sanskrit Texts*, ii. 454 ff.

[3] *Die Nachrichten des Ṛig und Atharva-Veda über Geographie, Geschichte und Verfassung des alten Indien*, pp. 36 ff.; *Transl. of the RV.*, iii. 237–43, &c.

[4] *Religion des Veda*, pp. 373 ff.; cf. *Zeitschrift der Deutschen Morgenländischen Gesellschaft*, li. 267 ff.

[5] *Vedische Studien*, ii. 146 n.

[6] For the arguments that diminish the force of Geldner's view, see *V. I.*, ii. 250–2.

[7] *RV.*, x. 33; Geldner, *Vedische Studien*, ii. 150, 184. [8] See above.

[9] Geldner, *op. cit.*, ii. 144, thinks that several *Purohitas* were possible. The grounds given are not sound. The example of Asamāti and the Gaupāyanas cited by him cannot be relied on as to the number of priests (Oldenberg, *Religion des Veda*, p. 375, n. 3), while the simultaneous *Purohita*-ship of Viśvāmitra and Vasiṣṭha is not probable (Hopkins, *J. A. O. S.*, xv. 260 ff.). Everywhere else *Purohita* is mentioned in the singular, and as there was one *Brahman* priest at the sacrifice, the *Purohita* was one only. (See *V. I.*, ii. 5, n. 4.)

The same *Purohita* for more than one king.

A single *Brāhmaṇa* could have acted as priest for more than one king simultaneously. Devabhāga Śrautarṣi appears as the 'domestic priest' of both the Kurus and the Sṛñjayas,[1] while Jala Jātūkarṇya for the three kings of Kāśī, Kośala, and Videha.[2] Such a simultaneous *Purohita*-ship could not but be rare, depending as it did to a great extent upon amity among the kings supplied with the priestly ministration.

Purohita's office, whether hereditary.

It cannot be ascertained with certainty whether the office of the *Purohita* was hereditary in a particular family. It is clear, however, from the relations of the *Purohita* with King Kuruśravaṇa and his son Upamaśravas that the priest of his father was sometimes kept on by the son.[3] In course of time the priest's connexion with the sovereign appears to have assumed permanency, and probably became hereditary.[4]

Brāhmaṇas excluded from kingship.

The *Brāhmaṇas* as a class became ineligible to kingship from very early times.[5] It was from the time of Mahāpadma Nanda that disregard of the bar is traditionally recognized as commencing.[6]

The exclusion is differently interpreted.

The exclusion of *Brāhmaṇas* from royalty has been differently interpreted. James Mill remarks, for instance, that 'it appears somewhat remarkable that the *Brāhmaṇas*, who usurped among their countrymen so much distinction and authority, did not invest themselves with the splendour of royalty. It very often happens that some accidental circumstances, of which little account was taken at the time, and which after a lapse of ages it is impossible to trace, gave occasion to certain peculiarities which we remark in the affairs

[1] *Śatapatha-Brāhmaṇa*, ii. 4. 4, 5.

[2] *Śāṅkhāyana-Śrauta-Sūtra*, xvi. 29. 5, 6.

[3] *RV.*, x. 33.

[4] Oldenberg, *Religion des Veda*, p. 375, compares the permanency of the relation between the king and his priest to that of husband and wife as shown in the rituals in the *Aitareya-Brāhmaṇa*, viii. 24.

[5] The *Skanda-Purāṇa* mentions Paraśurāma's gift of conquered lands to the *Brāhmaṇas* who became *monarchs* thereby; but this statement appears neither in any other of the *Purāṇas* nor in the epics:

> Tato niḥkṣatriye loke kṛtvā hayamakhaṃ ca saḥ,
> Prāyacchat sakalām urvīṃ brāhmaṇebhyaś ca dakṣiṇām.
> Atha labdhavarā viprās taṃ ūcur bhṛgu-sattamaṃ,
> Nāsmadbhūmau tvayā stheyam eko rājā yataḥ smṛtaḥ.
>
> *Skanda-Purāṇa* (*Nāgara-khaṇḍa*), lxviii. 9, 10.

[6] See the chapter 'The Education of the Prince', n. 1, p. 71.

and characters of nations. It is by no means unnatural to suppose that, to a people over whom the love of repose exerts the greatest sway and in whose character aversion to danger forms a principal ingredient, the toils and perils of the sword appeared to surpass the advantages with which it was attended; and that the *Brāhmaṇas* transferred to the hands of others what was thus a source of too much labour, as well as danger, to be retained in their own.'[1] Sir W. W. Hunter is of opinion that 'from very ancient times, the leaders of the *Brāhmaṇa* caste recognized that if they were to exercise spiritual supremacy, they must renounce earthly pomp. In arrogating the priestly function, they gave up all claim to the royal office. They were divinely appointed to be the guides of nations and the councillors of kings, but they could not be kings themselves.'[2]

It is very difficult, if at all possible, at this distance of time to ascertain how far the exclusion of *Brāhmaṇas* from regal office was of their own choosing and how far it was the result of compelling circumstances. It is better to be silent than to read into the phenomenon any motives which would be either unjust or erroneous.

EPIC PERIOD AND LATER. Qualifications.

The importance of the position occupied by the royal priest made it imperative that he should be selected for his marked qualities, both natural and acquired. Some of the Sanskrit works furnish lists of these qualities, the more detailed of which generally emphasize that he should be of good family, gentlemanly, self-controlled, and religious; versed in Trayī (the three Vedas, &c.),[3] six Aṅgas,[4] polity, *mantras* and rituals, including the *śāntika* (propitiating), *pauṣṭika* (invigorating), and such other rites of the *Atharva-Veda* specially for averting calamities human and providential; eloquent; and devoted to the welfare of the king and the state.[5] To these are added

[1] James Mill's *History of British India* (1820), i. 189, 190.

[2] W. W. Hunter's *Indian Empire* (3rd ed.), p. 136.

[3] See for its explanation ch. ix.

[4] i.e. the science of proper articulation and pronunciation, rules for rituals, grammar, explanation of difficult Vedic words, prosody, and astrology. (Monier Williams, *Sanskrit-English Dictionary*.)

[5] *MBh.*, i. 170. 74-7; *Kauṭilīya*, I. ix. 15; *Gautama*, xi. 12; *Agni-*

by some of the lists other attributes, which may or may not be subsumed under those already mentioned, e.g. knowledge of the *arthaśāstra* (science of man's material concerns), *dhanurveda* (science of archery), military arrays (*vyūha*) and weapons (*astra*), and reading of portents.

Duties: Religious; The aforesaid qualities are required in the royal priest in view of the duties he is called upon to perform. He is entrusted with the supervision of all religious, as well as socio- or politico-religious ceremonies for the royal family or the State, which make it of paramount importance that he should be thoroughly versed in the Vedic *mantras* and the attendant rites. His personal officiation at the ceremonies by the utterance of *mantras* and performance of all other minutiae of the rituals may not have been needed in all cases, for there were the subordinate priests (*ṛtviks*) for the purpose. General attention to the strict conduct of the whole ceremonial and participation in its more important functions were his look-out. Vasiṣṭha, the royal priest in the *Rāmāyaṇa*, for instance, conducts Daśaratha's *Putreṣṭi* sacrifice,[1] the many *saṃskāra* rites of the four princes,[2] and Rāma's coronation, in which he appears as personally anointing and crowning Rāma.[3] Dhaumya, the *Purohita* of the Pāṇḍavas, officiates at the *śāntika* and *pauṣṭika* ceremonies for the achievement of their objects and their general welfare on the eve of their departure to live *incognito*.[4] The more important of the rituals are performed by him on the occasion of Yudhiṣṭhira's coronation, which leads us to infer that upon him rested the most onerous of the duties.[5] At the *Rājasūya* of the same prince, Vyāsa officiates as the *Brahman* priest and Dhaumya as *Hotṛ*.[6] As already pointed out,[7] the *Purohita* ought to have filled the

Purāṇa, cxxxix. 16, 17; *Garuḍa-Purāṇa*, cxii. 12; *Kāmandakīya*, iv. 32; *Śukranīti*, ii. 78–80; *Yājñavalkya*, i. 313; *Nītivākyāmṛta* (by Somadeva Sūri), xi. 43, 44 (*purohita-samuddeśa*); cf. *J. A. O. S.*, xiii. 156.

1 *Rām.*, i. *sargas* 8 ff. Here Vasiṣṭha is expressly mentioned as officiating as *Brahman* priest.

2 *Ibid.*, i. 18. 21–4. Cf. *Raghuvaṃśa*, iii. 18 for the performance of Raghu's *saṃskāra* rites by the royal priest.

3 *Rām.*, vi. 128.

4 *MBh.*, iv. 4. 51, 52, with Nīlakaṇṭha's commentary.

5 *MBh.*, xii. 40. 1 ff.

6 *MBh.*, ii. 33. 32–5.

7 See the first paragraph of this chapter.

first position; but an exception seems to have been made in favour of Vyāsa, in view perhaps of his relationship to the Pāṇḍavas and his deeper scholarship.[1] In the horse-sacrifice performed by the emperor Bali, his *Purohita* Śukrācārya figures as its *Brahman* priest.[2] Garga was asked by Vasudeva to perform the naming ceremony of his sons Balarāma and Śrīkṛṣṇa because he was the domestic priest of the Yādavas and versed in sacred lore and astrology.[3]

The *Purohita* is sometimes appointed to be the prince's tutor (*guru*) for instructing him in the *śāstras* and conducting the necessary rites up to *cūḍā-karaṇa*[4] (tonsure). It is the *Ācārya* who performs his *upanayana* (investiture with the sacred thread) and thereby undertakes his education thenceforward.[5] The *Purohita* at times happens to be both the *Guru* and the *Ācārya*, as instanced in the case of Vasiṣṭha completing all the rites of Daśaratha's sons up to the *upanayana* inclusive.[6] Śukrācārya, the domestic priest of Hiraṇyakaśipu appears as appointed by the king to conduct the education of his sons Prahlāda and others in the first capacity of *Guru*.[7] Tutorial;

The royal priest nowhere appears as a judge in a court of justice. According to Āpastamba,[8] cases of non-observance on the part of *Brāhmaṇa* householders of penances prescribed by the *Ācārya* for breaches of caste-rules according to sacred law were referred by the king to his *Purohita* for trial. The latter issued a fresh order for compliance with the proper penances, and, if this order was still disobeyed, the offenders were brought to reason by penalties other than corporeal punishment and servitude. The *Purohita*, according to Vasiṣṭha again, has to share with the king penances for certain Punitory

[1] Sudharman was the *Purohita* of the Kauravas (*MBh.*, xii. 40. 5, with Nīlakaṇṭha's commentary).
[2] *Bhāgavata-Purāṇa*, viii. 23. 14.
[3] *Ibid.*, x. 8. 1–6.
[4] *Manu*, ii. 142; *Yājñavalkya*, i. 34.
[5] *Manu*, ii. 140; *Yājñavalkya*, i. 34. For the duties of *upādhyāya* (sub-teacher) and *ṛtvij* (sacrificial priest), see *Manu*, ii. 141, 143, and *Yājñavalkya*, i. 35.
[6] *Rām.*, i. 18. 22–5, with Rāmānuja's commentary.
[7] *Bhāgavata-Purāṇa*, vii. 5. 1 ff.
[8] *Āpastamba*, ii. 5. 12–16.

prescribed cases of miscarriage of justice, viz. if the latter sets free a criminal deserving punishment, or punishes an innocent man.[1]

Negotiatory; The *Purohita* is appointed at times to carry on negotiations between the sovereign and other parties for various purposes, political or otherwise. King Drupada of Pañcāla, for instance, sent his *Purohita* as *dūta* to the Kurus with a political message,[2] and, on a previous occasion, to the Pāṇḍavas, to ascertain particulars about their parentage with a view to his daughter's marriage.[3] To cite a later instance, Śuddhodhana sent his *Purohita* to Daṇḍapāṇi to negotiate the marriage between the latter's daughter and Gautama.[4]

Political. The royal priest is never a minister (*mantrin*) *ex officio*, either in the Vedic period or later, though there is no bar to the combination of the two functions in the same person except the practical difficulty it involves. The duties attached to each of these offices are heavy enough, and their amalgamation would but make it impossible for a single person to perform the combined duties efficiently. The two offices appear separate from the lists of offices of the Vedic period;[5] and there is no evidence on record pointing to their identity in earlier times. The Vedic state-council was not so exclusive as it was in later times, and, even if it were so, the presence of the *Purohita* there, as also in the secret conclave of the later epic and the Paurāṇic periods, might not have been productive of any positive evil; but the practice appears to have been otherwise. So far as the evidences go, nowhere is he seen to occupy, or recommended to have, a seat in the state-council, though the use of the same name *Sabhā* both for the royal court and the state-council may give rise to this misleading impression. The non-didactic portions of the *Mahābhārata* show the kings arriving at important decisions in matters of State without much regard for Brāhmaṇic or ministerial advice, and much less, if at all, for that of their *Purohitas*.[6]

[1] *Vasiṣṭha*, xix. 40–43.
[2] *MBh.*, v. 5. 18.
[3] *MBh.*, i. 193. 14–17.
[4] *Lalitavistara* [transl. by R. L. Mitra (Bibl. Indica)], ch. xii, p. 203.
[5] See the chapter 'Evolution of the Principal State-Officials'.
[6] See the chapter 'The State-Council'.

The didactic parts of the epic recommend complete dependence[1] of the sovereign upon his *Purohita*. We are not in a position to infer from this recommendation, as Prof. Hopkins has done,[2] that it indicates the wholesale subjection of the sovereign to the former's will in all matters, including political. Had it been so, references of political questions by the king to the members of the state-council, regarded by Hindu statesmen from very early times as of paramount necessity for the conduct of government, would not have found a place in the works on polity. The royal priest was no doubt much respected by the king, and his opinions also carried weight in the latter's estimation. But versed as the *Purohita* was in the rules of polity, he knew well the limits to the range of his duties, which would have rendered it a transgression on his part to thrust his political views upon the sovereign, and to try to deflect him from the course incumbent on him by the resolution of the state-council. It is true that the king could consider any resolution after it had been passed, and suggest to the councillors any alteration that he might think fit, and that according to Yājñavalkya the resolution had actually to be referred to the royal priest for his opinion. This does not mean, however, that under the rules an opening was left for the king at this stage of deliberation to decide upon any course of action he liked, or give effect to the advice of the royal priest in opposition to the resolution of the council. The reference of the resolution to the royal priest was, it should be held, not for giving him an opportunity of setting it aside, or changing it as he pleased, but for judging of the time and place of the contemplated action and such other matters connected therewith from the astrological point of view. Under the circumstances, though the royal priest exercised much influence with the king, yet he was debarred under the constitution from prevailing over him to follow in political matters decided on by the state-council a course of action that ran counter to the advice of the political councillors. So long as the state-council existed, able to exercise its prescribed powers, it cannot be fairly held that

[1] e.g. *MBh.*, i. 170. 77, 78.

[2] *J. A. O. S.*, xiii. 155.

the monarch was but a puppet in the hands of the royal priest in State matters.[1] The causes of extension of the authority of the *Brāhmaṇas* are to be sought not so much in the influence directly exerted upon the king by the royal priest, to which there was a constitutional bar, as in the powerful hold of the *Brāhmaṇas* upon the intellect of the nation, of which the king and his ministers were but individual members. Anything that would tend to detract from that authority would as a rule be repulsive to their thoughts and feelings as well as to the public opinion reared and moulded under the Brāhmanic culture. The interference of the royal priest, therefore, in the business of the state-council for the preservation or extension of Brāhmanic interests was not necessary in view of the wider and more powerful forces that were at work outside the council to procure the very same objects.

Conclusion. The above limit to his constitutional powers does not mean that the personal influence wielded by the royal priest and the reverence commanded by him were not very great. He and all his *confrères* were looked upon as divinities [2] in human form. As a depositary of knowledge and wisdom, he was recommended to be the king's guide, confidant, and companion.[3] He was looked upon as a source of strength to the State, and his very appointment to the *Purohita*-ship, not to speak of his active participation in the duties attached to it, were regarded as conducive to the prosperity of the realm.[4] Side by side with this reverence for the domestic priest is found a counter-current of feeling—not perhaps very strong—tending to belittle him. He is put in *Manu* [5] in the middling rank of the states caused by activity (*rajas*), and his position is looked upon as a curse in the *Mahābhārata*.[6] But on the whole his influence predominated and grew ever greater.

[1] For the basis of the above inferences, see the chapter 'The State-Council'.

[2] This point has been adverted to in the last chapter.

[3] *J. A. O. S.*, xiii. 152; *Baudhāyana*, i. 10. 18. 7, 8.

[4] Cf. *Vasiṣṭha*, xix. 4.

[5] *Manu*, xii. 46.

[6] *MBh.*, xiii. 93. 130; Muir, *Sanskrit Texts*, i. 128, and *J. A. O. S.*, xiii. 161.

CHAPTER IV

REGAL SUCCESSION

THE selection of the eldest son as successor to the kingdom appears to have been the normal mode of disposition in ancient times. A review of the lists of kings of the Solar and Lunar dynasties as given in the epics and *Purāṇas* shows that the eldest son as a rule succeeded his father as heir to the kingdom, while deviations are noticed in cases in which the eldest son became civilly dead or legally incapable through physical defects. Among the six sons of Nahuṣa of the Lunar Race, the second, named Yayāṭi, succeeded to the kingdom in place of the eldest, Yati, who had turned an ascetic.[1] Pāṇḍu became king because his elder brother Dhṛtarāṣṭra was blind when the succession became open.

The normal mode of disposition.

In Rāma's case, the normal rule had almost been carried into effect when Daśaratha proposed to have Rāma formally declared as his successor in the presence of the priests, nobles, and the people, who cheerfully assented to the proposal. The installation of Bharata as crown-prince to the exclusion of Rāma, the eldest brother, at Kaikeyī's instance is an exception to the normal rule. This deviation was only possible for the reason that Rāma himself, the subject of the exclusion, instead of making any protest like Lakṣmaṇa, voluntarily gave up his right. Otherwise, the citizens would have risen in revolt against the commission of an act not sanctioned by practice. There had been such an outburst of active opposition when Yayāti, a king of the Lunar Race, declared his intention to make Puru, his youngest son, heir in supersession of

Rāma's case no deviation from the normal rule.

Instances of people' oppositio to deviations.

NOTE.—For Prof. Hopkins' writings on the subject, see *J. A. O. S.*, xiii. 139–44, and for Paṇḍit Jagannātha Tarkapañcānan's, see Colebrooke's *Digest*, i. 414–20 [reprinted separately in the *Asiatic Annual Register*, ii. (1800), 345 ff.].

[1] *Harivaṃśa*, xxx. 1–3.

the eldest, Yadu. The citizens in a body headed by the priests came to the king and protested against his action, 'A younger son cannot overstep the elder; this we make known to thee; see that thou do thy duty.' The king mollified them by saying, 'A son who disobeys his father is looked upon by sages as no son at all. All my sons have slighted and disobeyed me, whereas Puru alone has carried out my wishes. The sage Śukra also enjoined me to declare as heir the son who would obey me. Hence I entreat you to have Puru installed as heir.' The people were convinced, and submitted, saying that, as Puru was obedient to him and Śukra had sanctioned the king's action, they had nothing to say. This shows that the king could not make an arbitrary disposition of his kingdom. The king's will was not law in this matter, and the people retired, not because of his will, but because of his reasoning, which convinced them.[1]

The account of Devāpi and Śantanu in its epic form [2] may be cited to show the strength of the people's decision in its conflict with the will of a king to interfere with the established rules of succession. Pratīpa, a Kuru king, had three sons, Devāpi, Bālhīka, and Śantanu. The eldest suffered from skin-disease (*tvagdoṣa*), but he was much beloved by all. The king desired to install him as his heir-apparent, and made all preparations therefor; but the people opposed. The priests, the seniors, and the inhabitants of the city and the country in a sudden uprising objected to have a leper as sovereign, and they succeeded in making good their objection without a word of displeasure on the part of the king. The youngest son, therefore, was installed as heir-apparent, while the eldest son retired into the woods, the second son having already left the realm,[3] and having been adopted by his maternal uncle.

[1] *MBh.*, i. 85. 17–35; v. 149. 2–13; *Viṣṇu-Purāṇa*, iv. 10. 1 ff.; *Vāyu-Purāṇa*, xciii. 74–87; *Harivaṃśa*, xxx.

[2] *MBh.*, v. 149. 14–29.

[3] There are several accounts of Devāpi and Śantanu. In the *Ṛg-Veda*, x. 98. 11, the brotherhood of the two persons does not appear. The *Nirukta* account (ii. 10) relates that Śantanu got himself anointed, whereupon a drought ensued. This was attributed by the *Brāhmaṇas* to his having superseded his elder brother. Śantanu therefore offered the kingdon to Devāpi, who declined it, but, acting as domestic priest, obtained

Vasiṣṭha's speech to Rāma in the *Rāmāyaṇa* corroborates the above mode of disposition of the kingdom. 'Among all the descendants of Ikṣvāku, the first-born becomes king; you are the first-born, O Rāma, and should be consecrated to the kingdom. A younger brother should not be installed as king to the exclusion of the elder. You should not reject this prescriptive law followed by your family.'[1] Vasiṣṭha's speech.

Even if this speech be taken as pointing to a practice confined to the Ikṣvāku dynasty, and not general in its application, it cannot but be admitted that this practice has been followed by the dynasty for no less than fifty-five generations.

Mantharā's words addressed to Kaikeyī regarding Rāma's consecration agree with Vasiṣṭha's speech. 'Rāma will be king and his son after him. Kaikeyī! Bharata will be excluded from the royal race. All the sons of a king do not remain in the kingdom. If they are made to do so, it leads to a very great harm. Therefore, kings commit the affairs of government to their eldest sons, or to others qualified (i.e. according to the commentary, the competent younger sons, if the eldest son be incompetent).'[2] Among the sons, the senior, it appears, is chosen as heir by his father, the reigning sovereign, for, according to Mantharā's assertion, all the sons together cannot get the kingdom without giving rise to a very great harm. In support of her statement that harm ensues if all the sons remain in the kingdom, she points out that 'Rāma, after his installation as king, will either banish Bharata or kill him'.[3] Mantharā's notion of succession

Kaikeyī's statement that 'Bharata also will surely receive the hereditary kingdom from Rāma after the lapse of a hundred years' does not appear to point to any regular succession of the brothers to the kingdom every hundred Kaikeyī's statement.

rain for him. The epic and later accounts give two divergent stories. According to one, Devāpi was passed over for his leprosy, while according to the other, for his asceticism in youth. *V. I.* i. 378; also Hopkins, *J. A. O. S.*, xiii. 140 n. I quote here only one reference to Devāpi's exclusion through asceticism, viz. *Bhāgavata*, ix. 22. 12, 13. Though there are differences in the accounts, their bearing, if at all, is on the one or the other rule of succession.

[1] ii. 110. 35-7. [2] ii. 8. 22-4. [3] *Ibid.*, 27.

years by rotation, but to Kaikeyī's confident expectation, born of her good opinion of Rāma's nature, that, ruling, as he will do, the kingdom with paternal benignity towards his younger brothers, he cannot but install Bharata as his heir, be it at the end of even a hundred years.[1] The ruling of a kingdom by brothers in rotation has, so far as we see, nowhere been recorded as having taken place in the dominions of the Solar and Lunar kings in ancient times; and there is no reason to suppose that Kaikeyī is pointing to an actual mode of succession instead of a mere sanguine expectation.

Paṇḍit Tarka-pañcānan's inferences.

Paṇḍit Jagannātha Tarkapañcānan draws out some rules of succession inferentially from the royal succession in the *Rāmāyaṇa*, and from the silence of Miśra and other legal authorities on the point. Daśaratha, he argues, declared to commit his kingdom to Rāma, in the presence of Vasiṣṭha and many other sages, as well as the citizens at large, which, according to him, shows that he had the power to give away the whole of his kingdom to the eldest son to the exclusion of his other virtuous sons. But, afterwards, excluding Rāma and the rest, he gave away the entire kingdom to Bharata as a boon to Kaikeyī. This also, according to him, points to the king's power of giving away his kingdom to a younger son in supersession of the eldest without any offence on the part of the latter. Such a disposition of the kingdom by a king according to his own sweet will is held by him to have the tacit sanction of judicial authorities like Miśra and others; for the gift of a kingdom is not included by them in their lists of invalid gifts.

He puts forward one other argument in support of the king's power of disposition of his kingdom, not only to one of his sons, but also to others mentioned below. He starts with the proposition that a father has absolute power to give away even the person of his son, from which he draws the inference that it is not proper to assert that the father cannot, without the assent of the excluded son (or sons), give away

[1] ii. 8. 16, and Rāmānuja's commentary thereon. Paṇḍit Jagannātha Tarkapañcānan's remarks (Colebrooke's *Digest* i. 417) are obscure, and it is difficult to be certain what inferences he draws from the passage.

immovable property not yet owned by him (or them). The inference is pushed to its farthest logical limits. The king, he argues, can, in exercise of his aforesaid absolute power, give away the kingdom to his daughter's son, or other remote heir, or even to a stranger, to the exclusion of his sons though devoid of offence, there being no special prohibition nor usage to the contrary. But no father, he adds, who distinguishes right from wrong would be so disposed.

In all these cases of exclusion of virtuous sons, the king their father is bound to make provision for their subsistence.[1]

In the last three cases of disposition by a subordinate king of his kingdom, viz. to a daughter's son, remote heir, or stranger, the paramount sovereign has, according to Paṇḍit Jagannātha, the right to interfere. He can, of his own accord, set aside the dispositions, and give the whole kingdom to one of the sons of the subordinate king without meaning any injury to the rest; for a paramount sovereign is equal to a father. But if the paramount sovereign be asked by the excluded sons to do them justice, and he sets aside the disposition, but, without choosing a particular son as king, leaves the matter to be disposed of according to law, then, in the opinion of the aforesaid author of the *Digest*, it does not appear consistent with the reason of the law that one of the sons should take the whole kingdom without the assent of the rest.[2]

Criticism of Paṇḍit Tarkapañcānan's inferences

The above position of Paṇḍit Tarkapañcānan does not appear to be sound law for the following reasons:

(1) From the constitutional point of view [3], the promise of

[1] For details regarding 'subsistence', see subsequent portions of this chapter.

[2] The paragraph, which I have made out as above, is extremely obscure. Its context alone helps to some extent to clear up its meaning.

[3] To understand the legal significance of the chapters bearing on this subject, we should not study the passages apart from their relation to the general trend of the whole argument and apart form the context and the special circumstances in which the passages occur. The conversation between Rāma and Lakṣmaṇa is a better index to the main points at issue than the conversation of Rāma with his mother. To his mother, Rāma merely speaks words of obedience and consolation governed by his sacred relationship to them. To Lakṣmaṇa, he applies arguments which may satisfy a logical mind that is fully alive to legal rights, which the latter is

Daśaratha to Kaikeyī regarding kingship is itself invalid. That promise cannot override the constitutional law of succession. It is purely a private domestic matter, which can have no influence on such an important public matter as the succession to the throne.

Paṇḍit Tarkapañcānan supposes that Kaikeyī secured the succession of Bharata in supersession of the legal heir-apparent, Rāma, on the strength of the promise of which she took an undue advantage, and the legal inference he draws from this is that the king has constitutionally the power to give effect to his mere wishes, whims, or promises regarding the succession in contravention of the normal constitutional practice. Was Bharata's succession really brought about by the promise of Daśaratha to Kaikeyī? I hold that it was not so. If we consider all the circumstances in that truly complex situation from the strictly legal standpoint, we shall find this incontrovertible, fundamental fact standing out clear and definite from the maze of confounding events, viz. that it was Rāma's willing and cheerful resignation of his right to the crown-princeship that really paved the way for another. For that crown-princeship, Rāma alone was pre-eminently eligible by both nature and custom; and unless the legal incumbent, of his own accord, gives up the right, the way is barred for anybody else. What led Rāma to this voluntary self-sacrifice is another matter, which belongs to the domain of morality and religion, and has no constitutional significance whatever. The whole epic, indeed, is based on this supreme act of self-sacrifice on the part of Rāma—a self-sacrifice which was not forced upon him by the mandate of an autocratic sovereign, but was the spontaneous outcome of Rāma's unfettered, individual decision which placed some things higher than an earthly kingdom. The credit of this self-sacrifice belongs wholly and exclusively to Rāmacandra, the hero of the epic, who took upon himself the load of untold suffering to save his father from the sin of violating his 'plighted troth'. This

even prepared to assert by force of arms. In the light of what has been explained above are to be interpreted passages like those, which may otherwise be misleading: ii. 20. 30; 21. 30.

lends its charm and ethical value to the epic, of which it is indeed the starting-point. To ignore this is to forget the very basis on which the epic rests, and is to misunderstand utterly the character of the hero.

To sum up: Daśaratha was legally incompetent to make or keep any promise in respect of succession. When Kaikeyī extorted Daśaratha's sanction to Bharata's succession, Rāmacandra was the only person who could secure its observance, and he cheerfully sacrificed himself to prevent his father's fall from truth. To regard him as the victim of Daśaratha's absolute power both as father and sovereign, as the learned Paṇḍit supposes, is, I repeat, to misunderstand the epic and to lose sight of the real point of the law.

(2) The people at large as a constitutional factor have been altogether ignored.

(3) The legal authorities are silent on regal succession. They treat of the validity or otherwise of gifts of various sorts, but omit, as Paṇḍit Tarkapañcānan mentions, to speak of 'the gift of a kingdom by a king'. The instances of succession furnished by ancient Sanskrit literature, so far as I see, give us cases which only to a small extent make up for the silence of the legal texts. Nearly all of them illustrate the devolution of kingdom on the eldest or other sons of the retiring or deceased sovereign, and not on daughter's sons, other remote heirs, or strangers. The silence of legal authorities cannot be construed into a support of Paṇḍit Tarkapañcānan's position, while the absence of recorded instances of such cases leaves us quite in the dark as to what the law was.

(4) The inference from the premiss that a father, as having 'power to give away the person of his son', has also by implication power to give away immovable property (even supposing that the kingdom is an immovable property to which the son has a prospective right) without his consent may be sound logically, but not legally; for law is often a negation of logic.

(5) The attribution of powers of disposal, in two different classes of cases, to the paramount sovereign, who is said to

stand *in loco parentis*, is a very far-fetched extension of the previous inferences, in support of which again no law or example has been quoted.

Professor Hopkins' conclusion.

The position as it now stands agrees with the conclusion drawn by Professor Hopkins: 'If there are two (or more) sound sons, the king had no allowed right to select other than the eldest as heir, and, if he exceeded his right in this regard, the people openly and threateningly called him to account for his departure.'

As to the order of succession, therefore, no ancient work, so far as I see, throws any light on any other than the very first group of heirs, viz. the king's sons.

Legal disabilities to succession.

As regards legal incapacity arising from physical defects, we meet with examples of blindness and leprosy operating as grounds for exclusion from the throne. The case of Dhṛtarāṣṭra is an instance of the former disability[1] and Devāpi of the latter.

Criticism of Professor Hopkins' opinion regarding legal disabilities.

Professor Hopkins holds that these physical defects were not felt to be an infrangible legal bar, drawing this inference, I suppose, from the following facts regarding Dhṛtarāṣṭra and Dyumatsena (father of the well-known Satyavat, husband of Sāvitrī[2]): Dhṛtarāṣṭra after his brother Pāṇḍu's death wielded political power virtually as a king for some time, and Yudhiṣṭhira was consecrated to *Yauvarājya* (crown-princeship) a year after his father Pāṇḍu's decease.[3] This consecration to crown-princeship is an anomaly, and appears to have been dictated by policy on the part of Dhṛtarāṣṭra and his sons. Yudhiṣṭhira ought to have been installed as a full-fledged king, and not as a mere crown-prince or successor to a kingdom not yet to hand. The tender age of the heir of the deceased king was no bar to his coronation. Janamejaya, for instance, was a mere child at his father's death, and yet

[1] 'Dhṛtarāṣṭras tv acakṣuṣṭvād rājyaṃ na pratyapadyata' (i.e. Dhṛtarāṣṭra did not get the kingdom for his blindness) *MBh.*, i. 109. 25.

[2] *J. A. O. S.*, xiii. 144; also p. 143.

[3] See *MBh.*, i. 139. 1 ff. Prof. Hopkins regards it as an act of righteousness on Dhṛtarāṣṭra's part to have Yudhiṣṭhira installed as crown-prince. He does not seem to notice that by this the latter was given less than his due.

he was installed *as king.*[1] Yudhiṣṭhira's consecration to the crown-princeship does not relatively imply kingship in Dhṛtarāṣṭra. He was never formally crowned as such, and whatever power he wielded as king of the whole ancestral kingdom was reserved to himself partly by force and cleverness and partly by his relationship to Yudhiṣṭhira, who, out of respect, was reluctant to oppose his uncle's will. The slow process in which the right law asserted itself and the seeming submission of the people for some time to Dhṛtarāṣṭra's yoke should not be construed into an acknowledgement that congenital blindness was not an infrangible legal disability. In disputes between princes and kings, there is no tribune for administering a speedy justice; and if the law remains in abeyance for a time, the abeyant state of things should not be mistaken for the lawful one. It is therefore incorrect to hold that Dhṛtarāṣṭra reigned as sovereign of the paternal kingdom in spite of his physical defect.

It is equally incorrect to draw the same conclusion from facts regarding Dyumatsena. He was king of the Śālva[2] kingdom, became blind in course of time, and was dethroned by a usurper. The minister after some time slew the usurper, upon which the people went to the forest hermitage, where the king had taken refuge, to fetch him to his dominions, saying, 'Blind or not, he will be our king.' The account says that he had already been restored to sight, about which the people knew nothing.[3] It was therefore actually a case of restoration to kingdom of a king without any physical defect. Even if the king had been blind at the time of his restoration, it would not have constituted an illustration sufficient to justify Professor Hopkins' inference. It does not speak of either congenital blindness or even blindness prior to accession to the throne. The king appears to have reigned after he had turned blind and before he was dethroned. This only shows that a physical defect of the kind arising subsequently

[1] *MBh.*, i. 44. 5–7.

[2] It was near Kurukṣetra (see *MBh.*, iv. 1, 1 ff.), comprising portions of the territories of Jodhpur, Jaipur, and Alwar. (Mr. N. L. Dey's *Geographical Dictionary*, 2nd ed., in the press.)

[3] *MBh.*, iii. 293. 7–9; 298. 3–9.

to the opening of succession cannot deprive a king of the kingdom already vested in him.[1]

Provisions for excluded princes.

We now turn to the question of the sons who though virtuous are excluded from the throne to make room for the eldest. It has been already stated that the king their father is bound to make provision for their subsistence. This subsistence does not mean 'barely enough to support life', for a man may support life on leaves, roots, and the like; nor does it mean an 'appanage that would enable him to live like the brother upon whom has devolved the kingdom'. The subsistence should, therefore, mean enough for a decent living.[2]

Though this is the general rule, we find some provision made for the excluded princes. The descriptions in the *Purāṇas* relating to the devolutions of kingdoms are generally silent as to such provisions, mentioning the name of the crown-prince as such and either only stating barely those of the other princes or giving their total number without reference even to their names. We have to gather our information, therefore, from the occasional cases in which the descriptions either in the *Purāṇas* or other Sanskrit works are more detailed.

The kind of provision most considerate towards the excluded princes is found in the case of dispositions in favour of Rāma's sons and nephews. The two sons of Bharata were installed kings of Takṣaśilā and Puṣkalāvata in Gāndhāra conquered by Bharata,[3] the two sons of Śatrughna, kings of Madhurā and Vaidiśa, the former having been subjugated by Śatrughna,[4]

[1] Kings Kalmāṣapāda and Kalaśa were not deprived of their vested kingdoms on account of disabilities. (See *MBh.*, i. 176, for Kalmāṣapāda, and *Skanda-Purāṇa*, *Nāgara-Khaṇḍa*, xlix, for Kalaśa.) Veṇa was attacked with leprosy, for which he also was not deprived of his vested kingdom. (See Cunningham, *Ancient Geography of India*, p. 336, referring to the *Viṣṇu-Purāṇa*. The *Skanda-Purāṇa*, *Nāgara-Khaṇḍa*, lxxxiii, alludes to the disease, and, unlike the above account, describes it as having proved fatal to Veṇa.).

[2] See Colebrooke's *Digest*, i. 419, 420.

[3] *Rām.*, vii. 101. 11; for the conquest of Gāndhāra by Bharata, see *ibid.*, 4–11.

[4] *Rām.*, vii. 108. 9–11; for the conquest of Madhurā by Śatrughna, see *Ibid.*, lxix. 36 ff.; lxx. 1 ff.

while the two sons of Lakṣmaṇa, kings of two cities in Kārupatha newly subdued by Bharata and Lakṣmaṇa.[1] In the case of Rāma's two sons, Kuśa and Lava, the former, the first-born, obtained Southern Kośala, comprising Ayodhyā, while Lava, Northern Kośala with its chief town at Śrāvastī.[2] From this it appears that Rāma's nephews were given regions that were accretions to the paternal kingdom. Only as regards Vaidiśa we do not find when it was subdued, but all the other places were newly conquered. Rāma's nephews therefore obtained regions, not as mere estates from which to draw their appanages, but as kingdoms of which they were consecrated kings; but these regions were not part of the ancestral kingdom. In regard to Rāma's sons, the younger was given a portion of the hereditary kingdom while the elder the remainder. The portion of the elder was of course the more important, being superior in extent and riches, and containing the metropolis of the former empire. The most striking feature of this provision is division of the ancestral kingdom. Kuśa does not obtain the ancestral kingdom *in toto*, but has to part with a portion, of which his brother is installed the king.[3]

A second kind of provision is met with in some accounts of Yayāti's sons. It has been already explained how the youngest of them, Puru, succeeded his father to the exclusion of his elder brothers. To these excluded princes were allotted portions of the empire, where they ruled, but under the control of Puru. It is not clear whether they were placed there as viceroys of Puru, or as tributary princes.[4] Some of

[1] *Rām.*, vii. 102; for conquest of Kārupatha by Bharata and Lakṣmaṇa, see *ibid.*

[2] *Rām.*, vii. 107. 17.

[3] This kind of provision appears to have been made for the sons of King Ikṣvāku (*MBh.*, xiv. 4. 3, 4), as also for those of King Uparicara (i. 63. 29–32).

[4] The *Bhāgavata-Purāṇa* (ix. 19. 21–3) mentions the following allotments, viz. south (i.e. of the empire) to Yadu, west to Turvaśu, south-west to Druhyu, and north to Anu. *Puru was installed emperor of the 'whole world' and the elder brothers were placed under his control.*

The *Viṣṇu-Purāṇa* (iv. 10. 16–18) mentions in substance the same arrangement, but is not so explicit. Some of the *Purāṇas* refer only to the allotments to the sons without alluding to the superior control of Puru, e.g. *Vāyu*, xciii; *Harivaṃśa*, xxx.

the accounts are silent as to the superior control of Puru over his brothers, from which we may hold that the elder brothers were independent of the youngest. If this was the case, it was the same as that in regard to Rāma's sons and nephews. Had it been otherwise, i.e. Puru holding the superior control, we can differentiate it as a second kind of provision for the excluded princes.

A third kind of provision is one in which no portion of the kingdom is given to the princes as appanage. They live jointly with their royal brother, the State bearing all their expenses. We notice this in the case of the five Pāṇḍavas.

The evidence of the *Rāja-Dharma-Kaustubha* on regal succession.

Though the ancient texts do not furnish express rules for regal succession, the *Rāja-Dharma-Kaustubha*,[1] a later Sanskrit work, enters into a discussion of the subject thus:

(1) Of the many classes of sons of a king, viz. *aurasa*, *kṣetraja*, *dattaka*, *kṛtrima*, *gūḍhotpanna*, *apaviddha*, *kānīna*, *sahoḍha*, *krīta*, *paunarbhava*, *svayaṃdatta*, and *dāsa*, the last three are excluded from kingship, the remaining nine have right to inherit the throne in the order of their enumeration.[2]

(2) If the eldest son of the senior queen be junior to that of a junior queen, the former cannot be superseded.

(3) Of the two princes born of two queens at the same moment, the son of the senior queen will have preference.

(4) Of twins, the first-born obtains priority.

(5) and (6) A prince with organic defect is always excluded from the throne, giving place to the one next to him in seniority. The latter's line continues on the throne in spite of the existence of able-bodied sons of the excluded prince. Provision should be made for the maintenance of the excluded princes and their families.

Terms of kingship.

Kingship held for a certain term appears to have been the practice in a few countries in early times. There were octennial, triennial, annual, and even diurnal tenures, at the

[1] The manuscript is in my possession. The subject is dealt with in the beginning of pt. iii.

[2] This statement is based on the *Kālikā-Purāṇa*, lxxxviii. 34–7.

end of which the monarch was either deposed, put to death, or passed through some substituted ceremony. The reign of the ancient Spartan kings appears to have been limited to eight years, the term being perhaps determined by the octennial cycle of the early Greek calendars, which attempted to reconcile solar and lunar time.[1] The same seems to have been the term of regal office of the king of Cnossus in Crete. At the end of each period, the king had to renew his sacred powers by intercourse with the godhead at the oracular cave on Mount Ida, without which he forfeited his throne.[2] A triennial tenure of kingship was in vogue among the chiefs of the Remon branch of the Ijebu tribe of Lagos in Southern Nigeria.[3] Traces exist of a custom of killing the kings of Hawaii at the end of a year's reign,[4] while the Sacaea festival at Babylon perhaps points to a similar practice among the Babylonian kings.[5] The still more dreadful diurnal tenure of kingship seems to have been the practice in a certain kingdom which still exists. In Ngoio, a province of the ancient kingdom of Congo in West Africa, the custom is that the person who is consecrated king should be put to death on the night after his coronation. The head of the Musurongo possesses the right of succession, but does not exercise it, and the throne stands vacant.[6] In cases like this, it may be naturally supposed that people would be reluctant to exchange their life for a short-lived glory on the throne, and the supply of kings would be very meagre, or nil. To maintain a regular supply, traces exist in legends of a custom of compelling men to accept the fatal sovereignty.[7] In some races and at some periods of history, the fear of death was not so great as we suppose, and the recruitment of candidates for the fatal crown was at no time a difficult matter. In many places, the rigour of the acceptance of the deadly crown was softened by the appointment of nominal kings during the substituted temporary abdications of the real kings, who would otherwise have been

'Nominal' kings.

[1] Sir J. G. Frazer's *Golden Bough*, third ed. (henceforth indicated as *G.*), pt. iii, pp. 58–68.

[2] *Ibid.*, pp. 70, 71.

[3] *Ibid.*, pp. 112, 113.

[4] *Ibid.*, pp. 117, 118.

[5] *Ibid.*, pp. 113–15.

[6] *Ibid.*, pp. 118, 119.

[7] *Ibid.*, pp. 134–47.

put to death.[1] The nominal kings were sometimes relations of the royal family—even the king's sons, and were in many instances put to death.[2]

Kings killed when old or feeble.

Among many peoples there were no fixed terms of kingship, and sovereigns were killed on approach of old age or failing health, e.g. to name only a few, among the people of Congo, Fazoql on the Blue Nile, Unyoro and other parts of Africa, the Ethiopians of Meroe, the Shilluks of the White Nile.[3]

Indian examples: duo-decennial tenure of regal office in Quilacare near Cape Comorin.

The tenure of regal office was fixed at twelve years in the province of Quilacare, about twenty leagues to the north-east of Cape Comorin. There, an old traveller[4] records, a great festival was held every twelve years in honour of an idol. The kings of the province had no more than twelve years to reign, i.e. the intervals between the festivals. On the day of the jubilee, there assembled there innumerable people, and much money was spent in giving food to *Brāhmaṇas*. A wooden scaffolding was made, spread over with silken hangings. After bathing at a tank with ceremonies and music, the king came to the idol, prayed to it, mounted on to the scaffolding, took some very sharp knives, and began to cut off his nose, ears, lips, all his members, and as much flesh off himself as he could, until through loss of blood he began to faint, when he finished himself off by cutting his throat himself. During this sacrifice to the idol, the next candidate, who wished to reign during the ensuing twelve years and undertake similar martyrdom for love of the deity, had to be present. And they raised him up from his place as king.

Duo-decennial tenure of kingship at Calicut.

The Zamorin (lit. god on earth) of Calicut on the Malabar coast had also to cut his throat in public at the end of a twelve years' reign. This practice was modified towards the end of the seventeenth century, according to Alexander Hamilton, who did not personally witness the festival, but heard from

[1] *G.*, pt. iii, pp. 148–59. [2] *Ibid.*, pp. 160–95.
[3] *Ibid.*, pp. 14–46.
[4] *Ibid.*, pp. 46, 47, quoting Duarte Barbose, *A Description of the Coasts of East Africa and Malabar in the Beginning of the Sixteenth Century* (Hakluyt Society, London, 1866), pp. 172 ff.

a distance the sound of guns fired day and night in connexion with the ceremony, of which he has left an account.[1]

Mr. W. Logan, with the help of the reigning sovereign of Calicut, examined, in the latter part of the nineteenth century, the records of these festivals as preserved in the royal archives. From his description, we can have an accurate conception of the modified practice that was in vogue up to 1743, when it took place for the last time.[2] It was known as *mahā-makha* (Great Sacrifice). It took place every twelfth year, when Jupiter was in retrograde motion in the sign of the Crab, and lasted twenty-eight days. The ceremony was observed with great pomp at the Tirunavayi temple on the north bank of the Ponnani River. From its western gateway a straight road ran for half a mile to a high ridge with a precipitous bank, on which were three or four terraces. On the topmost terrace the king took his stand on the last day of the festival. The plain below swarmed with troops numbering about forty thousand, gathered there to defend the king. The road cutting across the plain from the temple to the king's stand was kept clear. It was barred by palisades on each side, and long spears, held by strong arms and projected through the palisade on either hand, met in the middle of the road, making a glittering arch of steel. When all was ready, the king waved his sword, and a large chain of massy gold enriched with bosses was placed on an elephant at his side. This served as a signal, and the very moment a stir might be seen near the gate of the temple. A number of swordsmen decked with flowers and smeared with ashes stepped out of the crowd. They had just partaken of their last meal on earth, and were receiving the blessings and farewells of their friends. A moment later, they were coming down the lane of spears, winding, and writhing, and stabbing right and left at the spearsmen. One after another they fell, some nearer the king, some farther off.

[1] Alexander Hamilton, 'A New Account of the East Indies,' in Pinkerton's *Voyages and Travels*, viii. p. 374. (*G.*, pt. iii, pp. 47, 48.)

[2] W. Logan's *Malabar* (Madras, 1887), i. 162–9. The writer describes in particular the ceremony of 1683 when fifty-five men perished in their attempt to kill the reigning sovereign in the manner described above. (*G.*, pt. iii, pp. 49–51).

The example from Bengal criticized.

The next example cited by Dr. Frazer is from Bengal under its Muhammadan rulers. Here, he has evidently been misled.[1] The extract from the *Tuzak-i-Bābarī* upon which he bases his statement does not in fact refer at all to any ceremony like that at Calicut.

The story of Vikramāditya. Its affinity with the custom of fatal kingship for a term criticized.

The legend about King Vikramāditya of Ujjain, the ancient capital of Malwa, has it that once on a time an arch-fiend with a number of devils at his command took up his abode in the city and began to devour the people. The city was fast losing its inhabitants. To stop it, the principal citizens requested the fiend to reduce his daily rations to one man only, who would be duly delivered up to him. The demon agreed, but stipulated that the person so delivered should mount the throne and exercise royal powers for a day. The names of the citizens were entered on a list, and every day one of them in his turn ruled from morning to night and was devoured by the fiend. Now, it happened that a caravan of merchants from Gujrat halted on the banks of a river not far from the city. They had a servant, who was no other than

[1] *G.*, pt. iii, p. 51. The example has been cited from H. M. Elliot's *History of India as told by its own Historians*, iv. 260, 261 (extract from the *Tuzak-i-Bābarī*). The *Tuzak* says, 'It is a singular custom in Bengal that there is little of hereditary descent in succession to the sovereignty.... Whoever kills the king, and succeeds in placing himself on the throne, is immediately acknowledged as king. All the amīrs, wazīrs, soldiers, and peasants instantly obey and submit to him.... The people of Bengal say, "We are faithful to the throne; whoever fills the throne, we are obedient and true to him." As, for instance, before the accession of Nusrat Shāh's father, an Abyssinian (Muzaffar *Sh*āh Habs*h*ī), having killed the reigning king, mounted the throne and governed the kingdom for some time. Sultan Alauddīn killed the Abyssinian, ascended the throne, and was acknowledged as king. *After Sultan Alauddīn's death, the kingdom devolved by succession to his son*, who now reigned.' John Dowson, the editor of Elliot's work, wrongly thinks it to have been the custom among the Muhammadan rulers of Bengal to succeed to the throne by killing the reigning sovereign, and parallels it with the Malabarian custom just now described. (See Elliot, *op. cit.*, p. 260 n.) This has evidently misled Dr. Frazer. The above instance from Bengal is no custom at all. It is but a disorderly state of royal succession. Any one who happened to have had power in hand, and managed to kill the ruler, was obeyed by the State officials and the people, because they had no other alternative. It would be observed also that Sultan Alauddīn was succeeded by his son in the normal way. Had there been a custom like that of Malabar, a ceremony for killing Sultan Alauddīn ought to have been held. In fact there was no such ceremony that we hear of, and it was never observed by any of the Muslim rulers of Bengal.

Vikramāditya. To be brief, the next day, a potter's son was being carried in great pomp to the royal palace to rule for a day and die. Vikramāditya, on entering the city, saw the spectacle and proposed to accept the fatal sovereignty in his stead. The demon came to devour him as usual, and, after a terrific combat, was compelled by Vikramāditya to quit the city, never to return. Thenceforth Vikramāditya was accepted as sovereign by the people.[1]

It is difficult to gauge the amount of truth round which the legend has grown up. According to Dr. Frazer, the persistence of bloody rites at Ujjain, of which he gives an account, raises a presumption that the tradition of the daily sacrifice of a king there is not purely mythical.[2] Reminiscences of defunct customs survive in a diluted form in legends. The present story, however, does not speak of any fatal periodical ceremony *attached to kingship by the custom of the country*. Its principal point is *the daily slaying of a man*, of whom kingship is but an accident, an office that is fixed upon him after his selection to meet death in his turn. The difference between this story and the accounts noted already is very great; indeed, so great that it makes the question of affinity between them a matter of doubt. If this difference be the effect of extreme dilution of the ancient custom, of which the legend is supposed to be a reflection, Dr. Frazer is right. If not, it is risky to base on it the inference drawn by him.

Nominal king at Bilāspu.

It seems to have been the custom at Bilāspur in the Central Provinces that after a rājāh's decease, a *Brāhmaṇa* ate *khir* (a preparation of milk) out of the dead king's hand, and occupied the *gadi* for a year. At the end of the period, he was given presents and dismissed from the territory, apparently never to return. The spirit of the dead rājāh was believed to enter into the *Brāhmaṇa* after he had eaten the *khir*, for he was carefully watched and not allowed to go away.[3]

A similar custom is believed to be in vogue in the hill states about Kangra in the Punjab.[4]

[1] *G.*, pt. iii, pp. 122, 123. [2] *Ibid.*, p. 124.
[3] *G.*, pt. iii, p. 154, quoting *Punjab Notes and Queries*, i, p. 86, article 674 (May, 1884).
[4] *Ibid.*

The custom of banishing the *Brāhmaṇa* who represents the dead king at the beginning of the ensuing reign may, according to Dr. Frazer, be a substitute for putting him to death.[1]

The ideas that probably underlie the institutions.

Primitive peoples sometimes believe that their safety, and even that of the world, are bound up with the life of the king, whom they regard as a human incarnation of the divinity. Naturally, they take the greatest care for his life, to prevent the enfeeblement of his powers and their final extinction in death. The only way to avert these, they believe, is to kill the man-god on the very appearance of symptoms of decay and replace him by a vigorous successor to whom the soul of the former king is transferred before it is seriously impaired or has departed for good. Natural death means to them voluntary departure of the soul from the body and its refusal to return, or, more commonly, its extraction therefrom, or detention in its wanderings by a demon or sorcerer. Even capture of the soul of the dying man-god and its transference to the successor would not serve their purpose, for it would be enfeebled by the weakness and exhaustion of the body it leaves, and could but drag out a miserable existence in any new human frame supplied to it. Violent death of the king on the appearance of signs of decay was supposed to avert all these evils, and was preferred to a natural one. Some peoples appear to have thought it unsafe to wait for even the first symptom of decay, and have adopted a fixed term short enough to ensure full vigour of life during its continuance. In some places, this belief has been carried to an extreme, giving rise to such institutions as diurnal destruction of the king.[2]

Whether the ancient Indo-Aryans had such institutions.

Of the Indian examples cited above, two appear to belong to the Dravidian races of Southern India. The one regarding Vikramāditya cannot be safely relied on, while the other from Bengal is wide of the mark. The instances of nominal king-

[1] *G.*, pt. iii, p. 154. In Cambodia and Siam, the temporary king ruled for three days. For details of the institutions in these and other places, see *G.*, pt. iii, pp. 148–59.

[2] *Ibid.*, pp. 9, 10, 46. The motives for regicide reproduced here are doubted by Mr. Andrew Lang in his *Magic and Religion.* The one suggested by him, viz. old age as such, does not, I think, explain all the cases.

ship of Bilāspur and the hill-states about Kangra may imply preceding fatal kingships, of which they are relics; but from them it does not appear clearly whether they relate to Aryan or non-Aryan races. The ideas that are supposed to underlie the institutions have about them an archaic stamp and may date back to a remote antiquity, though the times when their accounts were recorded are recent. We do not find traces of such institutions in early Sanskrit literature in connexion with the many cases of succession that are described at length. In one place in the *Rāmāyaṇa* already noted, Kaikeyī, in course of her conversation with her maid-servant, seems at first sight to speak of kingship termed for a hundred years; but it is capable of another interpretation, which appears to be the right one in view of the fact that nowhere within the ancient Indo-Aryan political system do we meet with any such custom.

CHAPTER V

THE EDUCATION OF THE PRINCE

The importance of king's education in view of his responsibilities.

THE heavy responsibilities devolving on the monarch make it of paramount necessity that he should be thoroughly educated and trained in the art of government.

The Hindu king was ordinarily of the *Kṣatriya* caste.

From the hierarchy of the four castes and their respective duties, it follows that the warrior-caste should always supply the society with competent rulers. The exercise of the regal powers is not within the competency of the other three. The duties of the *Kṣatriyas* comprise, according to the *Kauṭilīya*, *adhyayana* (study), *yajana* (performance of sacrifice), *dāna* (making gifts), *śastrājīva* (military life), and *bhutarakṣaṇa* (protection of beings).[1] The last two items of duty are not prescribed for any of the other classes in a normal condition of society,[2] though, under abnormal conditions and in exceptional cases, taking up arms or pursuit of the military profession by the other castes is met with in literature.[3]

NOTE.—It is not my object to give an historical survey of the training of the ancient Hindu princes, but only to bring out a few of its aspects.

[1] I. iii, p. 7.

[2] The occupations of a *Brāhmaṇa* are: (1) *Adhyayana* (study), (2) *Adhyāpana* (teaching), (3) *Yajana* (performance of sacrifices), (4) *Yājana* (officiating at others' sacrifices), (5) *Dāna* (making gifts), and (6) *Pratigraha* (acceptance of gifts from proper persons). Those of a *Vaiśya* include (1), (3), (5), as also *Kṛṣi* (agricultural), *Pāśupālya* (cattle-rearing), and *Vaṇijyā* (trade). Cf. *Manu*, x. 75 ff.

[3] Cf. *MBh.* xii. 78. 34—'The *Brāhmaṇa* by taking up arms does not incur sin in three cases, viz. self-protection, quelling robbers and compelling the other castes to betake themselves to their duties.' In the *Kauṭilīya* (IX. ii, p. 343), however, a quotation from the previous *Ācāryas* as well as Kauṭilya himself speaks of soldiers belonging to all the four castes. The *Mahābhārata* (xii. 166. 34) allows a *Vaiśya* to use weapons in particular circumstances. Cf. *Śukra.*, ii. 276–80 (Prof. Sarkar's transl., S.B.H.); Hopkins, *J. A. O. S.*, xiii, pp. 76 ff.

In the pre-epic period, we naturally find lesser hardening of caste-divisions and greater mingling of caste-occupations. See *V. I.*, ii. 249, 251, 260, 263, 334, 390; also *Viṣṇu-Purāṇa*, iv. 19. 16; *MBh.*, xiii. 30, and ix. 40 for attainment of *Brāhmaṇa*-hood by lower castes.

Kauṭilya's assumption.

Kauṭilya, in dealing with the education of the monarch, goes upon the assumption that he is a *Kṣatriya*. As an orthodox *Brāhmaṇa*, he cannot but hold the opinion; and if Candragupta Maurya, whom he supported, was not really of *Kṣatriya* birth, he must have claimed to be and passed as such after his victories as a warrior and assumption of sovereignty,[1] on the supposition, of course, that the *Kauṭilīya* is really to be attributed to the minister of Candragupta.[2]

The lines of his education.

The education of the prince is entrusted to competent tutors from his infancy. After the ceremony of tonsure, which is generally performed in his third year,[3] he is taught the

[1] On scanning the dynastic lists of Hindu kings, we meet as a rule with monarchs of *Kṣatriya* blood up to the time of Mahāpadma Nanda, whose reign according to the *Viṣṇu-Purāṇa*, iv. 24. 4, 5, marked the end of *Kṣatriya* rule and the beginning of *Śūdra* kingship. Cf. *Bhagāvata-Purāṇa*, xii. 1. 8. This prophecy that there will be *Śūdra* kings after Mahāpadma Nanda has been fulfilled to this extent, that thenceforth India has seen many a monarch belonging to castes other than *Kṣatriya* and the supremacy of kings of foreign or non-Aryan descent. The Kāṇva dynasty (72–27 B.C.), for instance, established by the *Brāhmaṇa* minister Vāsudeva was of *Brāhmaṇa* blood. The caste of Candragupta Maurya is somewhat obscure, and if he be taken to have been related to the Nanda dynasty, he was no doubt a *Śūdra* with all his successors. But as one body of evidence points to his *Śūdra* origin, another, including the orthodox opinion of Kauṭilya as to the proper caste for kings, points the other way. The truth may perhaps be reached if we bear in mind that, on many occasions, the business of kingship has preceded *Kṣatriya*-ship rather than the latter preceding the former. This is an instance of the assimilative power of Hindu society by which clans or families, like some of the Hinduized Bhars and Gonds who succeeded in winning chieftainship, to cite an example of a recent date, were readily admitted into the frame of Hindu polity as *Kṣatriyas*. (See V. Smith's *Early India*, 3rd ed., pp. 322, 413.) So, whatever may have been the real origin of Candragupta Maurya, he seems to have ranked as a *Kṣatriya* (*ibid.*, p. 408). The caste of the rest of the ancient Hindu monarchs is more or less obscure, but it seems that Puṣyamitra and his successors were *Kṣatriyas*, also the famous Harṣa, so far as it can be guessed from his relationships. It appears that, in many cases, the deviations from the orthodox rule that a ruler must be a *Kṣatriya* were placed out of sight by the veneer of assumed *Kṣatriya*-hood. In some of the *Saṃhitās*, a *Śūdra* king is specially out of favour, though, of course, the wielding of sceptre by a *Brāhmaṇa* or *Vaiśya* does not receive its approval. The *Manu-Saṃhitā* enjoins a *Brāhmaṇa* not to dwell in a country where the rulers are *Śūdras* (*Manu*, iv. 61); cf. the *Viṣṇu-Saṃhitā* (lxxi. 64; Foy, *Die königliche Gewalt*, p. 8; Fick, *Die sociale Gliederung*, pp. 83, 84; Roth, *J. A. O. S.*, 16. ccxliii.

[2] For arguments against this view see Keith, *J. R. A. S.*, 1916, pp. 130–7; J. Jolly, *Zeitschrift der Deutschen Morgenländischen Gesellschaft*, lxviii. 355 ff., and elsewhere.

[3] Cf. *Raghuvaṃśa*, iii. 28.

alphabet (*lipi*) and arithmetic (*saṃkhyāna*); and after investiture with the sacred thread, which takes place in the case of a *Kṣatriya* in his eleventh year,[1] he becomes qualified to commence higher studies—the curriculum including:

(i) *Trayī*, and *Ānvīkṣikī*, (ii) *Vārttā*, and (iii) *Daṇḍanīti*,[2] the subjects under (i) being taught by eminent scholars (*śiṣṭāḥ*), those under (ii) by superintendents of government departments (*adhyakṣāḥ*) having not merely a theoretical knowledge but also a thorough practical experience of the subject, and those under (iii) by theoretical masters of statecraft (*vaktāraḥ*) as well as by practical statesmen (*prayoktāraḥ*).

Besides these subjects, he had to hear daily from competent professors the *Itihāsa*, which, as has been noted formerly, comprehends (a) *Purāṇa*, (b) *Itivṛtta*, (c) *Ākhyāyikā*, (d) *Udāharaṇa*, (e) *Dharmaśāstra*, and (f) *Arthaśāstra*.[3]

Along with these, he was also given lessons in the military art comprehending (i) *Hastividyā*, (ii) *Aśvavidyā*, (iii) *Rathavidyā*, and (iv) *Praharaṇavidyā*, i.e. the subjects bearing on elephants, horses, chariots, and weapons respectively.

During the period of studentship the prince has to live the austere life of a *Brahmacārin*, observing celibacy and undergoing the hardships involved in the study of the different subjects. His daily routine, as Kauṭilya records it, allots the forenoon to the military exercises noted above, the afternoon to the hearing of the *Itihāsa*, and the rest of the day and night to receiving new lessons (*apūrva-grahaṇa*), revising the old ones (*gṛhīta-paricaya*), and trying to master those not clearly made out.[4]

The necessity for this rigorous discipline was well realized by the ancient Hindu statesman; for the prince could not be

[1] *Manu*, ii. 36; *Yājñ.*, i. 14; *Āśvalāyana-Gṛhya-Sūtra*, i. 19; *Śāṅkhāyana-Gṛhya-Sūtra*, ii. 1; *Pāraskara-Gṛhya-Sūtra*, ii. 2; *Gobhila-Gṛhya-Sūtra*, ii. 10; *Hiraṇyakeśi-Gṛhya-Sūtra*, i. 1; *Khādira-Gṛhya-Sūtra*, ii. 4; *Āpastamba-Gṛhya-Sūtra*, iv. 10.

[2] For explanation of the subjects, see Chap. IX.

[3] For explanation of the subjects, see *Ibid.* Cf. Hopkins, *J. A. O. S.*, xiii. 110–12 for parallels in the epics.

[4] For the above information, see *Arthaśāstra*, I. v. p. 10. The *Kāmandakīya* and all the writers on polity lay great stress on the *vinaya*, i. e. discipline of the prince and the cultivation of his latent faculties; cf. *Raghuvaṃśa*, iii. 29.

a competent ruler without this period of disciplined probation. The success of a well-educated and self-controlled sovereign is thus indicated by Kauṭilya:

> Vidyāvinīto rājā hi prajānāṃ vinaye rataḥ,
> Ananyāṃ pṛthivīṃ bhuṅkte sarvabhūtahite rataḥ.

(A king, well disciplined by education and bent on his subjects' government and the good of all living beings, can enjoy the whole earth without a rival.)[1]

The period of studentship lasts up to the sixteenth year, after which the prince performs the ceremony of *godāna* on the eve of his *Return from School* and enters into the next stage of his life by marriage.[2]

On completion of education, the prince is associated with administration.

The prince now enters upon a more practical stage of his life, in which he is gradually brought into contact with all the difficult problems he will have to handle in his future position as king. He seems to have been charged with responsible duties in government departments, where he worked as a subordinate under the head of the particular department in which he was placed for the time being.[3] When found competent, he was made a commander of an army, or an heir-apparent associated with the reigning sovereign in the work of administration.[4]

Kauṭilya's correctives for an erratic prince.

Kauṭilya discusses at length the steps to be taken by the king to correct a prince turning rebellious or morally perverse,[5] and also the means to be adopted by the latter if treated in a cruel and unbecoming manner by the former. He does not accept the opinions of other authorities on these points *in toto* and suggests proper education and discipline of the prince from his very infancy, constant contact with wholesome influences, and timely dissuasion from evil as the means of bringing him round. When these fail, he may be confined

[1] *Artha.*, I. v, p. 11. (Cf. *Kāmandakīya*, i. 37. 63. 65). Here Kauṭilya gives examples, by way of warning, of sovereigns who ruined themselves by yielding to temptation.

[2] *Op. cit.*, p. 10.

[3] *Op. cit.*, I. xviii, p. 35.

[4] *Ibid.*, I. xvii, p. 34; cf. *Matsya-Purāṇa*, ccxx. 2. 3. 7, 8; *Agni-Purāṇa*, ccxxv. 2. 4. 21, 22; ccxxxviii. 9.

[5] e.g. Sagara banished his son Asamañjas, who had caused some children of the city to be drowned. (*MBh.* xii. 57. 8).

and kept under surveillance in a definite place. If this also proves abortive, he may be exiled. Extreme cases of rebellious attitude in a prince may justify, according to Kauṭilya, even the sacrifice of his life for the good of the State.

If the reigning monarch takes an unjustifiably hostile attitude towards a good prince, Kauṭilya advises the latter to take measures which are to be passively protective at first, rising to the more severe steps.[1]

[1] *Arthaśāstra*, I. xviii, pp. 35, 36.

CHAPTER VI

THE ROYAL DUTIES; THE KING'S DAILY ROUTINE OF WORK

King's duties and the literature thereon.

THE manifold duties that devolve on a king after his accession to the throne are treated of in a good many Sanskrit works both printed and manuscript. The lists of duties furnished by the works vary of course as to their details, but agree generally as to certain main points. They touch on personal duties under which may be classed moral discipline and such other virtues, together with the study of the *Vedas* and the sciences and arts, conducing to the improvement of his intellect and physique. These duties go towards making the sovereign a better man, while his public duties as enjoined by the *Śāstras* have a direct bearing on his relations with the people at large. They cover a very wide range, and the numerous lists of royal duties in the Sanskrit works generally reiterate one or other of his obligations regarding the following, viz. the law of the four castes, the maintenance of the four *stages of life* (*āśramas*), consultation regarding the affairs of the State, and adherence to the principles of the works on government (*nīti-śāstras*) in daily practices, the appointment of competent ministers and other officials, the officiation of competent priests (who were often associated with public functions), the supervision of the duties of the officials, the inspection of the finance, the administration of justice, inquiries into the economic state of the country, and the undertaking of works for the economic welfare of the people, the inspection and maintenance of the army, foreign relations, encouragement of learning, protection of the needy and helpless, and the establishment and maintenance of institutions of public utility.[1]

[1] For royal duties, the following works may be consulted: *Śatapatha Brāhmaṇa* v. 4. 4. 5; ix. 3. 3. 10, 11; xi. 2. 7. 17; ix. 4. 1. 1, 13; xiii. 1. 5. 4; xiii. 2. 2. 7; &c. *Manu*, vii. 2–3, 35, 80, 88, 111–12, 142–4, 203;

The duties are heavy and numerous, and the conscientious monarch who undertakes to follow the injunctions has to work very hard to discharge properly his responsibilities. Many of the aforesaid duties have religious sanctions at their back, making the task all the more heavy for one who wears the crown.

King's ideal, daily routine according to Kauṭilya.

The traditional ideal daily routine of a monarch for the performance of his heavy duties is laid down in a good many works going back to an ancient date. The one given by the *Arthaśāstra* divides the day and night into sixteen equal parts and allots to each part a particular item of his duties:

Day—(1) 6 a.m. to 7.30 a.m. is devoted to looking after the defence of the country and the supervision of the finances;

(2) 7.30 to 9 to the supervision of the affairs of the townspeople and provincials;

(3) 9 to 10.30 to ablution, dining, and study;

(4) 10.30 to 12 to the collection of State dues from the heads of the departments (*Adhyakṣas*);

(5) 12 a.m. to 1.30 p.m. to correspondence with absent ministers;

viii. 41–2, 46, 172, 303–9; ix. 253; x. 80, 119 (protection of the people under his care); vii. 54–9, 60–8, 81 (appointment of officials); vii. 146–83, 205–16; ix. 294–9 (consultation); vii. 79, 145 (giving audience); vii. 37–8, 79, 82–6, 88, 134–6, 145; viii. 395; ix. 313–23; xi. 4, 21–3 (encouragement and honour to *Brāhmaṇas*); viii. 27–9 (support of the helpless); vii. 127–33, 137–9; x. 118, 120; viii. 401–3 (financial and economic duties); vii. 14–34; viii. 302–3, 310–11, 335, 343–7; ix. 252–93, 312; viii. 1–8, 43; ix. 233–4; viii. 9, 10, 18, 19, 40–4, 126–9, 170–5; ix. 249 (judicial duties); vii. 78–9, 145 (appointment of priests, and sacrifice); vii. 39–42, 43, 44–53; ix. 301–11 (personal duties); vii. 69–76, 99–100, 201–3, 222; ix. 25, 223; x. 115, 119 (military duties); *Āpastamba*, ii. 10. 25. 1–15; ii. 10. 26. 1–17; *Gautama*, viii. 1 ff.; xi. 1–31; *Vasiṣṭha*, xix. 1–20, 22–48; *Baudhāyana*, i. 10. 18. 1–20; *Viṣṇu*, iii. 2–98; *Yājñavalkya* (M. N. Dutt's ed.), i. 309–68; *Parāśara* (*ibid.*), i. 56–9; *Śaṅkha* (*ibid*), i. 4; *Hārīta* (*ibid.*), ii. 2–5; *Atri* (*ibid.*), i. 14, 17, 22–4, 27, 28, 29.

The following *Purāṇas* speak also of royal duties: *Matsya-Purāṇa*, ccxv–ccxxvii; *Skanda-Purāṇa*, *Nāgara-Khaṇḍa*, xii. 6 ff. (scanty); *Bhāgavata*, iv. 14. 14–20; 20. 13–16; *Mārkaṇḍeya-Purāṇa*, xxvii; xxxiv. 113–17; xviii. 1 ff.; *Agni-Purāṇa*, ccxx, ccxxii–ccxxv, ccxxvii, ccxxxiii–ccxlii; *Garuḍa-Purāṇa*, cxi–cxiii; *Devī-Purāṇa*, ix. 10 ff.; *Bṛhaddharma-Purāṇa*, *Uttara-khaṇḍa*, iii; *Kālikā-Purāṇa*, lxxxiv, lxxxv; cf. also *Kāmandakīya-Nītisāra*, i; *Śukranītisāra* (Prof. B. K. Sarkar's transl., S. B. H.), pp. 4, 6, 7, 11, 23, 36, and 53.

(6) 1.30 to 3 to amusements or self-deliberation;
(7) 3 to 4.30 to the inspection of elephants, horses, chariots, and infantry;
(8) 4.30 to 6 to consultation with the commander-in-chief and evening prayers at nightfall;

Night—(1) 6 p.m. to 7.30 p.m. to interview with the secret agents;
(2) 7.30 to 9 to ablution, supper, and study;
(3), (4), and (5) 9 to 1.30 a.m. to entering the bed-chamber amid sounds of trumpets, and sleep;
(6) 1.30 to 3 to waking amid trumpet-sounds and calling to mind the *Śāstric* injunctions and the duties of the ensuing day;
(7) 3 to 4.30 to convening the council and sending out secret agents on their errands;
(8) 4.30 to 6 to receiving benedictions in the company of his tutors, and domestic and sacrificial priests, interview with the physician, head-cook, and astrologer, and entering the court after perambulating a cow with her calf, and a bull.

The above divisions of the time-table, however, admit of alterations to suit the capacity of a particular monarch. The routine does not leave much leisure to the king, but keeps him occupied with some State business or other, the greater part of the day. There are only three hours during which he is set free from the cares of the State (9 to 10.30, and 1.30 to 3). His labours come to a close at 7.30 in the evening, after which he has seven hours and a half at a stretch, of which about six hours are devoted to sleep. The rest of the day and night (viz. 24 − 10 hours, i.e. 13½ hours) is divided among the various State engagements. It should be noted that these hours do not all impose upon the monarch brain work or physical worry of the same intensity. The time, for instance, from 4.30 a.m. to 6 a.m. is of comparative rest, as also a few other time-divisions and their fractions during which his work is more passive than the rest of his working hours. The time expressly set apart for study recurs twice during day and night. Though it adds to the volume of his intellectual work, the period allowed to it is short, considering that it is to be snatched from the hours of ablution and dinner. However, the sort of life implied by the routine is one of much stress and strain and pressure of work, explaining the necessity of disciplined life essential to kingship.

The second division of time in the morning (7.30 to 9) is an important one, devoted as it is to giving audience to the public and considering a variety of matters affecting the people at large. The king is enjoined to make himself easily accessible to the petitioners and attend personally to the subjects of their applications in the following order, instead of entrusting everything to his officials: [1]

(1) Deities (*devatā*), (2) abodes of ascetics (*āśrama*), (3) heretics (*pāṣaṇḍa*), (4) *Brāhmaṇas* versed in the *Vedas* (*śrotriya*), (5) lower animals (*paśu*), (6) sacred places (*puṇya-sthāna*), (7) minors, as also (8) the old, (9) the diseased, (10) the distressful (*vyasanin*), (11) the helpless, and (12) women. The above order of business may, however, be changed owing to importance or urgency of a particular item.[2]

It is practically the same as in *Manu*, *Yājñavalkya*, and some *Purāṇas*.

The routine as set forth in the *Saṃhitās* is in substance almost the same as the one in the *Arthaśāstra*. Manu's [3] version is as follows:

'Having risen in the last watch of the night, having performed (the rite of) personal purification, having with a collected mind offered oblations in the fire, and having worshipped Brāhmaṇas, he (king) shall enter the hall of audience which must possess the marks (considered) auspicious (for a dwelling).'—vii. 145.

'Tarrying there, he shall gratify all subjects (who come to see him) by a kind reception and afterwards dismiss them; having dismissed his subjects, he shall take counsel with his ministers.'—vii. 146.

'Having consulted with his ministers on all these (matters), having taken exercise, and having bathed afterwards, the king may enter the harem at mid-day in order to dine.'—vii. 216.

[1] *Arthaśāstra*, I. xix, pp. 38, 39.
[2] *Ibid.*, 39.
[3] Bühler's version in *S. B. E.* xxv.

'Adorned (with his robes of state), let him again inspect his fighting men, all his chariots and beasts of burden, the weapons and accoutrements.'—vii. 222.

'Having performed his twilight-devotions, let him, well-armed, hear in an inner apartment the doings of those who make secret reports and of his spies.'—vii. 223.

'But going to another secret apartment and dismissing those people, he may enter the harem, surrounded by female (servants), in order to dine again.'—vii. 224.

'Having eaten there something for the second time, and having been recreated by the sound of music, let him go to rest and rise at the proper time free from fatigue.'—vii. 225.

'A king who is in good health must observe these rules; but, if he is indisposed, he may entrust all this (business) to his servants.'—vii. 226.

Yājñavalkya's account [1] runs thus:

'Having risen up early in the morning, he (king) should personally look after the work of collection and disbursement; next he should attend to law-suits, after which he should bathe and take his meal at ease.'—i. 327.

'He should then deposit in the treasury the gold brought by persons engaged in the work and then see the secret agents, after which he should with his ministers send the envoys on their errands.'—i. 328.

'Thereafter he should enjoy his leisure alone or in the company of ministers. Next, he should take counsel with his commander-in-chief after the inspection of the army.'—i. 329.

'Then after evening adoration, he should listen to the confidential reports of the secret agents. He should then enjoy singing and dancing, take his meal and study.'—i. 330.

'He should then go to sleep amid sounds of trumpets and get up from bed similarly, when he should cogitate the scriptural injunctions and all his duties.'—i. 331.

'Then with respectful welcome, he should send secret emissaries to the dominions of other kings as well as his own, after receiving blessings from his sacrificial priest, domestic priest and teacher. Next, he should see his astrologers and physicians and confer on the Brāhmaṇas learned in the *Vedas*, kine, gold, land, houses and their furniture.'—i. 332, 333.

The time-table in the *Agni-Purāṇa* [2] corresponds in its main features:

'Pushkara said, "I shall relate to you the daily routine of

[1] M. N. Dutt's version.

[2] ccxxv. 1–17.

the king. It is called *ajasra-karma*, i.e. incessant work. When there are only two *muhūrtas* (48 minutes) before the break of dawn, the king should get up from bed amid music and singing of panegyrists and see the secret emissaries so privately that no body can recognize them when on duty as his men. Next, he should attend to his income and disbursement and then after attending the calls of nature, he should go to his bathing-house. There, after cleaning the teeth and taking bath, he should perform the *Sandhyā* service, repeat prayers and worship Vāsudeva. He should then make sacred offerings to the fire and worship the manes of his ancestors, take blessings from the *Brāhmaṇas* and make gifts of gold and kine. Then after decorating his person and smearing it with unguents he should see the reflexion of his face in a mirror as also in clarified butter kept in a gold receptacle. Then he should hear the auspicious or inauspicious nature of the day, take the medicines prescribed for him by the royal physicians, touch the auspicious articles, make obeisance to his superiors and then enter his hall of audience where, Oh Highly Fortunate, he should receive the *Brāhmaṇas*, the ministers and the officers of the court as also such of his subjects as would be announced by the usher. Then having heard the reports of works, he should determine the steps to be taken, and then proceed to adjudicate law-suits, after which he should consult his ministers on important matters. A king should take counsel neither with a single minister nor with too many; nor with the ignorant and untrustworthy. He should carry into action those schemes that have been well thought over and will not therefore injure the State. He should not betray his secrets by looks and gestures, for the wise can gather others' intentions from those outward signs. A king, following the advice of his astrologers, physicians, and ministers, attains prosperity, for the latter are the custodians of the former's welfare. Council dissolved, the king should take physical exercise with a discus or sword, or on a carriage. Then he should bathe in a tank free from aquatic animals, and see that the God Viṣṇu has been duly worshipped, that the sacrificial fire has been duly lighted and offerings made to it, and that the *Brāhmaṇas* have been properly honoured with presents. Then having decorated his body, he should make gifts, and next take his meal which has been duly tested. Then he should take dressed betel and rest awhile on his left side. Then, after the inspection of the army, armoury and store-house, he should peruse the *Śāstras*. He should then finish his evening prayer and send the secret agents to the works previously thought over by him. Thereafter, he should take his supper and enter the seraglio. The king being well protected should do this every day amid songs and sounds of musical instruments." '

The *Devī-Purāṇa*[1] gives a similar programme of royal duties.[1] A portion of this routine up to the holding of court in the assembly-hall (the differences in details being excepted) is represented in the *Bhāgavata-Purāṇa*[2] as being followed by Kṛṣṇa in his capital at Dvārakā. The *Raghuvaṃśa* refers to the traditional routine upon which Mallinātha makes his commentation, adding some details.[3] Daṇḍin, in his *Daśakumāra-carita*, parodies the *Kauṭilīya* routine but hands down the tradition:

The routine is followed in part by Kṛṣṇa in the *Bhāgavata-Purāṇa*. It is also given in the *Raghuvaṃśa*, and also in the *Daśakumāra-carita* where Daṇḍin parodies the *Kauṭilīya*.

Day.—'The king risen from his bed in the *first of the eight divisions of the day* hears reports concerning his income and disbursement after having washed his face in a hurry and devoured a handful or half-handful of food. The cunning heads of government-departments of a king, who does not hear them attentively, rob him of double his wealth and multiply thousandfold the four hundred means of collection of wealth enjoined by Cāṇakya.

In the *second division* of the day, the king passes his life distressfully with his ears burnt so to speak by the hubbub of mutually quarrelling subjects. The judges decree or dismiss the cases of the suitors at will, bringing sin and disrepute upon their master, and wealth to themselves.

The *third division* is the time for bathing and eating. So long as his food is not fully digested, his fear of being poisoned does not leave him. After his meal, he stands up, in the *fourth division*, with his hands stretched out for gold.

In the *fifth division*, he suffers great pain from consultation with his ministers. Then also the ministers individually or collectively grow indifferent, and turn at will to their evil design the good or bad qualities of things, the reports of envoys and secret agents, the practicability or otherwise of actions, as well as the states of undertakings due to time and place, and are supported by the 'circles' of friendly, inimical, and neutral kings bringing their master under their control by secretly, and in the guise of peace-makers, inflaming the anger of people within and outside the kingdom.

[1] ii. 69–76. [2] x. 70. 4–17. [3] xvii. 49.

In the *sixth division* ($3\frac{3}{4}$ *dandas*, i.e. $1\frac{1}{2}$ hrs.) he engages either in amusements or conversation.

In the *seventh* comes the inspection of the military force composed of its four elements.

The *eighth* is devoted to consultation with his commander-in-chief regarding military matters.

Night.—Having performed the *Sandhyā* service, he sees the secret agents in the *first division of the night.* Through them the very cruel uses of weapons, fire, and poison are to be provided for.

In the *second*, after meal, he commences religious studies like a Brāhmaṇa versed in the *Vedas.*

In the *third*, he goes to bed amid sounds of trumpets, while the *fourth* and the *fifth* find him asleep—fast asleep, because of the incessant mental worry by which he enjoys the pleasure of sleep like an ascetic.

In the *sixth*, he cogitates the *Śāstras* and his own duties.

The *seventh* is devoted to the sending of secret informants on their duties after consultation. They by their sweet words gain wealth from the sender as well as the person to whom they are sent, and increase it by commerce through routes where they have not to pay any tolls, and roam about by skilfully creating works where there are none.

In the *eighth*, the priest and others come to him and say, &c.'

It is also found in Megasthenes.

The regular round of the king's daily duties is fragmentarily referred to by the Greek ambassador Megasthenes: 'The king may not sleep during the daytime.[1] . . . He leaves his palace . . . for the purpose of judging causes. He then remains in court for the whole day, without allowing the business to be interrupted, even though the hour arrives when he must needs attend to his person—that is, when he is to be rubbed with the cylinders of wood. He continues hearing cases while the friction, which is performed by four attendants, is still proceeding. Another purpose for which he leaves his palace is to offer sacrifice.'[2]

The traditional programme of diurnal duties, as we find it, is the result of evolution through centuries dating back to the Vedic times. The discharge of heavy responsibilities of the

[1] Cf. the Vedic injunction, '*mā divā svāpsīḥ* (or *suṣupthāḥ*)' found in several *Gṛhya Sūtras*, *Brāhmaṇas*, &c.

[2] See Megasthenes, Fragm. XXVII.

king ought to follow a method; and the method that was recommended to the monarch was one matured by the wisdom of statesmen. The monarch could no doubt alter it to suit himself, but the freedom was hedged in by limits which he could not overstep. The considerations by which the programme was framed are briefly stated in a *śloka* of the *Mahābhārata*,[1] viz. equable pursuit of *dharma*, *artha*, and *kāma* (for explanation of these terms, see *supra*).

The general principles behind the routine.

The general principles to guide the monarch in the regulation of his duties are found in both the *Rāmāyaṇa*[2] and the *Mahābhārata*,[3] and also in a Vedic injunction by Dakṣa with which the later developments seem to have a relation of direct descent.

The injunction is as follows:

Pūrvāhne cācared dharmaṃ madhyāhne 'rthamupārjayet,
Sāyāhne cācaret kāmam ity eṣā vaidikī śrutiḥ.[4]

(Forenoon is for religious duties, midday for acquisition of wealth, and evening for diversion: such is the Vedic saying.)

[1] ii. 5. 20. [2] ii. 100. 17 (cf. *MBh.*, ii. 5. 29). [3] ii. 5. 85.
[4] *Vide* Nīlakaṇṭha's comment on *MBh.*, ii. 5. 20.

CHAPTER VII

THE EVOLUTION OF THE PRINCIPAL STATE-OFFICIALS

THE next point for our consideration is the officers and departments of the State. In this connexion we may note the following passage of the *Kauṭilīya*:

Kauṭilya's reference to eighteen *Tīrthas*.

> Evaṃ śatrau ca mitre ca madhyame cāvapec carān,
> Udāsīne ca teṣāṃ ca tīrtheṣv aṣṭādaśasv api,[1]

where Kauṭilya advises the stationing of secret agents in the surrounding states, whether inimical, friendly, or neutral, to watch the movements not only of the people but also of the *eighteen* functionaries. This recognition of *eighteen Tīrthas* in a State is traditional and appears to be of very early origin. Not only is it referred to in the above passage as a matter of general familiarity, but also in the *Mahābhārata*, where Nārada asks Yudhiṣṭhira, 'Seekest thou to know every thing about the *eighteen Tīrthas* of the foe and *fifteen* of thy own, by means of three and three spies all unacquainted with one another?'[2] These *eighteen Tīrthas*, according to Nīlakaṇṭha, the commentator of the *Mahābhārata*, are:

Enumeration of *tīrthās* in the *Mahābhārata*.

(i) *Mantrin*—Councillor,
(ii) *Purohita*—Priest,
(iii) *Yuvarājan*—Crown-prince,
(iv) *Camūpati*—Commander-in-chief of the army,
(v) *Dvārapāla*—Chamberlain,[3]
(vi) *Antarveśika*—Superintendent of the ladies' apartments,
(vii) *Kārāgārādhikārin*—Overseer of prisons,
(viii) *Dravyasaṃcayakṛt*—Steward,

[1] I. xii, p. 21; the word *Tīrtha* also occurs at I. iv, p. 9.
[2] *MBh.* ii. 5. 38.
[3] For the translation of some of the names, I have received suggestions from Prof. Hopkins, *J. A. O. S.*, xiii. 128.

(ix) *Kṛtyākṛtyeṣv arthānāṃ viniyojaka*—Corresponding to *Sannidhātṛ*[1] in the *Kauṭilīya* list (see *infra*, p. 170),

(x) *Pradeṣṭṛ*—an officer combining both executive and judicial powers in the *Kauṭilīya*,

(xi) *Nagarādhyakṣa*—overseer of the city,

(xii) *Kāryanirmāṇakṛt*—Engineer,

(xiii) *Dharmādhyakṣa*—Judge,

(xiv) *Sabhādhyakṣa*—Overseer of the assembly,

(xv) *Daṇḍapāla*—Guardian of punishment,

(xvi) *Durgapāla*—Overseer of forts,

(xvii) *Rāṣṭrāntapāla*—Protector of the frontiers, and

(xviii) *Aṭavīpāla*—Guardian of the forests.[2]

The eighteen *Tīrthas*, according to the commentary on the passage in the *Rāmāyaṇa*,[3] differ only as to the two officers *Vyavahāranirṇetṛ* and *Senādhyakṣa*, the *Mahābhārata* mentioning *Sabhādhyakṣa*, and *Aṭavīpāla*, whom the former identifies with *Rāṣṭrāntapāla*. The existence of eighteen *Tīrthas* is echoed in works like the *Pañcatantra*,[4] *Raghuvaṃśa*,[5] and *Śiśupālavadha*.[6]

The *Tīrthas* according to the *Rāmāyaṇa*, *Pañcatantra*, *Raghuvaṃśa*, and *Śiśupālavadha*

[1] His principal duty was to exercise a check upon the following officials: (1) *Kośādhyakṣa*, (2) *Paṇyādhyakṣa*, (3) *Koṣṭhāgārādhyakṣa*, (4) *Kupyādhyakṣa*, (5) *Āyudhāgārādhyakṣa*, and (6) *Bandhanāgārādhyakṣa*.

[2] For another reference to the eighteen *Tīrthas*, see *MBh.*, xii. 69. 52; cf. *Nītiprakāśikā*, i. 52.

[3] The *Rāmāyaṇa* gives us some light on this point in the dialogue between Rāma and Bharata in ii. 100. 36.

> Kaccid aṣṭādaśānyeṣu svapakṣe daśa pañca ca,
> Tribhis tribhir avijñātair vetsi tīrthāni cāraṇaiḥ.

This *śloka* also mentions the eighteen *Tīrthas* explained by the commentator as follows: '(i) Mantrī, (ii) purohitaḥ, (iii) yuvarājā, (iv) senāpatiḥ, (v) dauvārikaḥ, (vi) antaḥpurādhikṛtaḥ, (vii) bandhanāgārādhikṛtaḥ, (viii) dhanādhyakṣaḥ, (ix) rājājñayā, ājñāpyeṣu vaktā, (x) prāḍvivākasaṃjño vyavahārapraṣṭā, (xi) dharmāsanādhikṛtaḥ, (xii) vyavahāranirṇetā sabhyākhyaḥ, (xiii) senāyājīvitabhṛtidānādhyakṣaḥ, (xiv) karmānte vetanagrāhiṇaḥ, (xv) nagarādhyakṣaḥ, (xvi) rāṣṭrāntapālaḥ ayam evāṭavikaḥ, (xvii) duṣṭānāṃ daṇḍanādhikārī, (xviii) jalagiri-vana-sthala-durgapālāḥ.

Etāny eva svapakshe mantri-purohita-yuvarājān hitvā ca pañcadaśa. Ekaikasmin viṣaye tribhis tribhir abhijñātaiḥ parasparam itaraiś cābhijñātair etāny aṣṭādaśa tīrthāni vetsi kaccit. Svadeśe 'py etair nyāyato vyavahāraḥ pravartyate na veti vicāraṇīyaṃ paradeśe ceti bhāvaḥ.'

[4] iii. 67–70 (F. Kielhorn's ed.). [5] xvii. 68. [6] xiv. 9.

The lists, it should be noted, mention the names of individuals as representatives of either the respective classes of officials or government-departments to which they belong, except when the individual stands by himself, e.g. *Yuvarājan.*

The *Kauṭilīya*,[1] in a similar context as the passages in the *Rāmāyaṇa* and the *Mahābhārata*, recommends the appointment of spies to watch in the king's own State the following people:

Kauṭilya's list of *Tīrthas.*

(1) *Mantrin*, (2) *Purohita*, (3) *Senāpati*, (4) *Yuvarājan*, (5) *Dauvārika*, (6) *Antarveśika*, (7) *Praśāstṛ*, (8) *Samāhartṛ*, (9) *Sannidhātṛ*, (10) *Pradeṣṭṛ*, (11) *Nāyaka*, (12) *Pauravyāvahārika*, (13) *Kārmāntika*, (14) *Mantripariṣadadhyakṣa*, (15) *Daṇḍapāla*, (16) *Durgapāla*, (17) *Antapāla*, (18) *Āṭavika.*

Agreement of the lists.

On comparing this with the previous list from the *Mahābhārata*, they appear to agree *in toto*, *Praśāstṛ* corresponding with *Kārāgārādhikārin*, *Samāhartṛ* with *Dravyasaṃcayakṛt*, *Sannidhātṛ* with *Kṛtyākṛtyeṣv arthānāṃ viniyojaka*, *Nāyaka* with *Nagarādhyakṣa*, *Pauravyāvahārika* with *Dharmādhyakṣa*, *Kārmāntika* with *Kāryanirmāṇakṛt*, *Mantripariṣadadhyakṣa* with *Sabhādhyakṣa*, the rest having correspondence even in names. As we proceed, we shall find that the agreement in names is supported by more or less similarity of functions.

The *Tīrthas* exhaust roughly the whole sphere of work of a State.

The reason for this traditional division of the State into eighteen *Tīrthas* probably lies in the fact that they exhaust, roughly at least, the whole sphere of work of a State and meet its indispensable requirements—providing for the deliberation of State-questions and assistance to the sovereign, both secular and spiritual, for his personal safety and convenience, for the administration of justice in the country, for its internal peace and external security, for the collection of State-dues and their application, and lastly for the supply of material needs of the people by the exploitation of its natural resources—by manufactures, commerce, and industries. The information gathered through secret agents regarding these *Tīrthas* is sufficient for ordinary purposes to show the inner workings of a State and the direction of its policy.

[1] *Kauṭilīya*, I. xii, p. 20.

We find some of the officials existing in the Vedic period, a few among whom having the same designations as those in later times. Some officials of the Vedic times figure among the lists of *Ratnins* found in several early Sanskrit works:

The *Taittirīya-Saṃhitā*[1] and *Taittirīya-Brāhmaṇa*[2] mention (1) *Brāhmaṇa*, (2) *Rājanya*, (3) *Senānī*, (4) *Sūta*, (5) *Grāmaṇī*, (6) *Kṣattṛ*, (7) *Saṃgrahītṛ*, (8) *Bhāgadugha*, and (9) *Akṣāvāpa*, excluding *Mahiṣī* (king's first wife), *Vāvātā* (king's favourite wife), and *Parivṛktī* (king's discarded wife), whom we need not notice for our purposes.

The *Śatapatha-Brāhmaṇa*[3] enumerates all the above officers, adding *Go-vikartana* and *Pālāgala*, while the *Maitrāyaṇī Saṃhitā* puts *Rājan* for *Rājanya* (perhaps implying the same person), gives *Grāmaṇī* the name of *Vaiśya-Grāmaṇī*, adds *Takṣa-Rathakārau*, and inserts *Go-vikarta* without interfering with the rest. The *Kāṭhaka-Saṃhitā*[4] only substitutes *Go-vyaccha* for *Govikarta* in the above list and omits *Takṣa-Rathakārau*.

The eight *Vīras* (i.e. heroes, friends of the king) figuring in the *Pañcaviṃśa-Brāhmaṇa*[1] are *Purohita*, *Mahiṣī*, *Sūta*, *Grāmaṇī*, *Kṣattṛ*, and *Saṃgrahītṛ*, adding nothing to the previous lists.

The two persons *Brāhmaṇa* and *Purohita* are perhaps the same, signifying the royal priest. It does not appear clearly whether *Rājanya* is a government-official or not. *Senānī* is the Commander of the Army, *Sūta* the Royal Equerry. It seems that *Sūta* was not a mere private servant of the king's household, but an official charged with the State duty of looking after the management of all the horses kept for the king's personal use as well as for military purposes. In later times, when differentiation of duties had progressed a good deal, we find his place occupied by the *Aśvādhyakṣa* (Superintendent of Horses) in the *Kauṭilīya* list.

[1] i. 8. 9. 1 ff. [2] i. 7. 3. 1 ff. [3] v. 3. 1. 1 ff.

[4] *Kāṭhaka-Saṃhitā*, xv. 4. The lists quoted by Weber in his *Über den Rājasūya* (pp. 21, 22) differ in a few places from those cited above, but add no official with a new designation. Stray references to the above officers occur in many other places, as will be evident from the *V. I.*

[5] *Pañcaviṃśa-Brāhmaṇa*, xix. 1. 4.

Grāmaṇī is the Village-Headman. His importance as a State-official is realized only when we bear in mind that in early times he had military duties to perform, for which he might be called a Troop-leader.[1] It is not clear whether he is the head-man of a particular village, in which case his importance would be considerably diminished. It is probable that he is the head of all the village-headmen in the realm.

Kṣattṛ is the Chamberlain.[2] It is difficult to define his duties, which may have been like those of the official called 'Chamberlain' in the later lists.

Saṃgrahītṛ appears in the *Kauṭilīya* with manifold duties. He has to attend to the collection of revenue and the checking of accounts, to the operations of the land-survey and the statistical department. He is principally connected with the collection of revenue and may therefore be termed 'Collector-General'.[3]

Bhāgadugha is variously translated into 'dealer out of portions', 'distributor of food'. Sāyaṇa renders it by 'tax-collector' in some places,[4] and by 'carver' in others,[5] thus making him either a revenue-officer or a court-official. In view of the existence of a principal collector of taxes in the Collector-General (*Saṃgrahītṛ*), if the term is so understood, the rendering by 'Treasurer' appears to be more reasonable, for otherwise there will be an overlapping of functions. The office of a treasurer is found in the later works.

Akṣāvāpa[6] was the 'superintendent of dicing'. It may be

[1] See *V. I.*, i. 96.

[2] *Ibid.*, ii. 200.

[3] Messrs. Macdonell and Keith are not sure about the functions of *Samgrahītṛ*, whom they render by 'charioteer or treasurer'. The clear definition of his duties in the *Kauṭilīya* leaves no doubt that he was a revenue-officer, but this evidence, of course, is not cogent for the Vedic period.

[4] *Taittirīya-Saṃhitā*, i. 8. 9. 2; *Taittirīya-Brāhmaṇa*, i. 7. 3. 5; iii. 4. 8. 1; and *Śatapatha-Brāhmaṇa*, v. 3. 1. 9.

[5] *Śatapatha-Brāhmaṇa*, i. 1. 2. 17. See *V. I.*, ii. 100, 200, 416, and cf. the next note as to the difficulty of defining the functions of these early officials.

[6] Messrs. Macdonell and Keith remark that he may either be a professional dicer who plays with the king or watches his play, or a public officer who superintends the gambling halls of the State and collects the revenue, as was regularly done later on. Early English history shows similar evolution of household officers into ministers of state; see *V. I.*, ii. 200.

that the officer, like the rest, was at first a private servant of the royal *entourage*, but later on he was a public official superintending the gambling halls and collecting revenue therefrom. Officers with similar functions are found in subsequent times, e. g. the *Dyūtādhyakṣa* in the *Kauṭilīya.*[1]

It is doubtful whether *Govikartana* signifies a 'huntsman', or 'slayer of cows'.[2] *Govikartana* is replaced by *Govyaccha* in the list of one text. Sāyaṇa interprets that term where it occurs in the list of victims at the Puruṣamedha as a 'driver out of cows', while the *St. Petersburg Dictionary* as 'tormenter of cows', Weber[3] as a 'knacker of cows', and Eggeling[4] as 'one who "approaches" cows', but this use of the word does not in all probability explain the sense of *Govikartana* as a *Ratnin.*

If, however, he could be taken either as a huntsman or a 'superintendent of the slaughter-houses' (by giving the word '*go*' the wider signification of 'cattle'), we find officers with like functions in the *Kauṭilīya* under the names of *Śūnādhyakṣa*[5] and *Vivītādhyakṣa.*[6] Slaughter of cows was looked down upon by the Hindus from comparatively early times, but earlier, cows were regularly slain for guests.[7] If there was a post for the purpose, it must have ceased to exist as soon as cow-slaughter came to be looked upon with aversion.

Of the *Takṣan* and *Ratha-kāra*, the *Takṣan* (carpenter)[8] had perhaps to do all those works in wood that did not fall within the range of duties of the *Ratha-kāra.* The latter officer was in special charge of the construction of chariots, which played a principal part in the wars of those days. The *Kauṭilīya* mentions a superintendent charged with several duties, including the construction of chariots for various purposes, military and other.

Pālāgala is a courier—the predecessor, I think, of such important officers as ambassadors in later times.

The *Ratnins*, among whom figure the aforesaid officers,

[1] III. xx. pp. 197 ff.
[2] *V. I.*, ii. 200.
[3] *Indische Streifen*, i. 82, n. 11.
[4] *S. B. E.*, xliv. 416.
[5] *Kauṭilīya*, II. xxvi. 122,
[6] *Ibid.*, II. xxxiv. 140, 141.
[7] See *V. I.*, ii. 145–7.
[8] See *V. I.*, i. 297.

were called the 'king-makers', i.e. though not kings themselves, yet they assisted in their consecration as kings. They no doubt wielded much power in those days, of which, as I have already noted, the making of offerings in their respective houses is an indirect proof. Weber says that 'they had a hand in the choice of the king through palace-intrigues'.[1] Whatever might have been the means, the fact remains that they were important personages in the State.

[1] *Über den Rājasūya*, p. 23.

CHAPTER VIII

THEORIES OF THE EVOLUTION OF KINGSHIP AMONG THE INDO-ARYANS

SECTION I.

The usefulness of hypotheses which after satisfying the necessary tests develop into theories.

MAN'S desire to probe into all problems, however obscure, prompts him to frame hypotheses for the explanation of phenomena even where the means of direct perception of the conditions that bring them about are absent. These hypotheses are very useful inasmuch as they often enable him at length to find out the right cause for the phenomenon of which an explanation is sought. Many of the present acquisitions to the domain of human knowledge had to pass through this hypothetical stage before they could be accepted as established theories after their passage of the necessary tests.[1] We make hypotheses of all sorts in our daily life, and these fulfil more or less satisfactorily the objects for which they are framed. The hypotheses of systematized thought, however, have to be tested as accurately as possible till they satisfy all the demands made upon them as explanations of phenomena.

The tests vary.

The tests are not the same in all cases, but vary with the nature of the phenomenon required to be explained. A physical reality that admits of observation, accurate mathematical calculation, and quantitative measurement, that repeats itself and can be subjected to experiments, will necessarily allow application of various tests which may not be possible for one of a different kind.

The phenomenon to be explained.

The phenomenon with which we are at present concerned is the evolution of kingship, i.e. how the supreme political power in a community first fell into the hands of a single man, giving rise to the primitive monarchy in the place of the previous

[1] The word 'theory' is sometimes loosely used for 'hypothesis', but, logically, a theory is an established hypothesis.

political organizations, such as government by elders, or still laxer systems, such as the leaderless unions of little bands of Bushmen for hunting or plunder.

It should be particularly noted that the 'rise of kingship' being a single expression does not in the strict logical sense stand for a single effect from a single cause. It is a general expression for several phenomena which, from the logical standpoint, are different and attributable to different totalities of conditions. To make it clear by an example: the expression 'rise of kingship' resembles the word 'death' in its relation to causes. Just as logically there cannot be *death in general*, but must always be some particular kind of death, e.g. death caused by a bullet should be distinguished from that by drowning, similarly kingship reached through military prowess should be distinguished from that secured by any other means. From this, it will be clear that one particular hypothesis for the rise of kingship can speak of only one of the many ways thereto, and many such hypotheses propounding different ways need not be mutually exclusive; for they are concerned with really different phenomena, though classed under the same general expression. Any two or more of these ways, if their nature permits, may work in combination through the same king, their strength being increased through this combination, while there may be others that may not be operative even in neighbouring localities or in distant parts of the same country.

It should also be kept in view that we are here concerned (i) with the primitive ways of elevation to the throne and not with those utilized by subsequent aspirants thereto, (ii) with the determination of such of the ways as were operative among the primitive ancestors of the Indo-Aryans.

The tests for verifying the hypotheses.

Many hypotheses have been framed to account for the first rise of kingship. The tests applicable to them must needs differ at least in some respects from those for verifying hypotheses about a different element of reality. The first rise of monarchy does not admit of observation, calculation, or experiment. It may be objected that, as history is said to repeat itself, the emergence of kingship should admit of experiments on the new monarchies that come into being. It should be borne in mind that these repetitions have only superficial and nominal resemblance, and take place in conditions far from identical with the primitive conditions of the first monarchies. If China, for instance, relapses into a monarchy, would it be such an exact replica of the past verity that inference from its observation might be applicable *in toto* to the latter? Far from it. Many elements and forces, political, social, religious or otherwise, now at work might not at all have come into existence then, or, even if existent, were not perhaps in the same state of relative strength and development. This makes a good deal of difference. The present totality of conditions might be taken as a possible road to the throne, but this might not, or perhaps owing to essential differences could not, be one of those resorted to by the first kings. If we leave aside this example from a modern civilized country, and turn for one to the lowest savages now on earth, we would not perhaps fare better. Many of the conditions operative among them may approach in similarity those of the past, and may thus have a suggestive or explanatory value; but it would be hazardous to treat them as reproductions of the particular conditions of the past and to take them as eligible for experiments. I shall have occasion to dwell upon this point hereafter; suffice it to say that the rise of monarchy does not by its very nature admit of experiment. What, then, are the means of verifying the hypotheses relating thereto? The answer lies perhaps in these conditions of a valid hypothesis:

(1) It should be reasonable, self-consistent, and in harmony with the laws included in the contemplated system of reality.

(2) It should furnish a basis for rigorous deductive inference of consequences.

The first condition requires that the new supposition should be in agreement with the accepted laws. It may happen that a supposition inconsistent with the received conceptions is proved to be true, demanding thereby a revision of the latter. This was the case with the new Copernican hypothesis of the heavens, which conflicted with the accepted Ptolemaic theory, but instead of being rejected, had to be substituted for the latter. Such instances are rare, and the probability of such a radical revision of the received conceptions is perhaps growing less with the advance of science.

These conditions will be followed throughout the subsequent portion of this chapter for the rejection or acceptance of the hypotheses, some of which, as will be found hereafter, were discussed long ago and found faulty, while some others already obtain as 'theories'. The rejected hypotheses will be but referred to in passing, those newly propounded, if any, will be discussed, while the 'theories' will be recorded, not without a critical eye thereon.

SECTION II.

Whether the Sanskrit and Buddhist literatures contain any hints on the evolution of kingship.

The *Mahābhārata*, as pointed out by Prof. Hopkins,[1] speaks of a three-fold origin of kings according to the more ancient *Śāstras* (codes), viz. (1) good family (*satkula*), (2) personal bravery (*śūratva*), and (3) skill in the leadership of armies (*senā-prakarṣaṇa*).[2] The prince Duryodhana cites the above śāstric passage to justify his installation of Karṇa to the throne of the Aṅga kingdom, in order to make him eligible to fight Arjuna by putting the former on a par with the latter in a tournament.

The *Mahāsammata* in the *Jātakas*.

The tradition about the *Mahāsammata* (Great Elect) in the *Jātakas* relates that he was the first king in the *Vivaṭṭa*[3] of the first *Kappa* (cycle), elected by the people from among themselves to remove the want of a ruler, which they had keenly felt.[4] The elect was 'handsome, auspicious, commanding, altogether perfect.'[5]

The above legend is much more detailed in the *Mahāvastu Avadāna*: 'Then, O, *Bhikṣus*! the men (lit. beings) hastened and assembled; after doing so, they held a consultation: "Let us elect that person from among us here present, who happens

[1] *J. A. O. S.*, xiii. 99, 100. [2] *MBh.*, i. 136. 35.

[3] Third division, in which the process of renovation of the world begins.

[4] See Ṭīkā on the word 'devadhammā' of a verse in the '*devadhamma-jātaka*' in the *Jātaka*, i. 132; also R. C. Childers's *Pāli-English Dictionary*, under 'Mahāsammata'.

[5] See the *Jātaka* (transl. by W. H. D. Rouse and ed. by E. B. Cowell), ii. 242 (*ulūka-jātaka*).

to be pleasing to all (*sarva-prāsādiko*) and hailed of all as lord (*sarva-maheśākhyo*), so that he may punish those deserving punishment, and support those worth supporting, and exact a share of paddy from each of our paddy-fields." Then, O, *Bhikṣus*! the men elected the person who was pleasing to all and hailed by all as lord, (saying): "Do you punish among us that person who deserves punishment, and support him who is worth supporting; we shall elect you as the foremost of all beings; and shall give you a sixth of the produce of each of our paddy-fields." Elected (*sammato*) as he was by a large (*mahā*) collection of people, he was termed the Great Elect (*Mahāsammata*).'[1]

The *Mahāsammata* in the *Mahāvastu Avadāna*.

This Buddhist tradition emphasizes the selection by the

[1] My best thanks are due to Mahāmahopādhyāya Paṇḍit Haraprasād Śāstrī, M.A., C.I.E., for kindly drawing my attention to the passage in the *Mahāvastu Avadāna* (ed. by É. Senart, 1882), i. 347, 348. It is as follows: 'Atha khalu bhikṣavaḥ te satvā saṃdhāvensuḥ saṃnipatensuḥ saṃdhāvitvā saṃnipatitvā saṃmantrensuḥ. Yaṃ nūnaṃ vayaṃ bhavanto yo asmākaṃ satvo sarvaprāsādiko sarva-maheśākhyo ca taṃ saṃmanyemaḥ yo asmākaṃ nigrahārahaṃ ca nigṛhṇīyā pragrahāraham ca pragṛhṇeyā deśaye cāyam svakasvakeṣu śālikṣetreṣu śālibhāgam. Atha khalu bhikṣavaḥ te satvā yo sānaṃ (p. 348) satvo abhūṣi sarva-prāsādiko ca sarva-maheśākhyo ca taṃ saṃmanyensuḥ. Bhavān asmākaṃ satvaṃ nigrahārahaṃ ca nigṛhṇātu pragrahārahaṃ ca pragṛhṇātu; vayaṃ te sarva-satvānāṃ agratāye saṃmanyema svakasvakeṣu śālikṣetreṣu ṣaṣṭhaṃ śālibhāgaṃ dadāma. Mahatā janakāyena sammato ti mahāsammato ti saṃjñā udapāsi. (Up to this translated above). Arahati śālikṣetreṣu śālibhāge ti rājā ti saṃjñā udapāsi. Sammak rakṣati paripāleti mūrdhnābhiṣiktaḥ . . . saṃjñā udapāsi. Mātāpitṛsamo naigama-jānapadeṣu tti jānapadasthāma-vīrya-prāpto ti saṃjña udapāsi tenāhaṃ rājā kṣatriyo mūrdhnābhiṣikto jānapadasthāma-vīrya-prāpto ti. (Translation of the remaining portion of the passage: 'Worthy as he was of the share of the produce of paddy-fields, he was called king. For protecting and maintaining adequately, he was called a 'Kṣatriya be-sprinkled on the head' [(Kṣatriyo mūrdhnābhiṣiktaḥ). The lacuna here has been supplied in the light of the subsequent portion of the passage]. Being like father and mother to the people of the town and the country, he was called the 'repository of strength and energy to the people' (Jānapada-sthāma-vīrya-prāpto).

There is a brief allusion to this tradition and some of its details in the *Catuḥśatikā* by Āryadeva (ed. as a Memoir of the A. S. B. by Mahāmahopādhyāya Paṇḍit Haraprasād Śāstrī, M.A., C.I.E, who has kindly drawn my attention to this passage also), ch. iv, p. 461.

The legend of the election of Manu as their king by the people to avert a state of anarchy, together with its attendant reference to a sixth of the produce and such other dues payable to the king, is mentioned in the *Kauṭilīya* (I. xiii, p. 22) for insertion in dialogue between spies.

This selection of the king looks very much like the 'social contract theory as applicable to monarchies' when supposed to have been historically applied.

Review of the above legends.

people at large of a competent ruler and ignores the aspiration and exertion on the part of the would-be ruler himself to make his way to the throne by dint of his virtues. This has given an artificial appearance to the elevation of the first king to the throne. What seems more plausible is that the person who towers over his fellows in the qualities more appreciated in a particular society, as, for instance, ability in sea-faring in the race living on the sea-coast, or strength, fleetness of foot, sureness of mark, &c., in a community of hunters, becomes gradually their chief.[1] It is not probable that the people felt the want of a ruler because they suffered the pinch of hunger for a few days, and met together to choose the best among themselves as their head. Such deliberate and collective choice of a ruler may have been possible in later stages of evolution, when kingship had already become a firm institution of the society, and when the vacant throne was felt as ominous and undesirable. The 'natural' races may not have felt it much, for living in small, detached, headless groups was so far in harmony with their temper as not to have been to them a source of inconvenience and anxiety. They had not yet, moreover, any experience of the conveniences of corporate life under a chieftain likely to excite their cravings therefor by contrast with their chiefless condition. The only truth, therefore, that the legend may furnish is that the first Elect had extraordinary personal virtues which influenced his elevation. The account from the *Jātakas* does not, however, mark out any special virtue or combination of virtues. He is no doubt described as 'commanding', which may be taken to suggest that he was brave, physically strong, and so forth; but an all-round perfection is next claimed for him, which is fatal to all suggestions as to the reality in its legendary megalogue.

The account from the *Mahāvastu Avadāna* fares little better in this respect. The first Elect is recognized by all as lordly, which enables him to reward and punish. The Elect is also 'pleasing' and hence popular to the people. It is not specified what words and deeds gained him popularity before his selection, and in what circumstances those words were

[1] Cf. Prof. F. Ratzel's *History of Mankind*, i. 131.

uttered and deeds done. The only facts that stand out are that the Elect was already recognized as a great lord by all; and hence the advantages that could be expected from such a man could be used for the people's benefit. He was expected to be just, and, as he was 'pleasing', it may be inferred that he had given indications to the people that he would not be unjust in the use of his lordship, but would administer justice among the people properly, which would be one of the factors for maintaining his future popularity. Justness alone could not perhaps have gained chiefship for a person devoid of other virtues; at least, as will appear from subsequent discussion, no one has yet claimed this power for it. The qualities denoted in the epithet *maheśākhya* probably include bravery, physical strength, military skill, and so forth, attributes, as will be shown, sufficient, especially when found in conjunction, to secure chieftainship for their possessor.

Hints from the *Mahābhārata*.

The hints from the *Mahābhārata* are much more definite and tangible. The qualities mentioned are *good family, personal bravery, and skill in the leadership of armies*. The first attribute is comparatively obscure; for the elements upon which the nobility of a family was considered to depend are not enumerated. They may have been wealth, seniority of stock, or any other factors, taken separately or combined. The second and the third attributes are clear enough. There is nothing in the three qualities that stands in the way of their union in the same person. The object, therefore, of making three-fold the origin of kingship seems to be that each of these, operating in isolation from the other two, may secure for its possessor the rulership over a community. It is not clear how far back this tradition of the three-fold origin of kingship dates. It is cited from the *śāstras* obviously more ancient than the time of their citation, though it cannot be asserted that the tradition was as old as the rise of the first Aryan kings.

Herbert Spencer's mention of the

The second and the third attributes are mentioned by Herbert Spencer[1] along with other king-making qualities of primitive times. The political headship, in his opinion, was

[1] See his *Principles of Sociology* (1902), ii. 333-4.

second and the third attributes. His enumeration of the above as well as other attributes. Whether unaided wealth is sufficient?

acquired by one whose fitness asserted itself in the form of superior prowess, greater physical strength, stronger will, wider knowledge, quicker insight, greater age, larger wealth. The first-named quality includes both personal bravery and military skill—the very attributes mentioned in the *Mahābhārata*. Good family may, as I have already said, depend upon various factors, among which wealth may be reckoned as one. I have some doubt as to whether wealth alone could procure kingship. It may create an influence which may not be in the direction of political headship. Spencer says that wealth (largeness of possessions) is an indirect mark of superiority and a direct cause of influence, and confirms his views by instances, two of which need be noticed: 'With the Tacullies, any person may become a *miuty* or chief who will occasionally provide a village feast',[1] and 'among the Tolewas in Del Norte County, money makes the chief'.[2] Wealth combined with one or a few personal virtues may be of help to the operation of the latter, but whether, unaided, it can achieve the aforesaid end is a question about which I have doubts. Even if the reports of the above two instances be correct, we cannot, I think, apply them to the early societies without further evidence showing that the temper of the primitive savage was such that it could unhesitatingly welcome a man, though devoid of all recommendations but that of wealth, to the chiefship of his community. There may be positive hindrances to the transpiration of such a state of things; for it is very likely that a *man possessed of wealth along with other virtues* may be the rival of the *man with mere wealth*. It would not be difficult for the former to beat the latter down and secure for himself what was passing into another's hand.

Should we suppose that the primitive man of wealth was always endowed in those days with some or other of the aforesaid qualities, we have to make another assumption—that the acquisition of possessions by heredity had not yet begun.

[1] *Op. cit.*, ii. 334. The manifestations of the abstract qualities or their combinations may be various, and impossible to be exhaustively enumerated.

[2] *Ibid.*

If this be true, the wealthy man would always be a maker of his own fortune and hence endowed with many qualities involved in its acquisition, which may count among them some of those requisite for elevation to the headship.

The greater experience generally accompanying old age commanded deference in early societies, though old men with senile incapacity were killed or left to die. The most energetic senior of a tribe could wield political superiority. Seniority

Of bravery, skill in leadership, and superior bodily strength, the first and the third may often be found together; and these when joined with the second become a powerful combination. The remaining attributes of stronger will, wider knowledge, and quicker insight could be more effective when co-operating with one or some of the qualities already mentioned; and it would be perhaps difficult for them to make headway in absolute isolation from one or other of the above group of attributes. The other qualities.

The actual operation of the above qualities may imply the existence of many subsidiary ones, e.g. the leadership of armies requires endurance. It contemplates also the creation of many favourable circumstances, the timely use of those already favourable, the occurrence of many unexpected events helping the purpose in view, and so forth. All these taken together would be the totality of conditions constituting the cause for the elevation of a person to the throne. The attributes, single or grouped, as the case may be, are the dominating forces in the field and have therefore been specially mentioned. War and unrest may be favourable for the play of some of them, while peace or other states of affairs for the rest.

Thus far about the personal attributes. There may be other forces which may also be specially mentioned and which may be said to lie more in the beliefs or institutions of the early societies than in the men availing themselves of those forces; though of course the utilization of the forces may require the possession of particular attributes by those men.

Such a force may lie, for instance, in the patriarchal institution. When men, says Herbert Spencer, passed from the The patriarch becomes a chief.

hunting stage into the pastoral and wandered in search of food for their domesticated animals, they fell into conditions favouring the formation of patriarchal groups. The growth of simple groups into those compound and doubly compound acknowledging the authority of one who unites family headship with political superiority has been made familiar by Sir Henry Maine and others as common to early Greeks, Romans, Teutons, Slavs, and Hindus.[1] The joint undivided family, wherever its beginning is seen in the Aryan communities, springs universally out of the patriarchal family, a group of natural or adoptive descendants held together by subjection to the eldest living ascendant, father, grandfather, or great-grandfather. In the more extensive assemblages of kinsmen constituting the joint family, the eldest male of the eldest line is never the parent of all the members, and not necessarily the first in age among them. There is always the impression that the blood of the collective brotherhood runs more truly and purely in some one line than in any other. Among the Hindus, the eldest male of this line, if of full mental capacity, is generally placed at the head of the concerns of the joint family. If he is not deemed fit for his duties, a worthier kinsman is substituted for him by election and the longer the joint family holds together, the more election gains ground at the expense of birth. The whole process may be described as the gradual transmutation of the patriarch into the chief, the general rule being that the latter is elected with a strong preference for the eldest line. Sometimes he is assisted by a definite council of near kinsmen, and sometimes this council takes his place. On the whole, where the body of kinsmen formed on the type of the joint family is a purely civil institution, the tendency is towards greater disregard of the claims of blood. But in those states of society in which the brotherhood is a political, militant, self-sustaining group, we can perceive from actually extant examples that a separate set of causes comes into operation and that the chief as military leader sometimes more than regains the privileges lost through the decay of the tradition connecting him with the common root of all the

[1] Herbert Spencer, *op. cit.*, pp. 342, 343.

kindred. Thus all the branches of human society may or may not have been developed from joint families, but wherever it was an institution of the Aryan race,[1] we see that the patriarch could rise into political headship.

The matriarchate.

The 'maternal system' is held by some to have preceded the paternal, but there are doubts as to this priority. 'If patriarchal reasons are enough to account for the custom as we find it', says Sir Frederick Pollock, 'we can hardly assume that in a given case it was formerly matriarchal, merely because, for all we know, it might have been so. This would be to assume the very thing to be proved, namely, that the society in question was in fact maternal at some earlier time.'[2]

Under this system, however, women have no personal power. If it at all confers political power on any person, like the paternal system, it is on a male rather than on a female. In many societies, again, in which this system is the rule, an exception is made in the case of the political head.[3]

The influence of the medicine-man as an origin of kingship.

Spencer mentions another influence as the origin of political headship. It operates alone in some cases and conjointly with that of military prowess in other cases. But 'that this arises as early as the other can scarcely be said; since until the ghost-theory[4] takes shape, there is no origin for it. But when belief in the spirits of the dead becomes current, the medicine-man professing ability to control them and inspiring faith in his pretensions is regarded with a fear which prompts obedience.'[5] Spencer has not elaborated the hypothesis by showing the various steps by which the medicine-man can acquire political superiority. He also remarks that the

[1] See Sir Henry Maine's *Early History of Institutions* (1905), pp. 115–18. I have retained his language as far as possible, with changes or omissions for the sake of brevity or adaptation to the present context, in order to allow him to state his own case with its necessary details. (See also his *Ancient Law*, ch. v, and its Note on patriarchal theory by Sir Frederick Pollock.)

[2] See Note K on ch. v, Maine's *Ancient Law*, p. 178.

[3] *Encyclopaedia Britannica*, 11th ed., xvii. 889; H. Spencer, *op. cit.*, pp. 344, 345.

[4] I.e., the fear of the ghosts of powerful men. Where many tribes have been welded together by a conqueror, his ghost acquires in tradition the pre-eminence of a god. (See H. Spencer, *op. cit.*, p. 363.)

[5] H. Spencer, *op. cit.*, p. 338.

operation of the influence of the medicine-man depends upon the ghost-theory which comes into being later than the 'attribute'-origin of chieftainship, but how much later he does not state. The supposed aid of supernatural powers as a strengthener of political authority already acquired by some means or other cannot be denied. But how a magician (medicine-man) can make his way to the throne requires to be shown. This has been done by Sir James Frazer in his *Golden Bough* with an industry in the compilation and presentation of materials that is indeed admirable. We shall postpone our remarks on it until we have glanced over his whole position.

SECTION III.

The hypothesis expounded by him may be summarized thus:

1. Ancient kings commonly combined in themselves both the administrative and priestly functions, and, in addition, the divine functions, for they were looked upon as gods incarnate. They were expected to confer upon their subjects blessings which lie beyond the reach of mortals. Thus rain and sunshine in proper seasons, growth of crops, removal of epidemics, in short, freedom from all scourges of humanity and bestowal of the essentials of public welfare were supposed to be dependent upon their will. A primitive man hardly perceived the difference between the natural and the supernatural, and conceived the world as worked to a great extent by personal beings moved by appeals to their hopes, fears, and compassion. Guided by this belief, he thought he could influence the course of nature by prayers, threats, and promises directed to none other than the god incarnate in the king, or, as he sometimes believed, in himself or any one of his fellow men.

2. Along with the view of the world as worked by spiritual forces, the primitive man had another and probably still older conception that contemplated nature as a series of events occurring without the intervention of any personal agency Such a conception was involved in the 'sympathetic magic' that played such an important part in those days. In early

society, the king was a magician, and he appears to have risen to the throne by his proficiency in the black or white art.

'Sympathetic Magic' and its branches explained.

3. The principles involved in 'sympathetic magic' are two:

(i) Like produces like, i. e. an effect resembles its cause.

(ii) Things once in physical contact continue to act on each other from distant places after the severance of the contact.

The accompanying table shows the branches of sympathetic magic, with their alternative names and the principles upon which they are based.

Sympathetic Magic
(Law of Sympathy)

Homoeopathic or Imitative Magic
(Law of Similarity)

Contagious Magic
(Law of Contact)

4. The magician infers from the first principle, the law of similarity, that he can produce any effect he likes by imitating it; and from the second, the law of contact, that whatever he does to a material object affects equally the person with whom it was once in contact, whether it formed part of his body or not. In practice, the two principles are often combined.[1]

5. From another point of view, sympathetic magic is divided into Private and Public, the former being practised for the benefit or injury of individuals, and the latter for public well-being, or injury to public enemies.

Examples of private homoeopathic magic of image and other things.

6. As examples (mostly private) of 'homoeopathic magic' (see the table, *supra*), Sir J. Frazer cites the uses of an image, which is subjected to magical treatment in the belief that sufferings caused to it will produce like sufferings to the intended enemy, and its destruction will cause his death. This practice was very widely diffused all over the world, and still persists. Only a few instances are described, viz. its practice among the American Indians, Malays, and Arabs of North Africa, as also in Torres Straits, Borneo, China, Japan, Australia, Burma, Africa, ancient and modern India, Egypt, Babylon, Scotland.[2] The magical image is also used in various countries for various ends, viz. to get offspring, procure

[1] For what precedes about magic, see Sir J. Frazer's *Golden Bough* (henceforth referred to as '*G.*'), 3rd ed., pt. i, vol. i, pp. 50–4.

[2] *G.*, pt. i, i. 55–70.

love, ensure food-supply, maintain domestic harmony, heal diseases, and so forth.[1]

7. Not merely images, but also various animals and objects, the tides, sun, moon, and stars, are magically treated to yield homoeopathically the desired results.[2]

Taboos come under sympathetic magic.

8. Not merely positive precepts, but also negative ones, i.e. prohibitions, form part of this magic, the latter being termed *taboos* and the former *sorcery*. Through these also operate the two principles of similarity and contact. To cite instances: Camphor-hunters of Malay refrain from pounding their salt fine. The reason is that owing to the resemblance of salt to camphor, they believe that by the taboo they ensure that the grains of the camphor he seeks for will be large like their coarse salt. The infringement of the taboo would make the camphor fine like the pounded salt they use.

9. In most parts of ancient Italy, women were forbidden by law to carry their spindles openly, for any such action was believed to injure the crops. The belief probably was that the twirling of the spindle would twirl the corn-stalks.[3] Hence, the taboo.

Examples of private contagious magic.

10. The second branch of sympathetic magic, viz. 'private contagious magic' is equally widespread. Only a few instances need be noted: it is customary in many parts of the world to put extracted teeth in a place where they might come into contact with a mouse or a rat, in the hope that through sympathy the teeth of their former owner would become firm and excellent like those of the rodents. This belief obtains in Africa, Europe, America, India, &c., with more or less modifications. Similarly, there are superstitious practices in various countries based on beliefs in sympathetic connexion between a wound and the weapon which inflicted it, a person and his clothes or foot-prints, and so forth.[4]

The 'public magician'. His elevation to

11. Thus far we have noticed instances of homoeopathic or contagious magic practised for private ends, i.e. for the benefit or injury of individuals. But side by side with this may be found the practice of public magic for the good of the whole

[1] *G.*, pt. i, i. 70–111. [2] *Ibid.*, pp. 136–174. [3] *Ibid.*, p. 111 ff.
[4] *Ibid.*, pp. 174–214.

community or for the injury of the inimical ones. The magician ceases to be a private practitioner and rises into a public functionary. He has to direct his attention to the properties of drugs and minerals, the causes of rain and drought, of thunder and lightning, the changes of the seasons, the phases of the moon, the diurnal and annual journeys of the heavenly bodies, the mystery of life and death and such other things, a knowledge of which is necessary to make up his peculiar outfit. He is expected, by his magical rites, to secure objects of public utility—supplying food, healing diseases, making and stopping rain, controlling the sun and wind, averting epidemics and other scourges of society, and so forth. The means that he adopts are the same sympathetic magic with its two branches. The examples have been imported from a large number of countries and peoples all over the world.[1] The evolution of such a class of functionaries is of great importance to political and religious progress in early society. The public welfare being believed to depend on the performance of magical rites, they attain to a position of much influence and power, and may readily step up to the rank of chiefs or kings. The profession draws to it the ablest men of the tribe, who, as in other professions, drive to the wall their duller brethren by dint of their superior intelligence. This superiority depends for the most part, however, on a command over the fallacies that impose upon their credulous and superstitious clients. Thus the ablest members of the profession become more or less conscious deceivers, though it is by no means the case that a sorcerer is always an impostor. He often sincerely believes in his own wonderful powers; but this sincerity renders him weaker than his roguish fellow-practitioners. It leaves him unarmed to meet the many perils that beset him. When his incantations fail, he is not ready to make plausible excuses like his knavish colleagues; and before he invents one, he may be knocked on the head by his disappointed and angry clients.[2] The result is that at this

sovereignty, a benefit to early society.

[1] *Ibid.*, pp. 244–331.
[2] *Ibid.*, p. 214. Among the Latukas of the Upper Nile, for instance, the unsuccessful rain-maker is often banished or killed. (*G.*, pt. i, i. 346.)

Supreme power in the hands of a public magician. The rise of monarchy and its beneficial effects in early times.

stage of the social evolution, supreme power tends to fall into the hands of men of the sharpest intellect but the most unscrupulous character. If we strike a balance between the benefits they confer and the harms they perpetrate, the former will be found to greatly outweigh the latter, for more mischief has been wrought in the world by honest fools in high places than by intelligent rascals. A change may also come upon the shrewd rogue, who, when at the height of his ambition, may turn his thoughts and powers to the service of the public. In the field of politics the wily and hard-hearted intriguer or victor may end by being a wise ruler, e.g. Julius Caesar and Augustus. The opposite has been the case with George III (who was of an opposite nature), under whom took place the heaviest calamity in English history, the breach with America. The elevation of a magician to power substitutes a monarchy for the primitive democracy, or the oligarchy of elders common in early societies. The concentration of power in one man helps him to break through the iron chain of custom that drags down even the ablest man to the dead level of his fellows. At this stage, even the whims of a tyrant may prove beneficial. Once the tribe ceases to be guided by the timid counsels of elders, and submits to the direction of a strong mind, it enters on a career of progress. Partly by force and partly by the voluntary submission of the weaker tribes, it acquires wealth and slaves, which serves to relieve some classes from their perpetual struggle for existence, affording them an opportunity to devote themselves to the pursuit of knowledge, the most potent instrument for ameliorating the lot of man. Intellectual progress follows closely on the heels of economic progress, which receives an immense impulse from conquests. The ancient Babylonians, Greeks, Romans, and Arabs may be cited as witnesses. Japan bids fair to be a similar illustration of our times. Nor is it an accident that in early epochs the first great strides of civilization were made under monarchic and theocratic governments, e.g. Egypt, Babylon, Peru. It appears, therefore, that in the early stages of social evolution, monarchy was the best friend of humanity.[1]

[1] *G.*, pt. i, i. 214–19.

12. This, then, is the line of the public magician's progress to the throne. Let us now examine the actualities of savage societies, which are but early societies crystallized, and which might supply proofs of the above process of the magician's elevation to kingship.

Illustrations of the various stages of the magician's progress to the throne.

13. The instances that Sir J. Frazer cites may be distinguished into two groups, one of which places before us persons who, starting as magicians in savage societies, have been noticed to have risen to chiefships or kingships, while the other is directed to show that chiefs and kings very often in savage, and even in many civilized societies of modern times, combine in themselves civil duties with those of public magicians. The latter comprises nearly all the examples given by Sir J. Frazer,[1] leaving only one or two for the other group.

Two groups of instances distinguished.

14. People supposed to be in close communication with spirits pass for omnipotent among the Dinkas of the Upper Nile. One of them became the richest and the most esteemed and dreaded chief of the Kič tribe through his skill in ventriloquism. He had a cage from which were elicited roars of lions and howls of hyaenas, which were believed to be guarding his house and awaiting his bidding to rush forth on enemies.[2]

First group of instances.

15. In the Lendu tribe of Central Africa, the rain-maker almost invariably becomes a chief.[3]

16. The aborigines of Central Australia are governed by elders, who have to perform magical rites, some for the supply of food for the tribe, others for rain-fall or such other services to the community. Their most important function is to take charge of the sacred store-house, containing the holy stones and sticks (*churinga*) with which the souls of all the people, both living and dead, are supposed to be bound up. Civil duties, such as the infliction of punishment for breach of tribal custom, are no doubt attached to their position as elders, but their principal functions are sacred or magical.[4]

Second group of instances.

17. In South-Eastern Australia, the head-men are often, sometimes invariably, magicians, magical rites being in-

[1] *Ibid.*, pp. 332–72.

[2] *Ibid.*, p. 347.

[3] *Ibid.*, p. 348.

[4] *Ibid.*, pp. 334, 335.

separable from their duties. Some of them are very powerful in their own and greatly feared by the neighbouring tribes.[1] The individuals possessing the greatest influence are the sorcerers. They are believed to have power to drive away wind and rain, heal the sick, and bring down lightning and disease upon objects of their own or others' hatred.[2]

18. In New Guinea, the natives are on a higher level of culture than the Australian aborigines. Among them the constitution is still essentially democratic or oligarchic, and chiefship is only in embryo. The only effective influence is that of the wizards, who domineer over chiefs. In the Toaripi tribe of British New Guinea, the chiefs have not necessarily supernatural powers, but a sorcerer is looked upon as a chief.[3]

19. Among the aborigines of the Melanesian Islands, the power of chiefs rests upon their supposed supernatural powers derived from the spirits or ghosts with which they hold intercourse. If a chief imposes a fine, it is paid because the people fear his ghostly power. As soon as they begin to disbelieve in this power, his authority to levy fines is shaken. Such belief having failed in the Banks Islands, the position of the chief tended to become obscure.[4]

20. In the Northern New Hebrides, the son does not inherit the chiefship, but does so if the father can manage to convince the people that he has transferred to his son his supernatural power, his charms, magical songs, stones, and apparatus, and his knowledge of the way to approach spiritual beings.[5]

21. At Tana, there are hosts of 'sacred men', among whom the disease-makers are the most dreaded. They rise to a position of immense wealth and influence. These rascals, according to Dr. Turner, appear to be on the high road to kingship and divinity.[6]

22. The African aborigines are still higher in the scale of culture, and chieftainship and kingship among them are fully developed, and the evidence for their evolution out of the

[1] *G.*, pt. i, i. 336. [2] *Ibid.* [3] *Ibid.*, p. 337.
[4] *Ibid.*, pp. 338, 339. [5] *Ibid.*, p. 339.
[6] *Ibid.*, pp. 341, 342.

magician, especially the rain-maker, is comparatively plentiful.[1] The respect shown to the magicians by those people is very great. Among the Ba-yakas, a tribe of the Congo Free State, the magicians enjoy the privilege of being exempt from justice.[2] The office of their chiefs is associated with, and appears to depend on, magical functions. The chiefs of the Ossidinge district in the Cameroons, to cite one among several instances, have, as such, very little influence over their subjects; but should they be fetish-priests as well, they wield a great authority.[3] Some chiefs in South Africa allowed none else to compete with them in rain-making, lest a successful rain-maker should acquire immense influence and ultimately displace them.[4] The Matabeles of South Africa have witch-doctors with as great a power as that of kings. The head of the tribe engages witch-doctors, with whom he busies himself a certain portion of the year in compounding potions for rain-making.[5] He is held responsible not only for rain but also for various other natural phenomena disastrous to the people—blight, locusts, drought, epidemics, dearth of milk in cows, &c. Cases are on record in which the chiefs have been exiled or put to death for failure to supply remedies for disasters.[6] Parallels of such punishments are found in the annals of ancient Scythia, Egypt, Corea, China, and Tonquin.[7]

The regalia of kings are but the talismans of their predecessors, the magicians.

23. The regalia, according to Sir J. Frazer, are the wonder-working talismans, which the kings even of several modern civilized countries appear to have derived from their predecessors the magicians, and were perhaps viewed in this light in former days.[8] In Malaya, a few talismans of the magicians are exactly analogous to the regalia of the king, and bear even the same names.[9] The royal authority in some countries depends entirely upon the possession of the regalia, which the rebels and deposed monarchs try to have by all means, e.g. in Southern Celebes.[10] The very existence of the kingdom is supposed to depend in Cambodia upon the regalia, which are committed to the *Brāhmaṇas* for safe-keeping. They were

[1] *Ibid.*, p. 342. [2] *Ibid.*, p. 348. [3] *Ibid.*, p. 349.
[4] *Ibid.*, p. 350. [5] *Ibid.*, p. 351. [6] *Ibid.*, pp. 353, 354.
[7] *Ibid.*, pp. 354, 355. [8] *Ibid.*, p. 364. [9] *Ibid.*, p. 362.
[10] *Ibid.*, p. 363.

supposed to have the same magical virtue in Egypt, Greece, Scythia, and several other countries.[1]

Belief in the supernatural powers of kings shared by the ancestors of all the Aryan races.

24. The belief in the magical or supernatural powers of kings to control the course of nature for the good of their subjects seems to have been shared by the ancestors of all the Aryan races from India to Ireland.[2] A noteworthy instance of a relic of this belief is the notion that English kings can heal scrofula by their touch. This gift of healing they are said to have derived from Edward the Confessor, while a similar gift of the French kings was transmitted from either Clovis or St. Louis.[3] But Sir J. Frazer suspects these derivations, and holds the real origin to be with the 'barbarous, nay savage, predecessors of the Saxon and Merovingian kings', who, according to him, possessed the same gift many ages before.[4]

The sum-total of the former evidences.

25. Kings appear thus to have often been evolved out of magicians. Corresponding to the great social revolution in the rise of the sorcerers into monarchs, there was an intellectual revolution affecting the conception and functions of royalty. For in course of time the fallacy of magic became apparent to the acuter minds, and religion emerged. In other words, the magician became priest, and performed now by appeals to the gods the things formerly done by him by his command over nature. The distinction between the human and the divine was, however, still blurred, or had scarcely emerged. Hence the priest-king was also looked upon as a god through the temporary or permanent possession of his whole nature by a great and powerful spirit.[5]

The priority of magic to religion in the evolution of human thought.

26. The priority of magic to religion, implied in the subsequent emergence of religion just mentioned, in the evolution of human thought is thus explained. By religion Sir J. Frazer understands a propitiation or conciliation of powers superior to man, which are believed to control the course of nature and human life. It consists of two elements, a theoretical and

[1] *G.*, pt. i, i. 364, 365.

[2] Sir J. Frazer cites instances from India, Sweden, Denmark, Ireland, and the Highlands of Scotland. (*Ibid.*, pp. 366–8.)

[3] *Ibid.*, pp. 366–8, 370.

[4] *Ibid.*, p. 370.

[5] *Ibid.*, pp. 371, 372.

a practical—a belief in the superior powers, and an attempt to please them. Of these, belief comes first, and leads to a corresponding practice. The belief without the practice is no religion but mere theology, while the latter alone cannot also constitute religion. It is not necessary that the religious practice should always be rituals; it may lie in merely pure conduct. The assumptions of magic and religion are radically conflicting. The former, like science, looks upon the course of nature as rigid, while the latter, by the implication of a conscious or personal agent who can be propitiated, contemplates the processes of nature as capable of modification. Magic, like religion, deals, no doubt, with spirits, but it treats them as 'inanimate agents, i.e. it constrains or coerces instead of conciliating or propitiating them as religion would do'. It takes all personal beings, whether human or divine, as subject in the last resort to impersonal forces which can be turned to account by one who knows how to manipulate them by proper spells and ceremonies. The opposition of principles between magic and religion had its counterpart in history in the antagonism between the priest and the magician, the former looking upon the latter as impious and blasphemous. But this antagonism seems to have appeared late in the history of religion. At an early time they co-operated and were confused with each other, e.g. in ancient Egypt, early India, modern Europe, &c., where the priest solicited the goodwill of the gods by prayer, and had also recourse to rites and forms of words believed to produce of themselves the desired result. This early fusion of magic and religion was not, however, the earliest phase of human thought. It was preceded by a still earlier one when magic existed without religion. The fundamental notions of magic and religion may confirm this view. The conception of personal agents is more complex than a recognition of the similarity or contiguity of ideas. The very beasts associate ideas of things that are like each other, or found together in their experience; but none attribute to them a belief that the phenomena of nature are worked by invisible animals or one prodigious animal. Three stages of evolution are therefore distinguished: First, a stage in which magic existed without religion; second, a stage in which the two co-operated and, to some extent, were confused; and third, a stage in which their radical difference was recognized.

Inductive proof confirming the deductive.

27. The deductive inference regarding the priority of magic is confirmed inductively by the fact that among the Australian aborigines—the rudest savages regarding whom we have accurate information—magic is universally practised, but religion is almost unknown. This is only a landmark of a primitive phase of human thought through which the savage as well as the civilized races of the world had all to pass. There had been an Age of Magic before religion emerged. The solid substratum of belief in the efficacy of magic among the ignorant and superstitious, who constitute the vast majority of mankind, may be an indication of this ruder and earlier aspect of the human mind.

Religion evolving out of the inefficacy of magic.

28. In course of time the inefficacy of magic became gradually apparent and religion evolved. Man could no longer believe that he was guiding the course of nature by his supernatural powers. He saw that it went on without him and without heeding his commands. It must, then, be worked by invisible beings superior to him To these beings he now resigned himself, beseeching and propitiating them for all good things, instead of depending upon his own supposed powers.[1]

SECTION IV.

The application of the magician-theory to India.

1. Sir J. Frazer makes the generalization, in his chapter on 'Magicians as kings',[2] that the belief that the kings possess magical or supernatural powers, by which they can confer material benefits on their subjects, seems to have been shared by the ancestors of all the Aryan races from India to Ireland, and it has left clear traces of itself in England down to modern times; and draws the conclusion from the supposed gift of healing by touch of English and French kings that they had magician-predecessors many ages ago.[3] He instances

[1] For the evolution of religion after magic, see *G.*, pt. i, i, ch. iv (pp. 220–43).

[2] *Ibid.*, ch. vi.

[3] *Ibid.*, pp. 366, 370.

some other countries which he also considers as coming within the application of his theory. With regard to the supposed supernatural powers of ancient Hindu kings, he quotes the *Laws of Manu*: 'In that country where the king avoids taking the property of mortal sinners, men are born in due time and are long-lived. And the crops of the husbandmen spring up, each as it was sown, and the children die not, and no misshaped offspring is born'.[1]

2. Under 'public magic' he refers to the magical control of rain among the Hindus of the Central Provinces, who believe that a twin can save the crops from the ravages of hail and heavy rain if only he paints his right buttock black and his left buttock some other colour, and thus adorned goes and stands in the direction of the wind.[2] Public magic in India.

3. He also refers to the rules observed by a *Brāhmaṇa* student, performing the *Śākvarī-vrata* (a kind of vow) for varying periods determined in each case, preparatory to his study of the *Mahānāmnī* verses of the *Sāma-Veda*. The virtue of the verses, the *Sūtra*[3] says, lies in water, and the performance of the vow involves, among many others, directions for touching water and refraining therefrom at certain times, eating dark food, wearing dark clothes, and so forth. After the accomplishment of this vow, the god Parjanya, it is stated, sends rain at the wish of the student. Prof. Oldenberg points out that 'all these rules are intended to bring the *Brāhmaṇa* into union with water, to make him, as it were, an ally of the water powers and to guard him against their hostility. The black garments and the black food have the same significance; no one will doubt that they refer to the rain-clouds when he remembers that a black victim is sacrificed to procure rain; "it is black, for such is the nature of rain". In respect of another rain-charm it is said plainly, "He puts on a black garment edged with black, for such is the nature of rain" We may therefore assume that here in the circle of ideas and ordinances of the Vedic schools, there have been preserved

[1] *The Laws of Manu* (*S. B. E.*), ix. 246.

[2] *G.*, pt. i, i. 269, quoting M. N. Venketswami, 'Superstitions among Hindus in the Central Provinces,' *Indian Antiquary*, xxviii (1899), 111.

[3] *Gobhila-Gṛhya-Sūtra*, iii. 2.

magical practices of the most remote antiquity, which were intended to prepare the rain-maker for his office and dedicate him to it.'[1]

4. Again, in Muzaffarnagar, a town in the United Provinces,[2] the people, during excessive rains, draw a figure of the sage Agastya on a loin-cloth and put it out in the rain, or paint his figure on the outside of the house in order that rain may wash it off. This sage is a great personage in the folklore of the people. It is supposed that as soon as he feels in effigy the hardships of wet weather, he exercises his power of stopping rain.[3]

When rain is wanted at Chatarpur, a native state in Bundelcund, they paint on a wall facing east two figures with legs up and heads down, one representing Indra and the other Megha-Rāja the lord of rain. It is believed that in this uncomfortable position they will be compelled to send down the showers.[4]

A sun-charm is held by Sir J. Frazer to consist in the offering made by the *Brāhmaṇa* in the morning, for it is written in the *Śatapatha-Brāhmaṇa* that 'assuredly the sun would not rise, were he not to make the offering.'[5]

Confusion of magic and religion in ancient India, representing the second stage in the evolution of magic. The confusion lasts up to modern times.

As indicative of the formerly explained second stage in the evolution of magic, reference is made to the earliest sacrificial ritual of which we have detailed information as being pervaded with practices that breathe the spirit of the most primitive magic.[6] The rites performed on special occasions such as marriage, initiation, and the anointment of a king are models of magic of every kind of the highest antiquity.[7] The sacrifices detailed in the *Brāhmaṇas* are interfused with magic. The *Sāmavidhāna-Brāhmaṇa*, the *Adbhuta-Bhāhmaṇa* which

[1] *G.*, pt. i, i. 269, 270, quoting H. Oldenberg, *Die Religion des Veda*, pp. 420 ff.

[2] Sir J. Frazer wrongly locates it in the Punjab.

[3] *G.*, pt. i, i. 296, quoting W. Crooke, *Popular Religion and Folklore of Northern India* (1896), i. 76.

[4] *Ibid.*, pt. i, i. 296, 297, quoting *ibid.*, p. 74.

[5] *Śatapatha-Brāhmaṇa*, translated by J. Eggeling, pt. i, p. 328 (*S. B. E.*, vol. xii).

[6] *G.*, pt. i, i. 228, quoting H. Oldenberg, *Die Religion des Veda*, p. 59.

[7] *Ibid.*, quoting *ibid.*, p. 477, &c.

forms part of the *Ṣaḍviṃśa-Brāhmaṇa*,[1] and the *Kauśika-Sūtra*[2] are really handbooks of incantations and sorcery. In the introduction to the translation of the last-named book, Dr. W. Caland remarks, 'He who has been wont to regard the ancient Hindus as a highly civilized people, famed for their philosophical systems, their dramatic poetry, their epic lays, will be surprised when he makes the acquaintance of their magical ritual, and will perceive that hitherto he has known the old Hindu people from one side only. He will find that he here stumbles on the lowest strata of Vedic culture and will be astonished at the agreement between the magic ritual of the old Vedas and the shamanism of the so-called savage. If we drop the peculiar Hindu expressions and technical terms and imagine a shaman instead of a *Brāhmaṇa*, we could almost fancy that we have a magical book belonging to one of the tribes of North American red-skins.'[3] So also Prof. M. Bloomfield: 'Witchcraft has penetrated and has become intimately blended with the holiest Vedic rites; the broad current of popular religion and superstition has infiltrated itself through numberless channels into the higher religion that is presented by the *Brāhmaṇa* priests, and it may be presumed that the priests were neither able to cleanse their own religious beliefs from the mass of folk-belief with which it was surrounded, nor is it at all likely that they found it in their interest to do so.'[4] The very name of *Brāhmaṇa*, according to some good authorities, is derived from *brahman*, 'a magical spell,' from which the *Brāhmaṇa* seems to have been a magician before he was a priest.[5] The *Mantra-śāstrī* claims to effect by mantras much more than any magician ever pretends to accomplish. He is even superior to the gods, and can make gods, goddesses, imps, and demons carry out his behests. Hence the following saying is everywhere current in India—'The whole universe is

[1] Sylvain Lévi, *La Doctrine du Sacrifice dans les Brāhmaṇas* (1898), p. 129.

[2] W. Caland, *Altindisches Zauberritual*, p. ix.

[3] As quoted in *G.*, pt. i, i. 229.

[4] M. Bloomfield, *Hymns of the Atharva-Veda*, pp. xlv ff. (*S. B. E.*, vol. xlii) quoted in *G.*, *loc. cit.*

[5] O. Schrader, *Reallexikon der indo-germanischen Altertumskunde* (1901), pp. 637 ff.

subject to the gods; the gods are subject to the *mantras*; the *mantras* to the *Brāhmaṇas*; therefore, the *Brāhmaṇas* are our gods.'[1] Even up to the present day, the great Hindu trinity is subject to the sorcerers, who by means of their spells exercise such a power over the mightiest gods that they are bound to do whatever they may please to order them.[2]

Incarnation of the deity, temporary or permanent.

Deification of the magician-king is the final step in his progress. The conception of human incarnation is, as already pointed out, common in early societies, and the divinity of the king is but one of its manifestations. No country in the world is perhaps so prolific of human gods, and nowhere else has the divine grace been poured out in so great a measure on all classes of society, from kings down to milkmen, as in India.

Temporary deification.

A *Brāhmaṇa* householder who performs the regular bi-monthly sacrifices is supposed thereby to become a deity for the time being.[3] 'He who is consecrated becomes both Viṣṇu and a sacrificer.'[3] Among the Kuruvikkaranas, a class of bird-catchers and beggars in Southern India, the goddess Kālī is supposed to descend upon the priest for a time.[4] The Takhas on the borders of Kashmir have prophets who become inspired and communicate with the deity.[5] Among the Todas of the Nilgiris, the dairy is a sanctuary and the milkman a god.[6]

Permanent deification.

'Every king in India is regarded as little short of a present god,'[7] and the Hindu law-book of Manu goes farther and says that 'even an infant king must not be despised from an idea that he is a mere mortal; for he is a great deity in human form.'[8] The same treatise lays down that a *Brāhmaṇa*,

[1] Monier Williams, *Religious Thought and Life in India* (1883), pp. 201, 202, and 202 n. (*G.*, pt. i, i. 225, 226).

[2] *G.*, pt. i, i. 225, quoting J. A. Dubois, *Mœurs, institutions et cérémonies des peuples de l'Inde* (Paris, 1825), ii. 60 ff.

[3] *G.*, pt. i, i. 380, quoting Eggeling's transl. of *Śatapatha-Brāhmaṇa*, (*S. B. E.*), pt. ii, pp. 4, 20, 29, 38, 42, 44.

[4] *Ibid.*, p. 382, quoting E. Thurston, *Castes and Tribes of Southern India*, iv. 187.

[5] *Ibid.*, p. 383, quoting C. F. Oldham, 'The Nagas,' *J. R. A. S.*, 1901, pp. 463, 465 ff., 467, 470 ff. The Takhas are, according to Oldham, descendants of Nagas of the *Mahābhārata*.

[6] *Ibid.*, p. 402, citing among others W. E. Marshall's *Travels amongst the Todas* (London, 1873), pp. 136, 137.

[7] *Ibid.*, p. 403, quoting Monier Williams, *Religious Life and Thought in India*, p. 259.

[8] *Ibid.*, *loc. cit.*, quoting *Manu* (*S. B. E.*), vii, ślk. 8.

'whether ignorant or learned, is a great divinity, just as fire, whether carried forth (for the performance of a burnt-oblation) or not carried forth, is a great divinity;'[1] and 'though he employs himself in all sorts of mean occupations, he must be honoured in every way; for every *Brāhmaṇa* is a very great deity.'[2] The *Śatapatha-Brāhmaṇa* records a similar view: 'Verily, there are two kinds of gods; for, indeed, the gods are the gods; and the *Brāhmaṇas* who have studied and teach sacred lore are the human gods. The sacrifice of these is divided into two kinds: oblations constitute the sacrifice to the gods; and gifts to the priests, that to the human gods—the *Brāhmaṇas* who have studied and teach sacred lore.'[3] The spiritual power of the priest (*purohita*) of a village community is described by Monier Williams as unbounded: 'His anger is as terrible as that of the gods. His blessing makes rich, his curse withers. Nay, more, he is himself actually worshipped as a god. No marvel, no prodigy in nature, is believed to be beyond the limits of his power to accomplish. If the priest were to threaten to bring down the sun from the sky or arrest it in its daily course in the heavens, no villager would for a moment doubt his ability to do so.'[4] A sect in Orissa some years ago worshipped the late Queen Victoria in her lifetime as their chief deity, and to this day all living persons noted for strength, valour, or miraculous powers run the risk of being worshipped as gods.[5] Nikkal Sen was the deity of a sect in the Punjab. He was no other than the brave General Nicholson.[6] At Benares, a celebrated deity was incarnate in Svāmī Bhāskarānandajī Sarasvatī, who was worshipped in temples during his life and had other temples erected to him since his death.[7]

[1] *G.*, *ibid.*, quoting *ibid.*, ix. 317.
[2] *G.*, *ibid.*, quoting *ibid.*, ix. 319.
[3] *G.*, *ibid.*, 403, quoting *Śatapatha-Brāhmaṇa* (*S. B. E.*), pt. i, pp. 309 ff.; cf. *ibid.*, pt. ii, p. 341.
[4] Monier Williams, *Religious Life and Thought in India*, p. 457.
[5] Monier Williams, *op. cit.*, p. 259. [6] *Ibid.*, 260.
[7] Sir J. Frazer (*op. cit.*, p. 404) borrows the description from the Rev. Dr. A. M. Fairbairn, who knew the *Svāmī* personally (*Contemporary Review*, June 1899, p. 768). Also Rai Bahadur Lala Baij Nath, B.A., *Hinduism Ancient and Modern* (Meerut, 1905), pp. 94 ff. The difference between a god and a madman, or a criminal, says Sir J. Frazer, is often merely a question of latitude and longitude.

The Liṅgāyat priests are worshipped as divinities and considered superior even to Śiva.[1] In 1900, a hill-man in Vizagapatam gave out that he was an incarnate god and gathered five thousand devotees, who resisted even to the shedding of blood the armed force sent by the government to suppress the movement.[2] At Chinchvad, a small town about ten miles from Poona [3] in southern India, there is a family of whom one in each generation is believed by a large number of Mahrattas to be god Gaṇapati in flesh and blood.[4] A Hindu sect which has many representatives in Bombay and Central India regards its spiritual chiefs or Mahārājas as incarnations of Kṛṣṇa, giving them homage including offering of incense, fruits, flowers, and waving of lights, just as they do to the god Kṛṣṇa.[5]

SECTION V.

Objections to the theory.

We should note first the objections to the general principles upon which the hypothesis is based and next those to the application of the hypothesis to India.

General objections. Alleged priority of magic to religion on *a priori* grounds.

A. Magic, according to Sir J. Frazer, is prior to religion on *a priori* grounds.[6] The fundamental conception of religion, viz. of superior personal agents able to direct favourably the course of nature in response to prayers, is more complex than the basic notion of magic—that the course of nature is subject in the last resort to impersonal forces, which can be turned to account by proper spells and ceremonies. It is added that magic, like religion, deals also with spirits, but treats them as inanimate agents, i.e. constrains instead of conciliating them as religion does.[7] In view of this exposition of magic and religion,

[1] E. Thurston's *Castes and Tribes of Southern India*, iv. 236, 280. *G.*, pt. i, i. 404).

[2] *Ibid.*, *Ethnographic Notes in Southern India* (Madras, 1906), p. 308. (*G.* pt. i, i, 405).

[3] Sir. J. Frazer (*ibid.*, p. 405) writes 'Poona in western India'. It should, of course, be 'in southern India'.

[4] Among other references, Captain Edward Moor's 'Account of an Hereditary Living Deity' in the *Asiatic Researches*, vii (London, 1803), pp. 381-95, and *Gazetteer of the Bombay Presidency*, xviii, pt. iii (Bombay, 1885), pp. 125 ff.

[5] *Monier Williams, op. cit.*, pp. 136 ff. Also *History of the sect of the Mahārājas or Vallabhāchāryyas* (Trübner Series, London, 1865). (*G.*, pt. i, i. 407.)

[6] See Sir J. Frazer's remarks on this subject, *supra*, sec. iii.

[7] For the references to Sir J. Frazer's work, see above.

I do not see how the latter can be held to be more complex than the former. The conception of nature is common to both, as also that of spirits. The course of nature is said to be variable in the one and uniform in the other. I fail to see how it is so. Had it been rigid, incapable of the slightest change, no spells could have altered it one way or the other. Thus, in the ultimate analysis, nature is somehow variable in magic. As to the propitiation or compulsion of the spirits, a religious man conciliates while a magician compels them. Conciliation implies a submissive attitude, while compulsion a domineering one. Thus the component elements of religion have either identical or corresponding elements in magic, but have nothing in them that marks the former as more complex or later in origin than the latter.

Sir J Frazer's descriptions of magic and religion analysed.

Besides, another point that should be considered is that we are here primarily concerned with public magic, through which the magician rises to the throne. The practice of this magic requires in the magician much cleverness, intellectual capacity, and power of swaying masses of people by various artful ways. Such magicians were not exceptions, but are said to have been abundant in early societies. Is it probable that the savage should develop so much his intellectual faculties, while remaining utterly stunted in the speculative and spiritual instincts implied in religion?

Public magic analysed.

Sir J. Frazer holds that religion has grown out of the inefficacy of magic. I do not understand why it should wait for its birth centuries, until the savages have despaired of magic; for, judging from its constituents, we see that there is nothing in it that cannot take root in a savage-mind as early as the conception of private magic.

Religion need not have grown out of the inefficacy of magic.

Dr. Marett looks upon religion and magic as two forms of an originally one and indivisible social phenomenon. The primitive man had *one* institution which dealt with the supernatural, and had in it the germs of both magic and religion, which were gradually differentiated. The priest and magician were originally one.[1]

Dr. R. R. Marett's view.

[1] *Encyclopaedia Britannica* (11th ed., vol. xvii, 'magic'); also Marett's *Anthropology*, pp. 209 ff. It is remarked by Mr. N. W. Thomas,

Professor D. G. Brinton's opinion.

'The principle', says Prof. Brinton, 'at the basis of all religions and all superstitions is the same . . . and the grossest rites of barbarism deserve the name of "religion" just as much as the refined ceremonies of Christian churches. The aims of the worshipper may be selfish and sensuous, there may be an entire absence of ethical intention, his rites may be empty formalities and his creed immoral, but this will be his religion all the same and we should not apply to it another name. . . . The Parliament of Religions announced these elements as essential to the idea of religion, viz. a belief in a god or gods, in an immortal soul, and in a divine government of the world. No mistake could be greater. Buddhism rejects every one of these items. Many religions have not admitted the existence of soul.'[1]

Mr. Andrew Lang's opinion:

Religion, according to Sir J. Frazer, consists of two elements, one theoretical and the other practical—a belief in the superior powers and an attempt to please them. The practical element, he adds, need not necessarily be ritual. It may be pure conduct alone. If so, the belief may not express itself in the asking of desirable things from the spirits at all. The belief accompanied by conduct influenced thereby may be enough for religion. Should the practical element consist in 'give and take'—'worldly good in exchange for religious practices'—piety, as Mr. Andrew Lang puts it,[2] becomes like that of

in the former work, that 'Dr. Frazer's theory is based on a selection of facts and not on the whole body of beliefs and rites recognized as magical, among which are many wherein spirits figure. Dr. Frazer's position appears to be that such rites are relatively late and may be neglected in framing a definition of magic. It may be perfectly true that the idea of magic has been progressively extended; but belief in transformation is also for Dr. Frazer magical. This belief is certainly primitive, yet sympathy will not explain it as it should if Frazer's theory is correct. . . . Frazer's method ignores the fact that magic, like religion, is an institution, i.e. a product of society, not of any single individual. There is no more reason to suppose that a child reared in isolation would develop any kind of magical practices than that it would invent for itself a religion; *but if this is the case, the associationist account of magic cannot be true.*'

[1] Brinton's *Religions of Primitive People* (American Lecture Series, 1897), p. 27.

[2] Mr. Andrew Lang's *Magic and Religion* (1901), p. 59:

Socrates.—'Sacrificing is giving to the gods, and piety is asking from them?'

Euthyphro.—'Yes, Socrates.'

Euthyphro in the Platonic dialogue of that name, a science of '*do ut des*'. He further adds that this principle of 'give and take' is not found in the most backward race, which believes in a Power but propitiates him neither by prayer nor sacrifice *for having earthly goods from him.*

the practical side of religion need not lie in 'give and take'.

B. As to the inductive proof from the actualities of the lowest savage societies, the opinions are far from being unanimous. Both the affirmative and the negative sides of the question are maintained with warmth by high authorities, travellers, bishops, missionaries, and others.[1] Mr. Andrew Lang holds that *the question of the relative priority of magic or religion cannot be historically determined.* Even if we find a race with magic but no religion, we cannot be certain that it did not once possess a religion of which it has despaired.

Opinions far from unanimous *as to the inductive proof.*

The remarks of Prof. Menzies [2] are very significant: 'It must not be forgotten that an adequate definition of a thing (here religion) which is growing can only be reached when the growth is complete. I propose, then, as a working definition of religion (of the savages), that it is "the worship of higher powers". This appears at first sight a very meagre account of the matter; but if we consider what it implies, we shall find it is not so meagre. In the first place it involves *an element of belief.* No one will worship higher powers unless he believes that such powers exist.* *This is the intellectual factor.* Not that the intellectual is distinguished in early forms of religion from the other factors, any more than grammar is distinguished by early man as an element of language. But something intellectual, some creed, is present implicitly even in the earliest worships. Should there be no belief in higher powers, true worship cannot continue. If it be continued in outward act, it has lost reality to the mind of the worshipper,

Professor A. Menzies.

Socrates.—'Upon this view, then, piety is a science of asking and giving.'

Euthyphro.—'You understand me capitally.'

[1] See Lord Avebury's *On the Origin of Civilization, &c.* (1902), Preface to the sixth edition, last paragraph.

[2] He has consulted the works of C. P. Tiele, P. D. Chantepie de la Saussaye, E. B. Tylor, and others, and come to the above conclusion after taking due note of the divergent opinions they might hold on the points under discussion, and their reasons therefor.

and the result is an apparent or a sham religion, a worship devoid of one of the essential conditions of religion. This is true at every stage. But in the second place, these powers which are worshipped are "higher". Religion has respect, not for beings men regard as on a level with themselves or even beneath themselves, but for beings in some way above and beyond themselves, and whom they are disposed to approach with reverence. When objects appear to be worshipped for which the worshipper feels contempt, and which a moment afterwards he will maltreat or throw away, there also one of the essential conditions is absent, and such worship must be judged to fall short of religion. There may no doubt be some religion in it; the object he worships may appear to the savage, in whose mind there is little continuity, at one moment to be higher than himself and the next moment to be lower; but the result of the whole is something less than religion. And in the third place these higher powers are worshipped. That is to say, religion is not only belief in the higher powers but it is a cultivating of relations with them, it is a practical activity continuously directed to these beings. It is not only a thinking but also a doing; this also is essential to it. When worship is discontinued, religion ceases; a principle indeed not to be applied too narrowly, since the apparent cessation of worship may be merely its transition to another, possibly a higher form; but religion is not present unless there be not only a belief in higher powers but an effort of one kind or another to keep on good terms with them.'[1] . . . 'Now of the things that all savages possess, certainly religion is one. It is *practically agreed that religion, the belief in and worship of gods, is universal at the savage stage; and the accounts which some travellers have given of tribes without religion are either set down to misunderstanding, or are thought to be insufficient to invalidate the assertion that religion is a universal feature of savage life.*'[2] . . . 'It (religion) would seem to be *a psychological necessity.*'[3]

[1] Prof. A. Menzies, *History of Religion* (1895), pp. 7, 8.
[2] *Ibid.*, p. 23.
[3] *Ibid.*, p. 24.

Mr. Lang and others oppose Sir J. Frazer regarding absence of religion among the modern Australian savages.

Regarding the existence of religion among the present Australian aborigines, Mr. Lang inclines to the affirmative view.[1] He also adds that Sir J. Frazer ignores without giving reason the evidence of Mr. Ridley, Mr. Greenway, Mr. Gason, Mr. Hale, Archdeacon Günther, the Benedictines of Nursia, Mr. Eyre, Mr. Roth, and Mr. Langloh Parker.[2]

Professor F. Ratzel.

'Ethnography', according to Prof. Ratzel, 'knows no race devoid of religion but only differences in the degree to which religious ideas are developed. Among some, these lie small and inconspicuous as in the germ or rather as the chrysalis; while among others they have expanded in a splendid wealth of myths and legends.'[3] Prof. Brinton, whom we have quoted in another connexion, adds, 'The fact is, that there has not been a single tribe, no matter how rude, known in history or visited by travellers, which has been shown to be destitute of religion under some form. The contrary of this has been asserted . . . by H. Spencer and Sir John Lubbock, not from their own observation, but from the reports of travellers and missionaries. I speak advisedly when I say that every assertion to this effect, when tested by careful examination, has proved erroneous.'[4]

Professor D. G. Brinton.

Importance of the definition of religion in this inquiry.

Sir J. Frazer states that amongst the lowest savages, magic is universally practised but religion is almost unknown, and turns for data to the Australian savages, who are regarded as still in the most backward state.[5] In this inquiry, the

[1] Mr. Ardrew Lang says that Dr. Frazer cites Mr. Howitt, Mr. Palmer, Mr. Oldfield, Mr. Dawson, and Mr. Cameron, all of whom testify to the existence of native religion among the Australian aborigines, for points other than the one where, if their reports be correct, they would invalidate his central theory.

[2] Andrew Lang's *Magic and Religion*, pp. 55, 57.

[3] Prof. F. Ratzel's *History of Mankind* (translated by A. J. Butler, 1896), p. 40. The above remarks have not been made without full knowledge of the American-Pacific group of races, including the Australians, Malays, &c.

[4] *Religions of Primitive People*, pp. 30, 31. 'The question has been carefully examined by G. Roskoff, in his work *Das Religionswesen der rohesten Naturvölker* (Leipzig, 1880). He conclusively refutes the assertion that tribes have been encountered without religion.' Brinton, *op. cit.*, p. 31 n.

[5] Dr. Frazer doubts the authenticity of the passage quoted by Hegel from Captain Parry's account for inductive confirmation of his view (*G.*, pt. i, vol. i, Appendix). Dr. Frazer has not been able to trace the

definition of religion is of vital importance. If too narrow, it will exclude those savage races who may be credited with a religion under a broader definition thereof. In order to find a religion among the Australian aborigines, in the opinion of Mr. Lang, we need not widen its definition so much as to bring it under the same category as the fear of a child at the sight of a dark room, the feeling of a horse towards its master, or the baying of a dog to the moon, which may have to be admitted under this widened definition as an act of worship.[1] 'If men believe', says he, 'in a potent being, who originally made or manufactured the nature of things or most things, that is an idea so far religious that it satisfies, by the figment of a supernatural agent, the speculative faculty. Clearly, the belief in such a being is a germ whence may spring the ideas of duty towards and an affection for the being.'[2] Again, ancestor-worship, belief in future life, and some practices which are liable to be classed as magical, but which should really form part of religion on account of the object of propitiation they subserve, are found among the Australian savages.[3] If these elements can make up religion, the Australians cannot be said to be without it.[4]

Religion of the aborigines in the

Sir J. Frazer has himself, in one of his Australian examples, given materials sufficient to establish the existence of religion among them from Mr. Lang's standpoint. He says, for

passage either in the English original or German translation of the captain's work. The expression 'empirical mode of existence' appearing in it 'savours', says he, 'rather of the professor's lecture-room than of the captain's quarter-deck.' Hegel relies upon Captain Parry and Captain Ross. If Dr. Frazer relies upon the philosopher, he should also like him rely upon what these travellers say. They state 'among other peoples (i.e. other than the Esquimaux) a mediation is already present', including, of course, the Australians. This opposes Dr. Frazer's view of the almost universal absence of religion among them. If the travellers' remark be impeached as too general for their range of personal observations, and hence erroneous, producing a corresponding error in Hegel in his reliance upon their wrong authority, it is no wonder that he might err similarly in the more slippery field of speculation, where mistakes are more insidious and difficult to avoid.

[1] See Lord Avebury, *On the Origin of Civilization, &c.* (1902), p. 219.

[2] Andrew Lang's *Magic and Religion*, p. 48.

[3] *Ibid.*, pp. 49, 51.

[4] The evidences adduced by Sir J. Frazer, in his *Totemism and Exogamy*, i, 141-53, in support of his opinion do not appear to carry his point farther than those of his *Golden Bough*, vol. i.

instance, that among the tribes of Central Australia the most important function of the headmen is to take charge of the *sacred store-house*, usually a cleft in the rocks or a hole in the ground, where are deposited *the holy stones and sticks* (churinga) *with which the souls of all the people, both living and dead, are apparently supposed to be in a manner bound up.*

examples cited by Sir J. Frazer.

In his examples from other countries there are many such materials. In Malo, one of the New Hebrides, the highest nobility consists of persons who have *sacrificed a thousand little pigs to the souls of their ancestors.* A man of exalted rank is never opposed, because *in him are supposed to dwell the souls of the ancient chiefs and all the spirits who preside over the tribe.*[1] In New Britain, a ruling chief was always supposed to exercise *priestly functions, that is, has professed to be in constant communication with the* tebarans (*spirits*).[2] Among the Masai of German East Africa, the chief is not so much a ruler as a *national saint or patriarch.*[3] The procedure of the rain-making chief amongst the Bari of the Upper Nile consists in *praying to the dead ancestor* which is religious and other rites which are magical.[4] In the Ossidinge district in the Camaroons in Africa, if the chief happens to be also the *fetish-priest*, as among the Ekios, he has not only powerful influence *in all fetish matters* (*and most of the vital interests of the people are bound up with fetish worship*), but also wields a powerful authority.[5] The old head-chief of Etatin in S. Nigeria in Africa performed many rites, but along with them *prayed to big deities* in order to make rain.[6] The king of the Matabeles of South Africa *had recourse to religion as well as magic for making rain.*[7] A successful medicine-man among the wild tribes of the Malaya peninsula has the best prospect of being elected a chief, and in the vast majority of cases *the priestly duties form an important part of a chief's work.*[8]

Sir J. Frazer's position is that the Australian savages, lowest

[1] *G.*, pt. i, i. 339. [2] *Ibid.*, p. 340. [3] *Ibid.*, p. 343.
[4] *Ibid.*, p. 347. Here Sir J. Frazer himself says that religion is combined with magic in the function.
[5] *Ibid.*, p. 349. [6] *Ibid.*, p. 349. [7] *Ibid.*, p. 351.
[8] *Ibid.*, p. 360.

Australian aborigines not absolutely free from religion even according to Sir J. Frazer's own standard.

as they are in the scale of civilization, are almost free from religion. All other savages, being higher in the scale, have religion, though it may be mixed with magic. But the Australians are not entirely free from it even according to his own standard of religion. If this standard be a little altered, as Mr. Lang suggests, it would not be difficult to find evidences of religion among the very savages whom Sir J. Frazer describes as almost free. Mr. Cameron, quoted by Mr. Lang,[1] says, for instance, 'As to religion, ghosts of the dead are believed to visit the earth and to be frequently seen. . . . The people of all these tribes appear to have a belief in a Deity and in a future state of some kind. The Wathi Wathi call this being Tha-tha-pali; the Ta-Ta-thi call him Tulong. . . . The being is regarded as a powerful spirit or perhaps a supreme supernatural being. They say that he came from the far north, and now lives in the sky. He told each tribe what language they were to speak. He made men, women, dogs, and the latter used to talk, but he took the power of speech from them.'[2] As to future life, he received this account from an intelligent member of the aforesaid tribe: 'the soul of a dead man is met by another soul who directs him to the path for good men.'[3]

More evidences of religion will be forthcoming if the above standard be a little altered.

Mr. Cameron's testimony.

Mr. Howitt's evidence.

Mr. Howitt, also cited by Mr. Lang, was initiated into the secret of the Kurnai religion. Before his initiation, the old men of the tribe satisfied themselves whether Mr. Howitt had been previously initiated by the Brojerak black fellows or not by seeing a particular token. The inmost secret of their religion was the belief in Mungann-gaur, the Great Father of the tribe, who was once on earth and now lives in the sky.

There are thus grave doubts about the inductive proof, which the future may remove.

It is needless to multiply such affirmative instances. Both the negative and affirmative opinions, as I have already mentioned, are held by quite a number of observers. Circumstanced as we are, we cannot at present finally determine the question of the relative priority of religion or magic from reports about the Australian aborigines—the lowest savages

[1] Andrew Lang, *Magic and Religion*, pp. 70–1.

[2] *Ibid.*, 70, 72. The extract appears above with two or three verbal alterations in order to make it shorter.

on the face of the globe. If these people cannot furnish definite proofs, the question cannot be inductively settled from other races of savages, stationed as they are on a higher scale of civilization. It may perhaps yet be hoped that the differences of opinion would be removed by greater scrutiny in observation and a more correct criterion of magic and religion at the hands of scholars trained to analyse the psychological processes of the savage-mind from the right standpoint. Upon the conflicting data at present at our command, it is unsafe to take one side or the other of the question and build on it any theory that cannot but be unsound.

C. Dr. Frazer makes no difference in the times of origin of the two classes of magic, private and public. From the nature of public magic—I mean the magic practised by professional magicians for the good of the whole community—it cannot, I think, be synchronous in origin with the other branch. It must be later in origin, and, if so, it is necessary to ascertain (*a*) how much later, and (*b*) whether in the *interim* any of the other methods of evolution of kingship may not have operated to give the early societies their kings, and also (*c*) what openings, if any, they left free for the operation of the method contemplated by the present theory; for Dr. Frazer says that 'magic is not the only or perhaps even the main road by which men have travelled to a throne.'[1]

There must be difference in times of origin of private and public magic.

Dr. Frazer has given instances of magicians as kings, which can be distinguished into two groups: (1) persons who, starting as magicians in savage societies, have been actually seen in their lifetime to rise to chiefships; (2) chiefs or kings who, from the supernatural qualities attributed to them and the magical functions attached to their office, are inferred to have come to the throne through public magic followed as a profession, or to have had ancestors who had done the same and from whom the supernatural qualities and functions have been inherited by transmission through generations.

D. (i). The question that demands an answer here is—If methods other than the magician-method of kingship really

Ways to kingship other than

[1] *G.*, pt. i, i. 332.

public magic. Possible origins of king's super-natural attributes and functions other than through public magic. First possibility.

operated, and supreme power came into the hands of a single man either by dint of his personal bravery, skill in leadership, any other personal quality, or any conglomeration of helpful circumstances, may not the king who thus came to the throne have acquired a halo of extraordinary and supernatural qualities, which by lapse of time gained in number and proportion, independent of any connexion whatever of the king with public magic? If the tendencies of the primitive mind are towards clothing anything extraordinary in a supernatural garb, it is only natural that the savage subjects of the king should attribute to him many extraordinary qualities in direct ratio to the nature and number of sterling attributes of mind and physique actually possessed by him. Royalty is itself awe-inspiring, and can perhaps without any other aid set the savage-mind a-working towards the attribution to it of supernatural qualities. In view of this, it is not correct to infer from the magical functions and supposed supernatural powers of the kings of the present savage societies (and even of many modern civilized societies, as Sir J. Frazer has done) that they or their ancestors in the past must have been public magicians who through their profession acquired the crown. It may be objected that many of the very qualities and functions of the public magician are associated with the royal office, e. g. rain-making, driving away storm, enemies, &c., from which it is justifiable to draw Sir J. Frazer's inference. The answer is to be found in the fact that the qualities and functions are by their nature associated with the public welfare, and the remedies are also by their character such as can and should be naturally expected by the people from the sovereign. If famine or pestilence decimates the land, crops wither for drought or rot for excess of rain, external or internal enemies cause havoc in the country, or other such calamities befall the people, they would naturally seek for relief from the head of the land. The latter would try his best to satisfy the subjects and would have recourse to means of all sorts; and, as the supernatural means were believed both by the prince and the peasant to be a potent one, it is no wonder that the sovereign might himself endeavour by such methods to remove the evil.

As very often happens in these matters, the people mark when the remedy hits, but do not note when it misses. If by a coincidence the king is successful in the eye of his subjects, his previous modicum of supernatural qualities receives confirmation and fresh accessions by leaps and bounds. The king may thus, without being a public magician, acquire supernatural attributes. The functions of the public magicians who appeared later may have been but subsequent borrowings of these attributes, which offered to the practitioners a fruitful prospect of earning a decent livelihood accompanied by public influence and power. According to this view, the magicians launched on their career of public usefulness by imitation of the functions and qualities of the king, who had first shown the way.

Second possibility.

There is also a second possibility. The king may have acquired the throne in ways other than through public magic, while the magicians may have developed their functions independently of the king, and then there was a gradual transference of the magicians' attributes to the king.

Third possibility.

According to a third possibility, the king may have attained to his position as described in the previous cases, and both he and the magicians may have developed supernatural qualities of public utility independently of each other, which by gradual intertransference might have become common to both later on.

The supernatural attributes and functions of modern kings cannot therefore be indubitably imputed to public magic as their only origin.

In modern societies, we may meet with supernatural attributes of sovereigns, but before imputing them to the only origin that the sovereigns or their first ancestors were magicians, we should make sure by indubitable proofs that the other three origins just mentioned were not responsible therefor.

The evidentiary value of the second group of instances, nil.

In the light of these possibilities, the value of the second group of instances reduces to nil.

D. (ii). Now, as to the first group, which comprises two instances, viz. a person among the Dinkas of the Upper Nile became the richest and the most esteemed and dreaded chief of the Kič tribe through his skill in ventriloquism, by which roars of fierce animals were made to emanate from

The first group of instances criticized.

a cage testifying to their stay there to guard the house of the ventriloquist. The other instance relates that the rain-maker almost invariably becomes a chief in the Lendu tribe of Central Africa.[1]

Sir J. Frazer appears to argue from the premisses that because the ventriloquist and the rain-maker have risen to chiefships in two particular savage societies at the present moment, the public magicians of whom they are types must have done so in the particular stage of evolution of human societies when monarchy came into existence, giving rise to a theory applicable by its logical extensions to a good many civilized societies of modern times also. It is a far cry from the conditions of two savage societies of the present time to the many societies brought within the application of the theory, separated as they are by ages and, in some cases, by extensive spaces. Before making an application of this sort, we should note the following points:

Does the collocation of sociological elements in existing savage societies represent the same or similar collocation in a particular epoch of the remote past?

D (ii), a. Is it certain that existing savage societies, or even the lowest savages now noticeable, represent the same or a similar collocation of sociological elements as those of remote antiquity, and, in the present case, of that particular epoch when the primitive political organizations were being replaced by monarchies? I do not mean to say that savage societies of to-day do not preserve customs and institutions that had their origin in the remote past; I wish it to be clearly understood that what I desire to ascertain is, Can it be asserted that the customs or institutions, beliefs or superstitions, of the existing aboriginal societies, to whatever spheres of mental or sociological activities they may belong, and in whatever state of development or degeneration they may be, are in the same or a similar state of relative progress or decay as they were in a particular epoch of antiquity? Is it not possible that some of them, though now seen side by side, did not come into being at all in the particular epoch, though the others were then existing? Is it not true that the societies, though now comparatively stationary, were at one time more changeful and dynamic? If this be conceded, we should

[1] See the first group of instances in sec. iii, *supra*.

admit that, though, in the two cases now under discussion, the ventriloquist and the rain-maker are reported to have risen through public magic to chiefship, the practice of this class of magic as a profession may not have developed at all at the time when the political organizations of the savages were being replaced by monarchies through non-magical methods of attaining kingship. It is one thing to assert that the customs and institutions of the extant savage societies are old or very old, and another to make, as in the present case, a particular political phenomenon dependent upon and synchronous with a particular socio-magical phenomenon.

It does not; and public magic may not have existed at all when kingships first came into being.

D (ii), b. Are the so-called magicians of Sir J. Frazer, who at last become successful in competition with their fellow practitioners in their endeavour to rise to the throne, really magicians? There are bona fide magicians in primitive societies who honestly believe in their own supernatural powers. But they lag behind in the competition. The persons who aspire to the throne, and are likely to meet with success, or ultimately do so, are of quite a different stamp. They are 'conscious deceivers' and 'intelligent rascals', their success varying with the roguishness they can bring to bear upon their clients.[1] In the first of the two illustrations noticed before, the 'magician' is nothing but a cheat imposing upon and terrorizing his credulous fellows principally by ventriloquism. The successful 'magicians' are not magicians proper, but impostors, who take to public magic as a convenient cloak to conceal their real character and acquire pelf and power from behind the disguise. If mere deception be the central principle that ultimately procures kingship for the men through whom it operates, and public magic be but a makeshift to guise its evil nature and make it appear decent and respectable, it need not have taxed Sir J. Frazer's genius and industry to convince us of the existence of the principle, access as it has to all quarters, perhaps at all times, in some of the primitive aspirants to kingship. But even here the question is whether it operated as the only dominant force, or mingled with other forces which occupied the principal position, and whether it

Sir J. Frazer's magicians are not magicians proper, but conscious deceivers.

If deception be the central operating principle and public magic a mere disguise, there cannot be a theory of kingship until certain questions

[1] See sec. iii, *supra*.

are satisfactorily answered.

could be incarnate as the aforesaid dominant force in the public magician whose very existence at the time of the origin of kingship is doubtful. Until these questions are satisfactorily answered, deception cannot be made into a theory.

So many cases of transformation of the roguish magician-king an impossibility.

D (ii), c. It appears unnatural that in so many cases the roguish nature of the 'magician' should be transformed into its opposite on his accession to the throne. Such transformations may happen in exceptional cases, but cannot be the general rule. In confirmation of the above view, Julius Caesar and Augustus are cited by Sir J. Frazer as two of the most conspicuous examples. To be thus transformed presupposes that the better side of the character should be exceptionally strong, though kept in abeyance for a while, and that it should be able to assert itself at the very period when stronger and additional influences come into operation by the obtainment of the royal office with all its attendant allurements. The higher nature, instead of being able to rise up, is very likely to be drawn down to the lower depths of evil. Caesar and Augustus may have had their better side strong in them, but they, as examples of the peculiar combinations of good and evil, are rare at all times and all places. Character of their stamp cannot be expected in every chief that developed out of a so-called magician among the savages, and such chiefs were not a few according to Sir J. Frazer.

A magician proper need not aspire to kingship.

D (ii), d. A magician proper need not aspire to kingship; his own supernatural powers in which he himself believes are to him a kingdom much greater perhaps than that of a king. He has effective powers over all things on earth and heaven; he can therefore make and unmake kings at will. Mentally he is a lord of much more than what earthly kingship can bring. It is an anomaly, and, indeed, it is depriving him of his character as a magician to impute to him a non-magicianly aspiration, as Sir J. Frazer does.

A magician proper unfit for kingship by his very nature.

D (ii), e. A genuine magician would most likely, by his very nature, be unfit for the performance of the civil, judicial, and military duties attached to royalty He would probably have to bear the joint burden of all these varied duties, differentiation of function not having yet commenced. Though the community or the State over which he rules be small, the personal attention he would have to pay to all sorts of public affairs would not make it an easy task to wear the crown in a primitive society. The primitive king has to decide upon all matters of public importance, settle disputes among his subjects, maintain internal peace, inflict punishments, regulate trading transactions, defend his own kingdom against external invasions, and attend to many serious and important works which presuppose his possession of serious intellectual and moral qualities. A magician who lives more in an imaginary world of his own fabrication, who is given perhaps to trances and hallucinations, and who busies himself more with spirits and demons than with the prosaic things of this earth, is not likely to have the capacity to be a king and keep on as such.

Sir J. Frazer's magician theory of kingship, therefore, is not a theory concerned primarily with the magicians properly so called, but with cheats and rascals; and in the latter case, as I have already said, there cannot be a theory of the principle of deception operating as the dominant force through the disguise of public magic to elevate a cheat to the throne until certain questions are satisfactorily answered.

The deification of kings in ways other than through public magic.

E. The public magician, according to Sir J. Frazer, attains divinity. He becomes a chief, then a sacred king, and lastly a god incarnate. It can by no means be contended that public magic is the only road to divinity. We have noted the various other ways in which supernatural powers may be attributed to the sovereign. It is but a step from these supernatural powers to his godhood, and the former easily leads to the latter. Thus, from the divinity of the kings of present savage societies, it cannot be inferred that it owed its origin to nothing but public magic.

SECTION VI

Objections to the Indian application of the hypothesis.

We have seen that a supernatural power attributed to the king of a modern civilized country cannot be indubitably taken as a relic of such powers possessed by his primitive predecessors who had attained to kingship through their careers as public magicians. Sir J. Frazer draws an inference of this sort when, from the supposed power of the English sovereign of healing scrofula by touch, which he looks upon as a relic of the aforesaid kind in the face of the tradition of its derivation from Edward the 'Confessor',[1] he comes to the conclusion that the sovereign's primitive predecessors were public magicians. He appears to draw the same conclusion in regard to France and many other modern civilized countries. He quotes the *Laws of Manu* as an evidence of the supernatural powers of the ancient Hindu kings, whose predecessors appear to be regarded by him as coming within the application of his hypothesis along with the first kings of all the Aryan races from India to Ireland.

Even if the preceding objections be ignored for the present, and the hypothesis granted for some societies, reasons and evidence are needed for extending it to other societies.

Even if we ignore the preceding general objections and assume for the present that public magicians are becoming kings in some modern savage societies and also in their prototypes in the particular epoch of the remote past, is it not reasonable to expect that, before applying the assumption to other societies, sufficient reasons and evidence should be given to show that they also come within its range? The concession that the existing savage societies, in which public magicians are seen to be becoming kings, had also seen similar elevations to the throne in the past, does not involve any implied admission of a similar origin of the kingship in any country in which we find any supposed supernatural power associated with kingship. The remark of Max Müller, made in a different connexion, is, with slight necessary alterations, very apposite in the present context and in regard to the application of the above assumption to India: 'We know,' says he, 'from the languages and from some of the complicated customs of uncivilized races, that those so-called sons of nature have had many ups-and-downs before they became what they are now; yet no one has attempted to prove that their ups-and-downs were exactly the same as the ups-and-downs of the Āryas. . . . Granted that the Aryans must have been savages, does it really follow that all savages, any more than all civilized races, were alike, or that

[1] See *G.*, pt. i, i. 370.

the Aryan savages . . . acted exactly like other savages (in a particular field of human activity)? Even modern savages differ most characteristically from each other. . . . Even if we were to admit that all human beings were born alike, their surroundings have always been different, and (the results of their influences upon actions) must have differed in consequence.'[1] It therefore lies on Sir J. Frazer, as I have already said, to adduce reasons and evidences before extending his hypothesis to India. While dealing, in the different chapters of his works, with the premisses that make for his final conclusion, he adduces Indian examples which appear to supply the evidences and arguments upon which the Indian application of his hypothesis is based. These instances have been collected, and put in their proper bearings as consecutive links in the chain of argument in a previous section. I shall now proceed to weigh their values *seriatim*, and see what they amount to.

The Indian examples have been collected before; their values should be weighed.

The instances[2] under public magic do not refer to it as a profession pursued by magicians for the good of the community. The *Brāhmaṇa* student who performs the *Śakvarī* vow for mastering the *Mahānāmnī* verses of the *Sāma-Veda* is regarded by Sir J. Frazer as a public magician who is preparing himself for his profession. This conclusion is very far from what can be gathered from the passages which lay down the rules for the performance of the vow. Some of its observances may not be explicable. It is better to leave them as such without forcing any interpretation upon them. The *Gobhila-Gṛhya-Sūtra* says that the performance of the rules procures rain at the asking. Be it so; but where is the evidence that the student utilized this power as a rain-maker for earning money and influence? The duties of a *Brāhmaṇa* are hard and fast, comprising only the following: (i) study, (ii) teaching, (iii) performance of sacrifice, (iv) officiating at others' sacrifices, (v) making gifts, and (6) acceptance of gifts

The Indian instances criticized. *Re* public magic. The *Śakvarī* vow.

[1] F. Max Müller's *Contributions to the Science of Mythology* (1897), ii. 441, 442. The changes required for fitting the extract in the present context have been put within brackets.

[2] For the references, see section iii, *supra*.

from proper persons. There may have been exceptions to this rule, which, however, do not negative the rule itself. How could then a *Brāhmaṇa* student become a professional rain-maker? The accomplishment of vows is said in a good many Sanskrit works to confer upon their observers many powers which may offer lucrative openings to the seekers of money and influence; but the inference that those powers were made into professions is as delusive as the powers themselves may have been visionary.

A few other points should be noted:

(I) The *Gobhila-Gṛhya-Sūtra* mentions the aforesaid power of rain-making as a result of the performance of the vow; but it appears only as a by-product of the performance, the principal object of the vow-maker being the mastery of the *Mahānāmnī* verses and not the acquisition of the power.

(II) The *Śāṅkhāyana-Gṛhya-Sūtra* does not refer to the power at all. Had it been a principal object to be achieved by the vow, it would not have been omitted.

(III) The *Gobhila-Gṛhya-Sūtra* itself makes the observance of the rules regarding the wearing of dark clothes and eating of dark food optional, which would never have been done, had the object been the development of the power of rain-making in the student, assimilating him to the dark clouds through his garments and food of the same colour.

(IV) In the story of Ṛṣya-śṛṅga in the *Rāmāyaṇa*,[1] no sooner did the sage enter Romapāda's dominion, where there had been a long-standing drought, than rains poured down in torrents. Here the power of rain-making was in the sage, but was dissociated from money-making.

We should therefore be on our guard against supposing that the power of rain-making was always utilized by its supposed possessor with an eye to the main chance.

(V) So far as I see, the *Mahānāmnī* verses themselves are not spells for causing rain, but relate to different matters altogether.

Rain-stopping at Muzaffarnagar. The next example comes from Muzaffarnagar, where the people stop rain by drawing the figure of Agastya on a loin-

[1] *Rām.*, i. 10, 11.

cloth, or the exterior of the house. It does not obviously speak of the existence of public magic in the locality as a profession. The people who use the charms are not professional magicians, and the ends for which the rain is stopped may not be public.

Rain-making at Chatarpur.

The same objections apply to the next instance of rain-making at Chatarpur.

A *Brāhmaṇa's* morning-offering.

The example from the *Śatapatha-Brāhmaṇa* merely expresses a belief as to the offering made by a *Brāhmaṇa* in the morning. The object for which the offering is made is more for the nourishment of the 'Sun-child' than for the good of the people to be derived from sunshine, while the *Brāhmaṇa* himself is not a public magician properly so called.

Re confusion of magic and religion as the second stage in the evolution of the former.

The object of the next illustrations is to show the mixture of magic and religion in India, and mark it as the second stage in the evolution of the former. It is not, however, certain, as already shown, what should be the ordinal number of the stage which the confusion of the two represents. There are differences of opinion as to the number and nature of stages that preceded it. It is, therefore, not at all sound to take the aforesaid mixture of magic and religion as the second stage and regard it as a witness of the first.

Objections to two side-issues: (i) Many religious rites classed as magical.

The magical character of many of the ancient Indian practices may not be denied, but it is objectionable that many of the religious rites and ceremonies should be classed as magical through the loss of the synthetic view in the analytic. If a ritual be detached from a sacrifice and dissected, it may appear magical, but if it be borne in mind that it is but a portion of a ceremony pervaded by the intention of propitiation of the higher powers, it cannot be classed as such.

(ii) Dr. Caland gratuitously shocked.

I do not appreciate Dr. Caland's shrugging of shoulders at what he calls the shamanism of the Vedic Hindus. If it is a fact that the remote ancestors of all the present civilized nations were, at some time or other in the past, tainted with aberrations of belief, more or less, a sober statement of facts would have been seemly and inoffensive.

(iii) Derivation of

Sir J. Frazer derives the word *Brāhmaṇa* from *brahman* = a magical spell', from which he concludes that the *Brāhmaṇa*

the word '*Brāhmaṇa*'.

had been a magician before he was a priest. The root, according to Monier Williams,[1] means 'swelling of the spirit or soul', from which the signification of 'pious effusion or utterance' may be derived. There is nothing in it to show that the utterances were magical rather than devotional and that the *Brāhmaṇa* had been a magician before he became a priest. Again, if the word be taken as indicating the special work that was coming to be marked as the *Brāhmaṇa's* own and none other's, or, in other words, if it be regarded as pointing to the beginning of the caste-system which was relegating to the *Brāhmaṇa* the monopoly of the pious utterances (which according to Sir J. Frazer were magical), it should be remembered that the same caste-system was precluding him from kingship and making the throne the monopoly of the *Kṣatriyas* (the warrior-caste).

Re the deifications of kings,—not a sure index to their elevation from public magicians.

The deifications mentioned next are not, on Sir J. Frazer's own showing, the exclusive possession of kings elevated from public magicians. If everybody, who is endowed with a measure of power more than the ordinary, runs the risk of being a deity in India, if General Nicholson can become a god and Queen Victoria a goddess, and if such instances can serve as an index to the mental proclivities of the ancient Hindu mind, it is obvious how difficult it is to infer from the divinity of an Indian king that he or his first predecessor in the past had been a public magician, the profession not being the only road to the Indian divinity.

What the Indian evidences amount to.

Thus the instances adduced by Sir J. Frazer for the Indian application of his hypothesis do not establish his point. To England he seems to apply his hypothesis merely on the ground of the English king's supposed power of healing scrofula by touch, which he regards as a relic of the supernatural powers of the king's magician-predecessors. I am not in a position to speak of England, but Sir J. Frazer's method of arrival at the aforesaid conclusion *per saltum* appears at the very first sight faulty. If more of belief than reasoning be the basis for the extension of the hypothesis to the Aryan races

[1] *Sanskrit-English Dictionary.*

from India to Ireland, or to other peoples, an assertion in its favour is only as good as another to the contrary.

SECTION VII.

Thus this hypothesis has been subjected to the tests. It assumes that magic precedes religion in the evolution of human thought. Its *a priori* arguments have been met by other such arguments of opposite tenor. Its inductive proof from the activities of the lowest savage societies is by no means certain in view of the differences of opinion obtaining on the subject. Again, as there should be a difference in the times of origin of private and public magic, the latter might be much later. It has not been shown that private magic must always be followed by public magic, and hence a place where there may be private magic may not see the emergence of magic of the other sort followed as a profession. If, again, religion be a psychological necessity of the savage, it is to be seen how far magic had become differentiated from religion in the epoch when kingship emerged. If the two were yet inextricably intermingled, it has also to be seen whether the so-called magician was not also a priest, or more a priest than a magician, and whether in the latter cases the priest had any chance of gaining kingship. The priest, as we have found in regard to India, may be precluded from kingship altogether, or may not aspire to it at all, for which we should be on our guard against fixing an unpriestly or unmagicianly aspiration upon them respectively. The inference of the magician-origin from the supernatural attributes and functions of the present kings either in savage or civilized societies is not sound, for these attributes and functions may have various possible origins and hence cannot invariably be imputed to the only origin accepted by Sir J. Frazer, viz. that the kings or their primitive ancestors were public magicians. Instances of so-called public magicians in the present savage societies actually rising to chiefships do not carry us far; for the collocation of sociological elements in those societies is not a sure indication that the same or a similar collocation existed in the particular epoch of the remote past under consideration. If it is so, public magic

Conclusion.

may not at all have been existent in the epoch when the first kings came into being. Then, again, Sir J. Frazer's magicians are not magicians properly so called. They are conscious deceivers; and the worst cheat defeats his rivals and becomes a chieftain. The hypothesis, therefore, is reduced to one that really contemplates deception as elevating a deceiver to the throne. It is not for all kinds of deception that the result is claimed, but only for that particular kind that works under public magic as its disguise. If so, there is difficulty in the way. The practice of this deception supposes that public magic plied as a profession existed in the place or the race in which it operated. Its existence in the particular place or race at the time of the emergence of the first kings has to be shown before the above alternative to which the hypothesis is reduced can be accepted. Some other difficulties have also been noted: cheats and rascals who are supposed to become kings have their rougish nature transformed into its opposite in so large a number of cases that it amounts to an impossibility. Finally, a magician proper need not, as I have already said, aspire to kingship, and may, besides, be unfit for the arduous duties of a primitive king. Again, as deifications of human beings or kings may take place in more ways than one, it has to be proved in every case that no other than supernatural attributes acquired through public magic were responsible for the divinity of a particular king before it could be admitted.

Even ignoring the above objections, and assuming that a public magician could become a king in particular primitive societies, we do not see sufficient grounds for applying the hypothesis to the primitive Indo-Aryans. The Indian illustrations of the various links of Sir J. Frazer's argument have been subjected to scrutiny and found wanting.

Let us now see what other hypotheses previously noted may apply to the Indo-Aryans. The hypothesis of the 'attribute'-origin of kingship has no obstacles in the way of its application to the aforesaid people or perhaps to any other. The mental and physical qualities enumerated are as old as man himself and may have operated to elevate one or many of the first kings. Of course, the particular combination of personal attributes that worked in any particular case cannot be determined. Deception is not mentioned by Spencer as operating by itself as a dominant force to raise a cheat to the throne. There is nothing impossible about it, but the hypothesis must be supported by strong grounds before it can be accepted as satisfactory. Wealth by itself has been mentioned as a factor, but it should, in my opinion, be subject to some limitation.

As to the patriarchal hypothesis of kingship, the Indo-Aryans are one of the peoples to whom it has been applied. So far as evidences—literary, philological, or otherwise—within our reach can point to a conclusion, it is thus that the families of the primitive Aryans rose into clans, clans into tribes, and so forth. That these assemblages of kinsmen were put to the necessity of self-protection and performance of administrative duties cannot be denied. As a sense of kinship pervaded the whole collection of kinsmen, it is probable that the burden of the political duties might be vested in one of these kinsmen, and that deference to the particular line to which he belonged might influence the convergence of power on him. It must not be thought that personal attributes did not come into operation in the elevation of a particular kinsman as the political head of the community; but the sense of kinship, deference to the purity or seniority of a particular line, might operate along with them, or at times independently of them, to bring about the centralization of the supreme powers. The application of the patriarchal hypothesis of kingship to the Indo-Aryans appears, therefore, to be justifiable.

[1] Dr. Brajendranath Seal, M.A., Ph.D., has very kindly helped me with suggestions on some points involved in this chapter.

CHAPTER IX

THE RELIGIOUS ASPECTS OF ANCIENT HINDU POLITY.

Points of contact between religion and political life.

It is not probable, judging from the religious bent of the ancient Hindus, that their political thoughts, aspirations, and activities should have remained in absolute isolation from religion. As a matter of fact, they were mixed with religious feelings and forms in a large measure. This is manifest principally in

(A) The conceptions of the State and its ideal, the monarch, the relations between the monarch and the people, &c.

(B) Minor ceremonials (mainly Atharva-Vedic) for the promotion of the welfare of the State either directly, or indirectly through that of the king's welfare.

(C) The politico-religious ceremonials of a more or less elaborate nature for the inauguration of the emperor, king, crown-prince, and State-officials to their respective offices, restoration to lost regal office, assertion of political power, and so forth.

The noteworthy features of the conceptions and ceremonials.

The conceptions and ceremonials were not synchronous in their birth. The former are examples of assimilation of political thoughts to religion, while the latter represent the inclusion of those thoughts within religious incrustations. Both represent the lines of touch between religion and politics, while among the latter may be noticed cases of competition for the attainment of the highest importance, evolution of one from another, fusion of two into one or mutual elimination, growth into complexity from simple origins, differences as to the eligibility of the performers and their objectives, and harnessing of purely secular or religious ceremonies to political purposes. An analysis of these can lay bare many political ideas and facts not discernible elsewhere perhaps in the whole range of evidences bearing on polity. Besides this inner significance, some of them had another in their outer influences upon the princes and peoples. An *Aśvamedha*, for instance, could shake the foundations of all those numerous states upon which its performer intended to assert his sway, each sacrifice being a source of anxieties and disturbances to a large number of princes with numerous subjects under their rule. The *Rājasūya*, when performed with a political end, proved to be a similar disturbing agency in later times by reason of its inclusion of the subjugation of territories as one of its rituals. The political significance of the other ceremonials need no explanation, obvious as it is from their immediate purposes, leaving out of account other aspects of their nature.

Re (A): (1) The conception of the State and its ideal; government according to the Hindu conception is an organization to promote the material and spiritual welfare of the people.

Government, like all other concerns of life, is associated in the eye of a Hindu with an ultimate spiritual purpose. A well-conducted government forms the basis, without which the aggregate spiritual progress of the people in an orderly and effective way is not possible. Hence comes the great responsibility of a monarch, who, as the head of a royal polity, works this important machinery, which, being out of order, affects not merely the material interests of the people but also their spiritual interests, the latter being regarded by them as far superior to the former. The successive links by which government is chained up to the *summum bonum* are: the four castes, viz. *Brāhmaṇa*, *Kṣatriya*, *Vaiśya*, and *Śūdra*, composing the society have arts and sciences to learn and duties to follow in and through the prescribed modes of life, which ultimately leads them to salvation. For a strict adherence to the duties, and for punishment of deviations[1]

[1] According to Kauṭilya (I. ii, pp. 6 ff.), there are four branches of learning viz. (i) *ānvīkṣikī*, (ii) *trayī*, (iii) *vārttā*, and (iv) *daṇḍanīti*. The first comprises the three branches of metaphysics, viz. *Sāṅkhya*, *Yoga*, and *Lokāyata*. The second literally means 'triple', i.e. the three Vedas, *Ṛg*, *Yajus*, and *Sāma*; but the signification is extended to include the *Atharva-Veda* and *Itihāsa-Veda*, which according to Kauṭilya's explanation (I. v. p. 10) consists of (*a*) *Purāṇa*, (*b*) *Itivṛtta* (history), (*c*) *Ākhyāyikā* (legends), (*d*) *Udāharaṇa* (illustrations), (*e*) *Dharmaśāstra* (codes of law and morals), and (*f*) *Arthaśāstra*, of which Kauṭilya thus marks out the scope—manuṣyāṇāṃ vṛttir arthaḥ; manuṣyavatī bhūmir ity arthaḥ; tasyāḥ prithivyā lābhapālanopāyaḥ śāstram arthaśāstram iti (XV. i, p. 424) which means '*artha* (wealth or 'goods') is man's means of

therefrom, as also for the protection and maintenance of order among the people, an organization is needed; and this is supplied by the ruler. Without him, anarchy[1] prevails, bringing in its train the evils *that are so much dreaded by mankind.*

The ideal of the State as set forth in the epics and later Sanskrit literature is therefore the attainment of the *summum bonum* '*mokṣa*' (salvation) through *dharma*, *artha*, and *kāma*. In other words, the State is the machinery for the collective attainment of salvation (*mokṣa*) by the people under its care, through the fulfilment of their legitimate desires (*kāma*) in a legitimate way (*dharma*), through *artha*, acquired also in a legitimate way, *dharma* regulating both *artha* and *kāma*.

life; *artha* is the land, with its people; that science which treats of the means of acquiring and preserving the said land is *Arthaśāstra* (science of man's material concerns)', which thus includes the ground covered by the modern sciences of economics and politics. The third is economics primarily concerned with agriculture, cattle-breeding, and trade, while the fourth is the science of government. The school of Manu recognizes three branches only, subsuming (i) under (ii), that of Bṛhaspati two, viz. (iii) and (iv), and that of Uśanas (iv) alone, viz *daṇḍanīti*, the other three being but its dependents. In the *Rāmāyaṇa* (ii. 100. 68) the divisions of learning are mentioned as three. In *Manu*, vii. 43, the *vidyās* are five if *ānvīkṣikī* and *ātmavidyā* be taken as separate, as some commentators have done, and in *Yājñavalkya* the *vidyās* are four (i. 311, M. N. Dutt's ed.). The *Kāmandakīya* (ii. 11) follows Kauṭilya in fixing the number at four, using *ātmavidyā* as explanatory of *ānvīkṣikī*. Cf. *Raghuvaṃśa*, iii. 30, which mentions four *vidyās*.

[1] Kauṭilya uses the pithy expression *matsyanyāya*, which reigns supreme in the absence of a ruler, the stronger destroying the weak like the large fishes preying on the small fry. In the *Rāmāyaṇa* (ii. 67. 31) the same idea occurs:

Nārājake janapade svakaṃ bhavati kasyacit,
Matsyā iva janā nityaṃ bhakṣayanti parasparam.

(Cf. ii. 61. 22, where the phenomenon is thus referred to—svayam eva hataḥ pitrā jalajenātmajo yathā.) The *Mahābhārata* in a similar context (xii. 67. 16) has:

Rājā cen na bhavel loke pṛthivyāṃ daṇḍadhārakaḥ
Jale matsyān ivābhakṣyan durbalaṃ balavattarāḥ.

Cf. *Matsya-Purāṇa*, ccxxv. 9; *Kāmandakīya*, ii. 40; *Manu*, vii. 20. The expression also occurs in the inscription of Dharmapāla at Khālimpura (*Gauḍa-lekha-mālā*, p. 12). Various meanings of the expression are given at pp. 148 ff. of the *History of Bengal* (in Bengali) by Mr. R. D. Banerjee, M.A.

The evils of anarchy are vividly depicted in *Rām.*, ii. 67, *MBh.*, xii. 59, 67, 68. Just as anarchy is deprecated, so is ruling with an iron hand or a mild one. Cf. *Arthaśāstra*, I. ii. 9, which has been versified almost *verbatim* in the *Kāmandakīya*.

The legitimate method of acquiring 'means' consists in the performance of duties in the stages of life prescribed for the four castes *Brāhmaṇa*, *Kṣatriya*, *Vaiśya*, and *Śūdra*. The branches of learning, which may be regarded as four, viz. *ānvīkṣikī*, *trayī*, *vārttā*, and *daṇḍanīti*, have a bearing on the attainment of the ideal. The first, as the *Kāmandakīya* has it, is intended to create non-attachment to this world, the second to show the difference between right and wrong, the third to teach the production, preservation, and improvement of wealth, and the fourth the conduct of government.[1] They are to be learnt by the first three castes alike, the practical application of *trayī* falling to the first caste, *daṇḍanīti* to the second (above all to the sovereign who comes from this caste), and *vārttā* to the third (according to Kauṭilya to the last also).[2]

The State, therefore, under the direction of the sovereign, leads the people under its protection to the final goal of human existence—emancipation—furnishing at the same time means therefor.

This conception of the ideal of the State, on the one hand, cannot be earlier than the development of the doctrine of emancipation[3] in the earliest *Upaniṣads*; on the other, it appears full-fledged in the epics. It must therefore have taken shape within these two chronological limits. It is not clear what the ideal had been before the addition of emancipation to the three other members of the quatern, found in use in pre-*Upaniṣad* Sanskrit literature, but, so far as I find, not expressly as the ideal of the State.

Re (A): (2) The deification of the monarch.

The conception of sovereignty was likewise religionized. The deification of kings has been observed by anthropologists to be common to the primitive peoples now extant, whatever may be the causes therefor; and some of them argue that, the tendencies of the primitive mind being the same irrespective of time and space, the primitive ancestors of the Indo-Aryans had also the same conception of their kings' divinity.[4]

[1] ii. 11; so *Agni-Purāṇa*, ccxxxviii. 9.
[2] *Kauṭilīya*, Bk. I, ii, p. 7.
[3] Prof. A. A. Macdonell's *History of Sanskrit Literature*, p. 389.
[4] See the chapter 'Theories of the Evolution of Kingship'.

The monarch, however, appears as human and not divine in early Vedic literature. In the *Ṛg-Veda*, for instance, the description of the monarch (x. 60, 173, 174) does not clothe him with divinity.[1] In the *soma*-sacrifices dealt with in the *Yajur-Veda* and its *Brāhmaṇas*, he, as the sacrificer, becomes identified with Prajāpati or other deities during their performance, but this is only *pro tempore*,[2] though it might have served as a factor towards the ultimate formation of the conception. I am not in a position to discuss the question why the divinity of the monarch, which, according to anthropologists, had its origin in primitive times and still continues among the extant savage races, does not find expression in the earliest record of the primitive ancestors of the Indo-Aryans. The conception emerges in the epics, and becomes the nucleus for several others allied to it in those as well as other works. He is identified with several divinities[3]—Śakra, Bṛhaspati, Prajāpati, Babhru (Viṣṇu), Fire, Vaiśravaṇa, Yama.[4] He is likened to a god,[5] or to Prajāpati,[6] and is the personification of Dharma[7] (right and law), and Daṇḍa[8] (punishment or government).

The deification of the *Brāhmaṇa* previous to that of the monarch.

The deification of the king was preceded as early as the *Śatapatha*[9] by that of the *Brāhmaṇas* who studied and taught the sacred lore, and thereby also of the royal priest. The divinity of the king and *Brāhmaṇas* is also echoed in the law-codes and later Sanskrit literature. In *Manu*, for instance, a *Brāhmaṇa* is an eternal incarnation of the sacred law, lord

Brāhmaṇa in *Manu*.

[1] Neither does the monarch appear therein as a magician able to carry out his intentions by bringing compulsion to bear upon the deities.

[2] Eggeling, *S. B. E.*, xli. 108–10, with nn.

[3] *MBh.*, iii. 185. 26–30; 139. 103. Cf. *Rāmāyaṇa* (Gorresio), ii. 122, 17 ff., and iii. 4. *Vide* Hopkins, *J. A. O. S.*, p. 153 n., for the references.

[4] *MBh.*, xii. 68. 41.

[5] *Ibid*, iv. 4. 22.

[6] *Ibid*, i. 49. 10.

[7] *Ibid.*, i. 49. 8.

[8] *Ibid.*, xii. 15. 34 = *Manu*, vii. 18. The *Purāṇas*, e.g. *Bhāgavata* (iv. 14. 26, 27), identify the king with all the divinities. As corollaries to his divinity may be mentioned the *Mudrārākṣasa* (ii. 7), which makes him husband of *Rājalakṣmī* (kingdom personified as a goddess), and *Raghuvaṁśa* (iii. 62–5), which makes him subduer of Indra.

[9] *Śatapatha-Brāhmaṇa*, ii. 2. 2. 6—'verily, there are two kinds of gods; for, indeed, the gods are the gods; and the Brāhmaṇas who have studied and teach sacred lore, are the human gods.' Cf. *MBh.*, xiii. 152. 16 = *Manu*, ix. 315 ff. = *Agni-Purāṇa*, ccxxv. 16, 18 ff., as quoted in *J. A. O. S.*, xiii. 153 n.

of all created beings, natural proprietor of all that exists in the world, others subsisting only through his benevolence.[1] Ignorant or learned, he is a great deity like Fire, whether carried forth for the performance of a burnt-oblation or not, or existing in a crematorium, or a place of sacrifice.[2] Though employed in mean occupations[3] he should be honoured. By his origin alone, he is a deity even for the gods.[4] He is the creator of the world, the punisher, teacher, and hence benefactor, of all creatures. He can create other worlds, other guardians of the world, and deprive the gods of their stations.[5]

King in *Manu*.

A king, again, is an incarnation of the eight guardian deities of the world, Moon, Fire, Sun, Wind, Indra, Kubera, Varuṇa, and Yama; the Lord created the king out of the eternal particles of those deities for the protection of the universe.[6] He is hence, like the sun, dazzling in lustre and able to burn eyes and hearts.[7] Through his supernatural power, he is the great Indra as well as the aforesaid eight guardian deities.[8] Even an infant king should not be despised, a great divinity as he is in human form.[9] The taint of impurity does not fall on the king, for he is seated on Indra's throne.[10]

Both king and *Brāhmaṇa*, though gods, have limitations.

Though the *Brāhmaṇa*, and thereby the royal priest, as also the king, are divinities, endowed with supernatural power, they have, like the gods in general of the Hindu pantheon, their own limitations. They are to observe the duties attached to their respective castes with the four stages of life, belonging as they do in their human aspect to the Hindu society with a framework of its own. They have, in addition, to observe the particular duties of the offices they hold. They are subject to transmigrations, bound like ordinary mortals to go to heaven or hell, and have despicable and agonizing births or otherwise as the results of their illegal and impious actions on this earth. The king and the royal priest constitute but the *middling rank* of the states caused by *rajas* (activity) in spite

[1] *Manu* i. 98–100; ix. 245. [2] *Ibid.*, ix. 317, 318; xi. 83.
[3] *Ibid.*, ix. 319. [4] *Ibid.*, xi. 85. [5] *Ibid.*, ix. 315, 316.
[6] *Ibid.*, vii. 3, 4; v. 96. Cf. *Śukranīti*, i. 72.
[7] *Ibid.*, vii. 5, 6. [8] *Ibid.*, vii. 7. [9] *Ibid.*, vii. 8.
[10] *Ibid.*, v. 93.

of their divinity.[1] The king, according to the *Śukranīti*, loses his claim to allegiance and reverence, and may even be dethroned, should he prove an enemy of virtue and morality.[2]

Re (A): (3) The public relations influenced by religious conceptions: (i) king.

The mutual public relations among the king and the four castes under his rule have been a good deal influenced by such and other religious conceptions, e.g., the origin of the four castes from the mouth, arms, thigh, and feet, which assign to each its particular rank.[3] The king, identified as he is with the aforesaid eight deities, has to emulate the actions of seven of them, excepting Kubera, with whom his identification is limited only to the possession of wealth. In addition, he has to emulate the Earth's action. Like Indra, pouring down copious rain during the rainy season, he should shower benefits on his kingdom; like the Sun, imperceptibly drawing up water during the remaining eight months, he should gradually draw taxes from his realm; he should through his spies penetrate everywhere like the Wind, present as vital air in all creatures; he should, like Yama (God of the Dead), exercise control over all his subjects, bringing under his rule both friends and foes; like Varuṇa, penalizing the sinner, he should punish the wicked; he should follow Moon's example by being a source of joy to his subjects; he should be Fire in his wrath against criminals and wicked vassals, and the all-supporter Earth in his support to all his subjects.[4]

The king's divinity does not place him above the observance of obligations attached to his office. In fact, his divinity requires that he should in reality possess a godly nature. The rules framed with this purpose in view perhaps contemplated a possibility of abuses of his power rendered indefinitely greater by the popular conception of his godhood, and hence considered it wise to deal minutely with the subject of his self-discipline,[5] hedging it in by several warnings and sanctions. His principal duties have also been similarly

[1] *Manu*, xii. 46. 51. 24 ff.

[2] See Mr. R. G. Pradhan's article in the *Modern Review*, Feb. 1916, pp. 154, 155.

[3] *Ṛg-Veda*, x. 90. 12.

[4] *Manu*, ix. 303–11. Cf. *Śukranīti*, i. 73–8.

[5] *Ibid.*, vii. 44, 46–51, 53.

treated. The king committed *sins* and *no mere infringements* of *salutary secular rules or conventions* by breaches of his principal obligations. *Daṇḍa* (Punishment), which the Lord created as his son for the king's sake for the protection of creatures,[1] destroys the king himself with his relatives for miscarriage of duties.[2] The king is enjoined to behave like a father towards his children in his treatment of the people, observe the sacred law in his transactions with them, and arrange for the collection of revenue by competent officials.[3] The protection of subjects is as sacred a duty as the performance of a sacrifice,[4] and secures the monarch from every person under his protection a sixth part of his spiritual merit. Remissness in this duty brings on him a sixth part of the demerit of each of his subjects, ruining his spiritual prospects, and depriving him of his right to revenue, tolls, duties, daily presents, and fines.[5] The ensurance of safety of his kingdom may involve him in battle in which death should be preferred to ignominious retreat.[6] Failures of justice throw him into perdition,[7] as also unjust seizure of property.[8]

(ii) *Brāhmaṇas.*

The *Brāhmaṇas*, though gods of gods, were not exempt from the king's control, though in the *Śatapatha-Brāhmaṇa* a *Rājasūya-mantra* repeated once or twice hints at such an exemption: 'This man (king), O ye people, is your king, Soma is the king of us *Brāhmaṇas.*'[9] They might not have enjoyed this immunity in practice, yet they had many privileges, and were treated with great respect and lenience. The king is enjoined to be lenient towards *Brāhmaṇas*,[10] give them jewels of all sorts and presents for the sake of sacrifices,[11] never to provoke them to anger which can instantly destroy him with his army and vehicles,[12] and not to levy taxes on *Śrotriyas* even in times of extreme want.[13] (The king should provide for the maintenance of those *Śrotriyas* that pine with

[1] *Ibid.*, vii. 14.
[2] *Ibid.*, vii. 28.
[3] *Ibid.*, vii. 80.
[4] *Ibid.*, viii. 303.
[5] *Ibid.*, viii. 304–9; ix. 253.
[6] *Ibid.*, vii. 87–9.
[7] *Ibid.*, viii. 18, 316, 317, 343, 344, 346, 386, 387, 420; ix. 249, 254.
[8] *Ibid.*, vii. 48; viii. 171; ix. 243, 244, 246, 247.
[9] *Śatapatha-Brāhmaṇa*, v. 3. 3. 12; v. 4. 2. 3.
[10] *Manu*, vii. 32.
[11] *Ibid.*, xi. 4.
[12] *Ibid.*, ix. 313–16.
[13] *Ibid.*, vii. 133.

hunger, for the kingdom would otherwise be afflicted by famine. The religious merit acquired by the *Śrotriyas*, thus maintained, procures for the king long life, wealth, and increase of territory.)[1]

(iii) Subjects.

The various differential treatments [2] pinned into substantive law and its administration, and proportioned to the grades of the castes, had also their roots in religious conceptions. Instances of these are met with in connexion with the right of personally interpreting the law to the court of justice,[3] order in which the suits were tried,[4] appropriation of treasure-trove,[5] punishments for false evidence,[6] infliction of corporeal punishments,[7] defamation,[8] insolence,[9] assault,[10] illicit intercourse,[11] and repayment of debt by personal service.[12] An exception to the ordinary rule is found in regard to the punishment for theft, which was severest for *Brāhmaṇas* and gradually lesser for the other three castes.[13] The condonation of some offences is also dictated by religious considerations,[14] e. g. forcible seizure of sacrificial articles. The *Śūdras* were interdicted from collecting wealth,[15] while the prohibitions imposed on them necessarily excluded as a rule their participation in the cadre of higher state offices.

It is the sacred duty of the subjects to submit to the king's orders,[16] and guard against showing him hate, or incurring his anger and displeasure, full of dire consequences.[17] Their co-operation in the administration of justice is enjoined in several rules with their usual warnings,[18] false evidence [19] being treated with the greatest emphasis. The distribution of sin incurred by unjust decisions takes place thus: 'One quarter

[1] *Manu*, vii. 134–6.
[2] It is not meant here to discuss whether or not these differential treatments were justified and balanced by the self-abnegation or responsibilities of the castes enjoying the preferences.
[3] *Ibid.*, viii. 20. [4] *Ibid.*, viii. 24. [5] *Ibid.*, viii. 37.
[6] *Ibid.*, viii. 123. [7] *Ibid.*, viii. 124, 125.
[8] *Ibid.*, viii. 267, 268. [9] *Ibid.*, viii. 270–2.
[10] *Ibid.*, viii. 279–81. [11] *Ibid.*, 374–85.
[12] *Ibid.*, ix. 229. [13] *Ibid.*, 337, 338.
[14] *Ibid.*, xi. 11–15, 21, 31; viii. 242, 339.
[15] *Ibid.*, x. 129. [16] *Ibid.*, vii. 13.
[17] *Ibid.*, vii. 9, 11–13. [18] *Ibid.*, viii. 13–16.
[19] *Ibid.* viii. 81, 82, 93–5, 98, 99, 111.

of the guilt of an unjust decision', says the code, 'falls on him who committed the crime, one quarter on the false witness, one quarter on all the judges, one quarter on the king. But where he who is worthy of condemnation is condemned, the king is free from guilt, and the judges are saved from sin; the guilt falls on the perpetrator of the crime alone.'[1] Just punishment of offenders purifies them like those who perform meritorious acts, and makes them eligible for heaven.[2] Mutual good relations between the *Brāhmaṇas* and *Kṣatriyas* are pointed out as essential to the welfare of both,[3] while the injunctions for each of the castes adhering to its duties, and thus securing the political harmony contemplated by the law-giver, attach formidable punishments to sins of deviations therefrom.[4]

Parallels to many of the above provisions are met with in other legal systems[5] and in the *Mahābhārata*.[6]

The extent to which religious ideas influenced polity and political thoughts will now be apparent. They coloured the whole system from the State-ideal to the innermost strata The caste-system, which was imbued with religion and had perhaps originated in religious exigencies, supplied the framework of Hindu society, not excluding its polity; the rights and privileges of the king and the people detailed above could not have had their origin except in that socio-religious institution, and subsequent politico-religious conceptions. Polity therefore received its religious colour and semblance through (1) the caste-system; (2) the politico-religious conceptions; (3) the inclusion of polity (*daṇḍa-nīti*) in the 'sacred law;[7]

[1] *Ibid.*, viii. 18, 19. [2] *Ibid.*, viii. 318. [3] *Ibid.*, ix. 320–22.

[4] *Ibid.*, xii. 70–72.

[5] *Baudhāyana*, i. 18. 7–8, 17, 18; 19. 8; 19. 12; ii. 1. 5–10; 1. 17; 3. 51. 52; *Gautama*, viii. 13; x. 9, 44; xi. 14; xii. 1–13, 15–17, 44–7; xiii. 11, 14–16; xiv. 45; xviii. 24–7, 32; *Vasiṣṭha*, i. 43, 44; iii. 14; xvi. 33, 34; xix. 3–6, 23, 43–5, 48; xx. 41; xxi. 1–5, 16; *Viṣṇu*, iii. 6, 26, 27, 44, 45, 50–2, 58, 70, 71, 79; iv. 96; v. 2–8, 19, 23–5, 33–5, 37–8, 40, 41, 43, 150, 196; xxii. 48–50; xxxv. 6; lii. 2; *Āpastamba*, i. 19. 16; 24. 22; 25. 4–5; ii. 25. 11; 26. 2–3; 26. 10; 26. 20; 27. 9; 27. 14; *Yājñavalkya*, i. 311–13, 321–3, 333, 334, 336, 353, 356; ii. 34, 43, 81, 163, 205–7, 215, 285, 286, 294; iii. 27, 28, 44, 244, 257.

[6] *MBh.*, xii. 56. 24, 25; 78. 21–3; 75. 7; 165. 4, 7–10, 13, 18–20; xiii. 61. 30; 152. 16, 21–3.

[7] Cf. *Manu*, i. 2.

(4) the treatment of breaches of many political rules as sins, and attachment thereto of those sanctions (of hell, &c.) that are prescribed for religious deviations proper. (This feature is not so much in evidence in special treatises of polity like the *Kauṭilīya*, *Kāmandakīya*, &c., as in the 'systems of sacred law' like *Manu*); and (5) the inclusion of *Arthaśāstra* in *Itihāsa*, which comprises along with it five other subjects[1] viz. *Purāṇa*, *Itivṛtta*, *Ākhyāyikā*, *Udāharaṇa*, and *Dharmaśāstra*. This *Itihāsa* constitutes the fifth *Veda*,[2] and *polity* dealt with as part of both *Dharmaśāstra* and *Arthaśāstra* assumes thereby a religious appearance by being one of the sub-constituents of the fifth *Veda*.

The minor politico-religious ceremonies mainly Atharva-Vedic.

(B). It was the special charge of the royal priest to perform the minor political ceremonials which had their basis principally in the *Atharva-Veda* and were intended to avert State evils and promote State welfare. According to *Gautama's* injunction, he should perform in the fire of the sacrificial hall the rites ensuring prosperity and connected with *śānti* (propitiation), festivals, march, long life, auspiciousness, as also those causing enmity, subduing, distressing, or destroying enemies.[3] Astrological forecasts and interpretations of omens should also share the king's attention.[4] The propitiation of the planets is expressly mentioned by *Yājñavalkya* as one of the duties of the royal priest, in addition to the performance of the other rituals.[5] Several other works mentioned in the previous chapter advert also to this portion of his charge. A few of the *mantras* from the *Atharva-Veda* intended to be used with appropriate rituals at the prescribed times are detailed below:[6]

Hymns I. 2, I. 19–21 were *sāṃgrāmika* (battle hymns), used in rites for putting enemies to flight, or avoiding wounds by arrows;

I. 9, 29, III. 3 for the restoration of a king;

I. 19–23, III. 6, 27, VI. 134, 135, VII. 62 against enemies;

[1] *Kauṭilīya*, I, v, p. 10. [2] *Ibid.*, I. ii. p. 7. [3] *Gautama*, xi. 17.
[4] *Ibid.*, xi. 15. [5] *Yājñavalkya*, i. 313.
[6] The references for the hymns and directions for their use are taken from Whitney's translation of *AV*. (Harvard Oriental Series).

III. 1, 2 for confounding enemy's army;

III. 19, IV. 22, VI. 65–7, 97–9, 103, 104, VIII. 8 for gaining victory over a hostile army;

V. 20 (addressed to the war-drum) and VII. 118 (used while arming a king or Kṣatriya) for terrifying the same, and

VI. 40 for inspiring it with courage;

VI. 125 (used with VII. 3, 4, 110) addressed to the war-chariot for its success, and

VI. 126 to the war-drum for success against the foe, and used in a battle rite either when the drums and other musical instruments were sounded thrice and handed over to the musicians or when the drum-heads were drawn on;

XI. 9, 10 for ensuring success in war;

XIX. 13 for use, according to Varāhamihira's *Yogayātrā*,[1] immediately before marching forth to war; and

XIX. 20 uttered by the *Purohita* while arming with a breastplate a king departing for battle. There are also hymns for wealth,[2] prosperity,[3] superiority,[4] rain,[5] victory in debate or deliberations of an assembly (*Sabhā* and *Samiti*),[6] for the king's safety at night (used by the *Purohita* on the entrance of the king into his sleeping hours)[7]; against wild beasts and thieves,[8] against king's evil-dreaming,[9] and the like.

The hymn (IV. 22) for the king's success and prosperity has been excerpted here to give an idea of the nature of the *mantras*: '(1) Increase, O Indra, this *Kṣatriya* for me; make thou this man sole chief of the clans (*viś*); unman all his enemies; make them subject to him in the contests for pre-eminence. (2) Portion thou this man in village, in horses, in kine; unportion that man who is his enemy; let this king be the summit of authorities; O Indra, make every foe subject to him. (3) Let this man be riches-lord of riches; let this king be people-lord of people; in him, O Indra, put great splendours; destitute of splendour make thou his foe. (4) For him, O heaven-and-earth, milk ye much that is pleasant, like two milch kine that yield the hot-draught; may

[1] Varāhamihira's *Yogayātrā*, viii. 6; *Indische Studien*, xv. 170.
[2] e.g. *AV.*, i. 15.
[3] e.g. *Ibid.*, ii. 5.
[4] e.g. *Ibid.*, vi. 15.
[5] *Ibid.*, iv. 15; vii. 18.
[6] *Ibid.*, vii. 12.
[7] *Ibid.*, xix. 16–19.
[8] *Ibid.*, iv. 3.
[9] *Ibid.*, xix. 57.

this king be dear to Indra, dear to kine, herbs, cattle. (5) I join to thee Indra who gives superiority, by whom men conquer, are not conquered; who shall make thee sole chief of the people, also uppermost of kings descended from Manu. (6) Superior (art) thou, inferior thy rivals, whosoever, O king, are thine opposing foes; sole chief, having Indra as companion, having conquered, bring thou in the enjoyments of them that play the foe. (7) Of lion-aspect, do thou devour all the clans; of tiger-aspect, do thou beat down the foes; sole chief having Indra as companion, having conquered, seize thou on the enjoyments of them that play the foe.'

The aforesaid hymns from the *Atharva-Veda* are sufficient to show the tendency of the king and the people to resort to rites and ceremonies for securing objects of desire and averting evils. The *Kauṭilīya*[1] and several other works[2] make it part of the king's daily routine to perform certain rites before entering the hall of audience in the morning. In the first of the aforesaid treatises, again, are presented certain rites securing the well-being of horses and elephants stabled by the king for domestic and military purposes: horses were regularly washed, bedaubed with sandal, and garlanded twice a day. On new-moon days, the sacrifice to the *Bhūtas* was performed; and on full-moon days, auspicious hymns were chanted. On the ninth of the month of Āśvina and also at the beginning and end of journeys, the priest invoked blessings on them by performing the waving of lights.[3]

This rite was also performed for the elephants thrice daily in the rainy season and at the periods of conjunction of two seasons. Sacrifices to *Bhūtas* were performed on new- and full-moon days, as also to the god of war Kārttikeya.[4] The rites mentioned in the same work[5] for the prevention or

[1] *Kauṭilīya*, I. xix, p. 38.

[2] *Manu*, vii. 145; *Agni-Purāṇa*, ccxxxv. 4–6; *Devī-Purāṇa*, ii. 71; *Bhāgavata-Purāṇa*, x. 70. 6–10; *Bṛhaspati-Sūtra* (edited and translated in an article by Dr. F. W. Thomas in *Le Muséon*).

[3] *Studies in Ancient Hindu Polity*, i. 51, 52.

[4] *Ibid.*, i. 66, 67; cf. *Kāmandakīya*, iv. 66.

[5] *Kauṭilīya*, IV. iii, pp. 205–8; IX. vii, p. 361. The meanings of many of the expressions for indicating the rites are very obscure.

removal of the several providential visitations in addition to the ordinary remedies are :—

(1) For fire, worship of the god Agni (Fire) on particular days with offerings, *Homa*, and prayers.

(2) For flood, worship of rivers, and performance of rites against rain by persons expert in magic or versed in the *Vedas*; and for drought, worship of Indra, Ganges, Mountain, and *Mahākaccha* (perhaps Varuṇa).

(3) For diseases, propitiatory and expiatory rites to be performed by *siddhas* and *tāpasas* (classes of ascetics); for epidemics, sprinkling of water from sacred places, worship of *Mahākaccha*, milking of cows on cremation grounds, performance of the *Atharva-Vedic* ritual called *kabandha-dahana*, and spending of nights in devotion to the gods; and for diseases or epidemics of cattle, waving of lights and worship of family gods.

(4) Rites for the extermination of 'pests' including rats, locusts, injurious birds, insects, and tigers.

(5) Rites for the destruction of demons to be performed by persons versed in the *Atharva-Veda* and magic; and on prescribed days, worship of *caityas*[1] by placing umbrellas, sweets, small flags, and goats on an altar, and with the cry of 'vaścharāmaḥ'[2] shouted a day and a night by all (engaged in the rites) while moving about.[3]

Closely connected with the ceremonies was astrology, which, judging from the place occupied by it as one of the complementary parts of the Vedas, exercised much influence. The auspicious moments for the rites connected with important acts in the conduct of State-affairs had to be determined in the light of this branch of sacred learning. The prediction of benign or malignant influences, not only on religious rites but also on all human acts, of the heavenly bodies, was one of its

[1] The expression in the text (p. 206) is corrupt.

[2] Perhaps sanctuaries, or sacred trees.

[3] Pandit R. Śyāma Śāstrī translates it by 'we drive thee'. The passage is obscure.

[4] The king has been enjoined by Kauṭilya to settle in his domain the *siddhas*, *tāpasas*, and persons versed in *māyāyoga* (magic) for applying remedies against the providential calamities.

important functions. The idea of the dependence of all the affairs of life upon heavenly luminaries might have tended to stop the spring of actions by deepening the belief in fatalism. This was perhaps counteracted to a great extent in public affairs by the doctrine preached in several Sanskrit works, e. g. *Manu*,[1] *Yājñavalkya*,[2] *Kauṭilīya*,[3] *Kāmandakīya*,[4] *Śukranīti*,[5] *Rāmāyaṇa*,[6] *Mahābhārata*,[7] *Agni-Purāṇa*,[8] and *Skanda-Purāṇa*.[9] According to this doctrine, human effort is superior to fate, which again is nothing but the outcome of human efforts accumulated through the past rebirths. Fate is never operative without exertion. It is only the cowards who look up to the former as the only dominant factor in life. Exertion can transform a malignant fate into a benign one; hence people should always be exertive and never dependent on fate.

This doctrine, however, did not preclude the performance of the rites and ceremonies; for their timely performance was regarded as a part and parcel of the exertion on which the doctrine laid so much emphasis. The *Kāmandakīya*, which is one of the works that recommended the pursuit of the doctrine, says, for instance, that the calamities (*vyasana*) afflicting a kingdom are of two kinds, human (*mānuṣa*) and providential (*daiva*): of these, the former should be averted by exertion (*puruṣakāra*) and wise measures (*nīti*), and the latter (consisting in fire, flood, diseases, famine, and epidemic) by exertion and *propitiatory rites* (*śānti*).[10] The *Kauṭilīya* also prescribes similar rites for the deprecation of providential calamities.[11]

The performance of rituals in connexion with State actions and the use of various means for ascertaining the divine will

[1] *Manu*, vii. 205. [2] *Yājñavalkya*, i. 349–51
[3] *Kauṭilīya*, IX. iv, p. 349 (see *Résumé* to this chapter).
[4] *Kāmandakīya*, v. 11; xi. 38–40; xiii. 3–11, 14–16, 19–21.
[5] *Śukranīti*, i. 48, 49, 53–7; 386.
[6] *Rāmāyaṇa*, ii. 23. 8, 18, 25; iv. 1. 121, 122; 49. 8; v. 12. 10; vi. 2. 6.
[7] *MBh.*, xii. 56. 15; 58. 14–16; 120. 45; 139. 82–4; xiii. 6. 7, 8.
[8] *Agni-Purāṇa*, ccxxv. 33; ccxxvi. 1–4.
[9] *Skanda-Purāṇa*, *Kāśī-khaṇḍa*, xxxii. 30, 31; 53. 46–9; 54. 53, 54. These references have been culled from the Hindu-Rāja-nīti in Bengali (2nd ed., 4th *stabak*) by Mr. Madhusudan Bhaṭṭācārya.
[10] *Kāmandakīya*, xiii. 20, 21. [11] *Kauṭilīya*, IV. iii, pp. 205–8.

in regard thereto were not confined to India alone. In ancient Babylonia and Assyria, 'astrology took its place in the official cult as one of the two chief means at the disposal of the priests for ascertaining the will and intention of the gods, the other being through the inspection of the liver of the sacrificial animal. . . . The liver was the seat of the soul of the animal, and the deity, in accepting the sacrifice, identified himself with the animal, whose "soul" was thus placed in complete accord with that of the god and therefore reflected the mind and will of the god. Astrology was (similarly) based on a theory of divine government of the world.' In its earliest stage, astrology had to do almost exclusively with the public welfare and the person of the king, upon whose well-being and favour with the gods, the fate of the country was supposed to depend. The Greeks and Romans came under the influence of Babylonian astrology in the middle of the fourth century B.C., and among the former, the liver divination was also introduced at an early date. In addition to these methods of reading the future, the consultation of the oracles and various omens other than those in the liver of the slaughtered animal should be taken into account. Astrology regulated the distinction of lucky and unlucky days and predicted future evils, while the oracle exercised its influence politically, not only by its occasional directions as to State matters, but also by inspiring in part, or at least furthering, the great colonial expansion of Greece. The influence of augury on politics was very great. Among the Romans the signs of the will of the gods were of two kinds: (i) in answer to a request, (ii) incidental. The latter had five sub-divisions: (a) *Signs in the sky*; on the very appearance of lightning, all business in the public assemblies was suspended for the day. As the reader of the signs was subordinate to no other authority who could examine his report as to the appearance of lightning, this became a favourite device for putting off meetings of the public assembly.

Some other countries compared.

(b) *Signs from birds*, with reference to the direction of their flight and their singing and uttering other sounds. With regard to public affairs, it was at the time of Cicero superseded by the observation of lightning.

(c) *Feeding of birds*, which consisted in observing whether a bird dropped a particle from its mouth on grain being thrown before it. It was in use particularly in the army when on service.

(d) *Observation of the course of or sounds uttered by quadrupeds and reptiles within a fixed area.*

(e) *Warnings of all unusual phenomena.* Their interpretation did not concern the augurs unless occurring in the course of some public transaction, in which case they operated as a divine veto against it.

The election of magistrates and their assumptions of office, holding of public assemblies to pass decrees, marching forth of an army for war, were subjects for which *auspicia publica* were *always* taken, while the crossing of rivers, founding of colonies, beginning of battles, mustering of an army, sittings of the senate, decisions of peace or war, were occasions for which they were taken frequently.[1]

'No public act,' adds Dr. Seyffert, 'whether of peace or war . . . could be undertaken without auspices. They were specially necessary at the election of all officials, the entry upon all offices, at all *comitia*, and at the departure of a general for war.'[2]

The divine will being ascertained through the signs, the undertaking to which they related was continued or postponed according as the will was favourable or unfavourable. In the latter case, no religious rites appear to have been performed forthwith to propitiate the divine power into a favourable attitude, and resume the postponed act; though, of course, a revision of the signs was permitted to remove any suspected flaw or error.

There were ceremonials for propitiating the gods and achieving objects of desire, as, for instance, the sacrifices, 'many of which were offered to Mars, the god of war, during the campaign and before battle'.[3]

[1] For all the above information, see *Encyclopedia Britannica*, 11th ed., under Astrology, Omen, Oracle, and Augurs; T. Mommsen's *History of Rome*, I. xii.

[2] *Dictionary of Classical Antiquities* (1902), by Dr. O. Seyffert—under 'Auspicia'.

[3] Seyffert, *op. cit.*, under 'Mars'.

Object of the performance of the *Rājasūya*.

(C). Of the more or less elaborate ceremonies belonging to this class, the *Rājasūya* will first engage our attention. The aims for the celebration of this ceremony are not identical, as stated in the several Vedic texts: the celebrant, according to the *Mahābhiṣeka* mantras in the *Aitareya-Brāhmaṇa*,[1] wishes to attain, by the performance of the sacrifice, *sāmrājya*, *bhaujya*, *svārājya*, *vairājya*, *pārameṣṭhya*, *māhārājya*, *sārvabhauma*,[2] and very long life, while according to the *Śatapatha-Brāhmaṇa*[3] he could attain by it mere royal dignity. The *Śāṅkhāyana-Śrauta-Sūtra*,[4] belonging as it does to the Ṛg-Vedic school, substantially agrees with the *Aitareya-Brāhmaṇa* in its enunciation of the objective of the *Rājasūya*, viz. to attain *śraiṣṭhya*, *svārājya*, and *ādhipatya* over heaven, sky, and the earth, while the *Āpastamba-Śrauta-Sūtra*[5] related to the *Taittirīya-Saṃhitā* puts heaven alone as its goal.

The aims as set forth here do not furnish any definite clue as to whether the spiritual ones were prior to the political. The *Śatapatha-Brāhmaṇa* limits the importance of the sacrifice by lowering it down to the position of an ordinary coronation. But as there was a separate ceremonial for the purpose, a difference must have been recognized between the *Rājasūya* and the *Rājyābhiṣeka* to avoid an anomaly. The difference lay in the great spiritual merit impliedly accruing from the former, not to speak of their distinctive ritualistic conformations. Moreover, the celebrant of the former was a consecrated *Kṣatriya* (i. e. *installed king*), while that of the latter a mere *Kṣatriya*.

The texts[6] agree in making a king (a consecrated *Kṣatriya*)

[1] *Aitareya-Brāhmaṇa*, viii. 12 ff.

[2] The terms have been explained in the chapter 'Forms and Types of States'.

[3] *Śatapatha-Brāhmaṇa*, v. 1. 1. 12. The passage 'rājā svārājyakāmo rājasūyena yajeta. *Taittirīya-Brāhmaṇa*' occurs as a footnote at p. 2 of Dr. R. L. Mitra's *Indo-Aryans*, ii, in his discourse on the imperial coronation in ancient India. So far as I see, the passage occurs in Sāyaṇa's commentary on the *Taittirīya-Samhitā* (Bibl. Indica), i. 8. 1, but not in the text of that work nor in that of the *Taittirīya-Brāhmaṇa*.

[4] *Śāṅkhāyana-Śrauta-Sūtra*, xv. 12. 1.

[5] *Āpastamba-Śrauta-Sūtra*, xviii. 8. 1.

[6] *Ṛg-Veda* school: *Aitareya-Brāhmaṇa*, viii. 12. 1 (appears inferentially from the text); *Āśvalāyana-Śrauta-Sūtra*, ix. 9. 19. *Yajur-Veda*

Eligibility for the performance of the *Rājasūya* and *Vājapeya*.

alone eligible to celebrate the *Rājasūya*. The *Vājapeya* was at first of lesser political importance than the *Rājasūya* and could be performed by the *Brāhmaṇa* or the *Kṣatriya* as well as by the *Vaiśya*, though of course with different purposes.[1] It was in the *Taittirīya* texts[2] that the *Vājapeya* obtained a higher rank than the *Rājasūya* for the reason that the former was declared to confer imperial position and the latter but royal dignity, from which followed the necessary prohibition that *Rājasūya* could not be performed after the *Vājapeya*.[3]

Object of the performance of the *Vājapeya*.

The goals reached by the celebration of the *Vājapeya* are thus set forth in the various Vedic texts: the position of an emperor and ascension to the upper region in the *Śatapatha*,[4] supremacy and *svārājya* in the *Taittirīya-Brāhmaṇa*,[5]

school:—(Of White Yajus): *Śatapatha-Brāhmaṇa*, v. 1. 1. 12; *Kātyāyana-Śrauta-Sūtra*, xv. 1. 1 (with Karkācārya's commentary); (Of Black Yajus): *Āpastamba-Śrauta-Sūtra*, xviii. 18. 1. *Sāma-Veda* school: *Lāṭyāyana-Śrauta-Sūtra*, ix. 1. 1.

[1] *Śāṅkhāyana-Śrauta-Sūtra*, xvi. 17. 2. 3. Cf. Weber's *Über den Vājapeya*, pp. 10 ff., and *V I.*, ii. 256.

[2] *Taittirīya-Brāhmaṇa*, ii. 7. 6. 1: 'That which is *Vājapeya* is a consecration to the dignity of a paramount sovereign (*samrāṭ*) and that which is *Rājasūya* is a consecration to the sway like that wielded by Varuṇa.' See *Taittirīya-Saṃhitā*, v. 6. 2. 1, with Sāyaṇa's commentary. According to the *Śatapatha-Brāhmaṇa*, v. 1. 1. 13, the performer of the *Rājasūya* becomes a king; but, as kingship is a condition precedent for its celebration, his political dignity remains but stationary. The *Vājapeya* secures imperial dignity, and is hence superior to the *Rājasūya*. The *Āśvalāyana-Śrauta-Sūtra* (ix. 9. 19) representing the *Ṛg-Veda* school of opinion directs that after performing the *Vājapeya*, the *Rājasūya* is to be performed by the king, and the *Bṛhaspati-sava* by the *Brāhmaṇa*. This shows that the *Vājapeya* was at one time inferior to the *Rājasūya*; for, as the *Śatapatha-Brāhmaṇa* (v. 1. 1. 13) argues, 'the *emperor* (i.e. the performer of the *Vājapeya*) would not wish to become *king* (the performer of the *Rājasūya*), for the office of king is lower and that of emperor the higher'. Cf. *V. I.*, ii. 256, and Eggeling, *S. B. E.*, xli, p. xxv. The reason why the *Vājapeya* was exalted lies, according to Profs. Macdonell and Keith (*V. I.*, ii. 256), in the fact that the *Rājasūya* was the monopoly of the *Kṣatriya*, while the *Vājapeya*, as the *Śatapatha* (v. 1. 1. 11) describes it, was the '*Brāhmaṇa's* own sacrifice'; and hence the *Brāhmaṇas*' interest to give it a higher position than the other.

[3] *Śatapatha-Brāhmana*. v. 1. 1. 13; *Kātyāyana-Śrauta-Sūtra*, xv. 1. 2. The *Bṛhaspati-sava*, performed for inaugurating a *Brāhmaṇa* to the office of royal priest, has been identified with the *Vājapeya* by the *Śatapatha* (v. 2. 1. 19). If this view be driven to its logical conclusion the *Vājapeya* should serve the same political end as the *Bṛhaspati-sava*.

[4] *Śatapatha-Brāhmaṇa*, v. 1. 1. 13 and v. 1. 1. 5.

[5] *Taittirīya-Brāhmaṇa*, ii. 7. 6. 1; i. 3. 2. 3.

annādya (i.e. food, &c.), and all desires in the *Śāṅkhāyana-Śrauta-Sūtra*,[1] *ādhipatya* [*ādhikyena svāmyam* (supremacy) according to the commentary of Nārāyaṇa] in the *Āśvalāyana-Śrauta-Sūtra*,[2] and prosperity in the *Āpastamba-Śrauta-Sūtra*.[3] *Lātyāyana*[4] holds, 'Whomsoever the *Brāhmaṇas* and kings (or nobles) may place at their head, let him perform the *Vājapeya*.'[5]

A general view of the *Rājasūya*, with special reference to its political aspects.

(C) (i). *Rājasūya*. The *Rājasūya*, strictly speaking, is not a single ceremonial, but a series of rituals several of which had independent existence. The completion of the whole ceremony was spread over about two years and three months.[6] There are minor differences among the Vedic schools of opinion[7] as to some of the rituals, but they have no importance from our present standpoint. The ritualistic details devoid of political significance and not required for a general view of the ceremonies will likewise be ignored.

The ceremony begins with the *Pavitra* sacrifice on the first

[1] *Śāṅkhāyana-Śrauta-Sūtra*, xv. 1. 11. 12.
[2] *Āśvalāyana-Śrauta-Sūtra*, ix. 9. 1.
[3] *Āpastamba-Śrauta-Sūtra*, xviii. 1. 1.
[4] *Lātyāyana-Śrauta-Sūtra*, viii. 11. 1.
[5] Eggeling, *S. B. E.*, xli, p. xxv.
[6] The *Rājasūya*, according to Dr. R. L. Mitra, spreads over a period of twelve months (*Indo-Aryans*, ii. 29). According to Eggeling (*op. cit.*, p. xxvi) it takes more than two years. Dr. Mitra must have made a wrong computation of the period, which even according to the *Taittirīya-Brāhmaṇa*, followed by Dr. Mitra, exceeds twelve months.
[7] The *Rājasūya* is dealt with in the *Aitareya-Brāhmaṇa*, vii. 13 to viii (begins with later ceremonies); *Āśvalāyana-Śrauta-Sūtra*. ix. 3. 3 to ix. 4. 23; *Śāṅkhāyana-Śrauta-Sūtra*, xv. 12–16; *Taittirīya-Saṃhitā*, i. 8. 1–21; *Taittirīya-Brāhmaṇa*, i. 6. 1 to i. 8. 4; *Āpastamba-Śrauta-Sūtra*, xviii. 8–22; *Vājasaneyi-Saṃhitā*, ix. 35 to x. 34; *Śatapatha-Brāhmaṇa*, v. 2. 3 to v. 5. 5; *Kātyāyana-Śrauta-Sūtra*, xv. 1–5; *Pañcaviṃśa-Brāhmaṇa*, xviii. 8–11; *Lātyāyana-Śrauta-Sūtra*, ix. 1–3; *Vaitāna-Sūtra* (of *A V*), xxxvi. 1–13; *Kauśika-Sūtra* (of same), xvii.

The three Vedic schools detail thus the duties of the sacrificial priests, viz. *Ṛg-Veda* of *Hotṛ*, *Yajur-Veda* of *Adhvaryu*, and *Sāma-Veda* of *Udgātṛ*. The *Brahman* priest acts as general supervisor of the rituals. Each priest has in theory three assistants. In the larger sacrifices, the sixteen priests take part. Sometimes, according to certain texts, another priest called *Sadasya* is added. To get an idea of all the details of the sacrifices in which the principal priests participate, all the three complementary schools of opinion should be consulted. The *Śatapatha-Brāhmaṇa* furnishes a general idea of the whole sacrifices, dealing as it does with the officiation of the *Adhvaryu* upon whom rests the manual work throughout the ceremonials.

The purificatory *Pavitra* sacrifice, an ordinary *Agniṣṭoma*.

day of the bright half of the month of Phālguna. This is a purificatory ceremony and, barring one or two additional features, an ordinary *Agniṣṭoma* which requires some words of explanation:

Agniṣṭoma explained.

Agniṣṭoma is a *soma*-sacrifice (i.e. a sacrifice in which *soma* juice is pressed out of the *soma*-plants supposed to be *Sarcostema viminale*, or *Asclepias acida*) belonging to the same class as *vājapeya*.[1] It took five days for its completion: *First day*: On a suitable place is erected an enclosed hall called *prācīna-vaṃśa*, containing among others three hearths called *Gārhapatya*, *Dakṣiṇāgni*, and *Āhavanīya*. Two *araṇis* (kindling sticks) heated on the fire at the sacrificer's house are brought to the hall to kindle the *Gārhapatya* fire from which again the other two fires are kindled. In the afternoon

Dīkṣā.

the sacrificer is consecrated (*dīkṣita*) after he has been duly cleansed. The ceremony contemplates him as an embryo in the womb awaiting rebirth as a deity, and the implements used in it are such as to symbolize and favour the same supposition. In the midst of this ceremony, oblations are offered to Agni, Viṣṇu, Ādityas, Purpose, Impulse, Wisdom, Thought, Initiation, Penance, Sarasvatī, and Pūṣan for helping him in the sacrifice with the gifts at their disposal and for elevating him to the gods.[2]

After sunset, the sacrificer takes fast-milk and sleeps after resigning himself to the care of Agni.[3] Certain restrictions as to food, speech, &c., are imposed on him for observance throughout the sacrifice.

Second day: He awakes in the morning, accepts some gifts

Prāyaṇīyeṣṭi.

and performs the *Prāyaṇīyeṣṭi* (opening sacrifice) in which offerings are made to Aditi (the earth), Pathyā Svasti (welfare on the road during a journey), Agni, Soma, and Savitṛ.[4]

Hiraṇyavatī offering,

Next comes *Hiraṇyavatī* (with gold) offering made to a cow to bring her formally into the sacrificer's possession. It is by this cow that king Soma (*soma*-plants) will be brought shortly

[1] *Rājasūya* and *Aśvamedha* are also regarded as *soma*-sacrifices, though they are complex ceremonials.

[2] *Śatapatha-Brāhmaṇa* (henceforth indicated as *Ś. Br.*), iii. 1. 1 to iii. 2. 1.

[3] *Ś. Br.*, iii. 2. 2.

[4] *Ibid.*, iii. 2. 3.

in pursuance of the legend that once on a time when Gāyatrī (metre) was carrying down Soma from the sky to the gods for their sacrifice, the latter was stolen by the Gandharvas. The gods gave them Vāc (speech) as a ransom for Soma and afterwards drew away Vāc to themselves by rapturous music. Similarly, the Soma cow identified with Vāc is after some higgling given to the seller of the *soma*-plants outside the enclosed hall in exchange for these plants, and taken back again in return for gold and a few other things. Gold is then wrested away from the seller by the *Adhvaryu* priest. King Soma thus purchased is brought to the hall in a cart drawn by two oxen, taken down therefrom, and given the guest-offering (*ātithyeṣṭi*).[1]

Agniṣṭoma 2nd day. (contd.)

purchase of Soma, and Guest-offering.

A solemn covenant (*Tānūnaptra*) is then made by the sacrificer and the priests to avoid any chance of dissension among themselves in imitation of the agreement made by the gods when they fell out with one another in the midst of a sacrifice, laying down the limits of their respective authorities. The *Avāntara* consecration is next performed in imitation of the expiation of offence committed by the gods by mutual abuses in the above dissension.[2]

Tānūnaptra (covenant) and *Avāntara* initiation.

Then follows a forenoon-*Upasad* consisting in three offerings of ghee to Agni, Soma, and Vishṇu preceded by *Pravargya* (offering of heated milk), and followed by *Homa* (oblation). This *Upasad* with the two attendant rituals is repeated in the afternoon. The two *Upasads* of this day symbolize the siege laid by the gods to the castle built by the *asuras* in this world for their supremacy, the *ghee* (clarified butter) used in the ceremony representing the thunderbolt hurled against the castle, Agni its point, Soma its barb, and Viṣṇu its connecting piece.[3]

Forenoon-*Upasad* with *Pravargya* and *Homa*.

The night is passed almost in the same way as already indicated.

After the performance of the morning *Upasad*,[4] the larger

3rd day.

[1] *Ś. Br.*, iii. 2. 4 to iii. 4. 1.
[2] *Ibid.*, iii. 4. 2 to iii. 4. 3.
[3] *Ibid.* iii. 4. 4.
[4] This, with the following *Upasad*, represents the gods' besiegement of the *asuras*' castle in the sky.

Upasads and preparation of the larger altar.

altar (*mahā-vedī* or *saumikī vedi*) is prepared with its *uttara-vedi* (high altar). The day is concluded with the afternoon-*Upasad*.[1]

4th day. Agni-Praṇa-yana.

After the completion of the two *Upasads* in the morning, with the accompanying rituals, some *firewood* from the *Āhavanīya* hearth in the *prācīna-vaṃśa* is taken to kindle the *Āhavanīya* fire of the high altar.[2]

Completion of the *Mahā-vedi.*

The cart-shed (*havir-dhāna*) with the inter-connected sound-holes[3] (*uparavas*), covered with two pressing-boards and a pressing-skin, is constructed in the middle of the larger altar, and two carts, one of which has been already noticed, are placed in it. The shed (*Sadas*) for the priests, with its six hearths (*Dhiṣṇyas*), and two other hearths called *Āgnīdhra* and *Mārjālīya* on the north and south of the cart-shed are also raised on the larger altar.[4]

Vaisar-jina offerings, Agni-Soma's journey.

Vaisarjina offerings come next, followed by the *Praṇayaṇa* of Agni and Soma in which Soma, preceded by Fire to clear the path of all dangers, is carried from the enclosed hall to the *Āgnīdhrīya* shed, and thence to the southern portion of the cart-shed.[5]

Animal and other offerings.

Eleven sacrificial stakes are fitted up in a row along the eastern limit of the *mahāvedi.* One animal victim is now killed preceded by eleven fore-offerings with the *Āprī*-verses (propitiatory), and the preparation of the cooking fire. Then follows a ceremony in which the sacrificer's wife participates and which is meant to revive symbolically the victim, in order that a living offering might reach the gods. The omentum (*vapā*) fixed on two spits is cooked on the above-mentioned fire and offered to Agni and Soma, the spits being offered to the *Ūrdhvanabhas* (*Vāyu*). A cake of rice and barley is also

[1] *Ś. Br.*, iii. 5. 1.

[2] *Ibid.*, iii. 5. 1 to iii. 6. 2. The *Āhavanīya* fire of the *prācīna-vaṃśa* is now regarded as the *Gārhapatya* fire of the *mahā-vedi.* The fourth day is called *upavasatha* day, i.e. preparatory to the last or *soma*-pressing day.

[3] So called because when *soma*-plants are pressed on them, they give out sounds.

[4] *Ś. Br.*, iii. 5. 2 to iii. 6. 2. The various parts of the enclosed hall and the larger altar correspond to the various components of the human body.

[5] *Ibid.*, iii. 6. 3.

given to Indra and Agni, followed by the offering of a preparation of gravy (*vasā*) to Air (identified with all the gods), to the Regions and Agni-Sviṣṭakṛt, and eleven by-offerings (*upayāga*) and the same number of after-offerings (*anuyāga*) of sour milk, clarified butter, &c., to various gods. Four *Patnīsaṃyājas* (offerings) to Soma, Tvaṣṭṛ, the wives of the gods, and Agni come next in order, after which the *Adhvaryu* priest throws away the heart-spit and takes the purificatory bath.[1]

Agniṣṭoma 4th day (cont.). Paśu-puroḍāśa.

Then to strengthen himself, the sacrificer, in imitation of Prajāpati, offers eleven animal victims to a number of divinities.[2]

The final preparations for the fifth day are now taken in hand. The *Adhvaryu* fetches the *Vasatīvarī* water supposed to be mixed with the blood of the first victim and make the sacrifice sapful. This water is kept in the *Āgnīdhra* for the night.

Agniṣṭoma 5th or soma-feast day. Morning prayer and preliminary ceremonies.

Before day-break, the preliminary arrangements for the ceremonies of the fifth (the most important) day are made and the morning-prayer said by the *Hotṛ*. The *Adhvaryu* fetches the water on which he has offered oblations of *ghee*, while the wife or wives of the sacrificer do the same in an uneven number of *ekadhanā* pitchers.

A portion of the *Vasatīvarī* water is kept in the *Hotṛ*'s cup (now called *nigrābhyā* water) for moistening the *soma*-plants at the time of pressing. The water brought by the *Adhvaryu* is mixed up in a trough (*ādhavanīya*) with the *ekadhanā* and *vasatīvarī* water for use in preparing the *grahas* (cups) to be mentioned shortly.[3]

The *Small* and *Great soma*-Pressings.

The morning pressing of *soma*-plants has two divisions, *small* and *great*. At the *Small Pressing* (*abhiṣava*), *soma*-plants[4] moistened with the *nigrābhyā* water are pressed on the covered boards of the sound-holes, and the issuing *soma*-juice collected in the *Upāṃśu* cup and offered to Sūrya (Sun). The *soma*-juice yielded by the *Great Pressing* (*mahābhiṣava*)

[1] *Ś. Br.*, iii. 6. 4 to iii. 8. 5.
[2] *Ibid.*, iii. 9. 1.
[3] *Ibid.*, iii. 9. 3.
[4] The *soma*-plants representing King Soma, though pressed with stones and thus slain, are supposed to be living for the reason given in *Ś. Br.*, iii. 9. 4. 2.

Agniṣṭoma 5th day (cont.). Grahas (cups).

is mixed up with some of the aforesaid waters and poured into the *droṇa* pitcher through a strainer. A large number of *grahas* (cups) is drawn from the *soma*-juice either when streaming into the vessel or when deposited in it.

The sacrifice is regarded as Prajāpati with a human form, the components of which have been already mentioned as represented by the different parts of the larger altar and the enclosed hall. Some of the *grahas* symbolize the functions of these components, and some others the energies operating through some of them. Thus, the high altar is the nose of the Sacrifice, cart-shed head, four sounding-holes passages of the ears and nose, *Āhavanīya* fire mouth, *Āgnīdhrīya* and *Mārjālīya* fires arms, *Sadas* belly, and *Gārhapatya* (old *Āhavanīya*) fires feet. The *upāṃśu-graha* is the out-breathing of the Sacrifice, *antaryāma*[1] in-breathing, *Aindravāyava* speech, *Maitrāvaruṇa* intelligence and will, *āśvina* hearing, *śukra* and *manthi* eyes, *āgrayaṇa* trunk, *ukthya* vital air, and *vaiśvānara* and *dhruva* front and hind vital airs.[2] The meaning of the offerings of these cups to the different gods is to be understood in the light of the Vedic belief that 'Prajāpati, the world-man, or all-embracing Personality, is offered up anew in every sacrifice; and inasmuch as the very dismemberment of the Lord of Creatures, which took place at the archetypal sacrifice (of the *Puruṣa-sūkta* of the *Ṛg-Veda*, x. 90), was in itself the creation of the universe, so every sacrifice is also a repetition of that first creative act. Thus the periodical sacrifice is nothing else than a microcosmic representation of the ever-proceeding destruction and renewal of all cosmic life and matter.'[3]

Of the *grahas*, the *maitrāvaruṇa* is associated with a legend of political significance. At first, Mitra and Varuṇa, representing the priesthood and nobility respectively, were disunited. The priesthood could stand without the nobility, but not the latter without the former. Hence Varuṇa asked Mitra for union, promising to give him the foremost place, and thence-

[1] The *upāṃśu* and *antaryāma-grahas* are offered immediately after preparation and the rest after the offering of *savanīya-puroḍāśas*.

[2] *Ś. Br.*, iv. 1. 1 to iv. 2. 4.

[3] *Ibid.*, *S.B.E.*, xliii, p. xv.

forth succeeded in all his deeds, from which followed the moral that a *Kṣatriya* should always have a *Brāhmaṇa* to advise him, and without this, all his undertakings would be utter failures. Hence the king should always have a *Brāhmaṇa* in the person of the royal priest for his guidance.[1]

Agniṣṭoma 5th day (cont.).

Viprud-homa, and Bahiṣpavamāna-stotra.

After the performance of the *Viprud-homa*, an expiatory oblation for the *soma*-juice spilt during the pressing, the priests and the sacrificer proceed to the *cātvāla* (pit) where the *Bahiṣpavamāna-stotra* is chanted. This *stotra* is mentioned as a ship bound heavenwards, the priests being its spars and oars. The *Agniṣṭoma* victim is then killed for Agni and cooked from that time till the evening *soma*-feast. Five sacrificial dishes (*puroḍāśas*) are also offered to particular deities.

Graha offerings and morning *soma*-feast.

After the offerings of some of the aforesaid *grahas*, which take place next, the priest and the sacrificer drink *soma*-juice left in some of the *grahas*, and eat the *iḍā*; twelve libations are made to the deities of the seasons, followed by the recitation of the *Ājya-śastra* and two more offerings of cups. The *Ājya-stotra* is next chanted. Those who take part in this ceremony drink the remnants of the *soma*-juice in the cups.[2]

The mid-day ceremonies.

The mid-day ceremonies are almost the same as those of the morning, with these noteworthy exceptions, that the libations[3] (some being different) are fewer, a separate *stotra* is chanted in the *Sadas* and *dakṣiṇā-homas* performed for making the prescribed gifts to the priests.[4]

The evening ceremonies.

The evening rituals are almost like the morning, differences being marked in regard to the *grahas* chanting of the *Ārbhava-stotra*, slaughter of the victim already mentioned, offering of *caru* (rice-pap) to Soma and *ghee* to Gandharvas, who had no share in the *soma*-drinking, *Pātnīvata-graha* to Agni and Tvaṣṭṛ, recitation of the *Āgnimāruta-śastra* and libation from the *Hariyojana-graha*.[5]

Concluding ritual.

The *Agniṣṭoma* is concluded with the offering of nine *Samiṣṭayajus* to bid farewell to the gods invited to the

[1] *Ś. Br.*, iv. 1. 4. 1–6. [2] *Ibid.*, iv. 2. 5 to iv. 3. 2.
[3] The *Māhendra* cup drawn previously is offered at the last libation.
[4] *Ś. Br.*, iv. 3. 3 to iv. 3. 4. [5] *Ibid.*, iv. 3. 5 to iv. 4. 3

Agniṣṭoma 5th day (cont.). sacrifice. This is followed by the *Avabhṛtha* bath, after which the sacrificer becomes as pure as a child, a rice-pap to Aditi as the concluding oblation, the *Udayanīyeṣṭi* like the *Prāyaṇīyeṣṭi* mentioned before, the offering of a barren cow (or a bullock) to Mitra and Varuṇa, the *Udavasānīyeṣṭi*, in which a cake is offered to Agni, and one or two other rituals.[1]

This brief sketch of the *Agniṣṭoma* will serve to explain not only the *Pavitra* which constitutes the opening ritual of the *Rājasūya*, but also many other sacrifices of which it forms the basis, and which will be dealt with hereafter.

Rājasūya (cont.). Pūrṇāhuti. Cakes to Anumati, Nirṛti, Agni, and Viṣṇu. After the *Pavitra* comes the *pūrṇāhuti* (full offering), in which a libation is made of a spoonful of *ghee*. In this ritual, the sacrificer formally resolves to be consecrated to perform the *Rājasūya*. On the following day, a cake is offered to Anumati (the personified approval of the deities) praying her to approve of his consecration, and another cake to Nirṛti (the goddess of evil) for averting her displeasure. Agni and Viṣṇu receive cakes the next day for assenting to the consecration.[2]

Offerings to Agni and Soma, and Indra and Agni. *Āgrayaṇeṣṭi.* On two successive days, Agni and Soma, and Indra and Agni, are given offerings, for gaining security from evil-doers from the first two, and vigour and energy from the next two deities.[3] This offering of new grain is also intended to secure the assent of Indra, Agni, *Viśvedevas*, &c., to the consecration, and obtain healthy crops.[4]

Cāturmāsya. The four Seasonal Offerings next commence, the first of which is held on the full-moon of Phālguna, and the other three at intervals of four months each. During the intervals the ordinary half-month sacrifices (*Darśa-pūrṇa-māseṣṭi*) are performed daily, either alternating the Full-moon sacrifice with the New-moon, or holding the former on each day of the bright fortnights and the latter on each day of the dark ones. The first seasonal offering, called *Vaiśvadeva* (All-gods), is

[1] *Ś. Br.*, iv. 4. 4 to iv. 5. 2. I am thankful to Prof. Rāmendra Sundar Trivedī, M.A., P.R.S., for kindly letting me have the use of his thoughtful MS. notes in Bengali on *Agniṣṭoma*, which have enabled me to apportion the several rituals to the five days covered by the sacrifice.

[2] *Ibid.*, v. 2. 3. 1–6. [3] *Ibid.*, v. 2. 3. 7–8.

[4] *Ibid.*, v. 2. 3. 9 and ii. 4. 3.

Rājasūya (cont.)

meant to secure the gods' approval to consecration by favouring the sacrificer with abundant food and creatures; the second, called *Varuṇapraghāsa*, is addressed to Varuṇa in order that he might express his assent by making the creatures free from blemish and disease. By the *Sākamedha*, i. e. the third seasonal offering made to Agni-Anīkavat (sharp-pointed Agni) and other gods, the sacrificer desires to have their assent through safety from his enemies, while by the last seasonal offering *Śunāsīrya* to Vāyu and Sūrya he seeks prosperity as an indication of their approval.[1]

Pañcāvattīya, Indraturīya, and Apāmārgahoma.

After the seasonal offerings, which occupy a year, follow *Pañcāvattīya*, *Indraturīya*, and *Apāmārgahoma*—all intended to procure safety and security for the sacrificer, to enable him to perform the sacrifice unmolested. The first ritual consists in the offerings of 'fivefold cut ghee' to the five winds or breaths, the second in offerings to Agni, Varuṇa, Rudra, and Indra, and the third in the performance of a *homa* by the *apāmārga* plants to kill or drive away the fiends.[2]

Trisaṃyuktāni.

The 'triply connected' offerings are (I) to Agni and Viṣṇu, Indra and Viṣṇu, and Viṣṇu for getting men, (II) to Agni and Pūṣan, Indra and Pūṣan, and Pūṣan for cattle, and (III) to Agni and Soma, Indra and Soma, and Soma for glory.

Here Agni is the giver, Viṣṇu guardian of men, Pūṣan protector of cattle, Soma glory, and Indra sacrificer.[3]

Oblations to Vaiśvānara and Varuṇa.

The oblations to Vaiśvānara and Varuṇa take place next, the first for abundance of food and creatures, and the second for making the creatures faultless.[4]

Twelve *Ratnahavis.*

These offerings, constituting the next item, have a special political significance. These *Ratnins* are (i) commander of the army, (ii) *Purohita*, (iii) *Kṣatra*,[5] (iv) queen, (v) *Sūta*,

[1] *Ś. Br.*, v. 2. 4. 1–4.
[2] *Ibid.*, v. 2. 4. 4–20.
[3] *Ibid.*, v. 2. 5. 1–12.
[4] *Ibid.*, v. 2. 5. 13–17.
[5] *Kṣatra* corresponds to *Rājanya* in the *Taittirīya-Saṃhitā*, i. 8. 9. 1, and *Taittirīya-Brāhmaṇa*, i. 7. 3. 3. Eggeling has identified *kṣatra* with the abstract 'ruling power'. Profs. Macdonell and Keith (*V. I.*, ii. 199, 200) explain *Ratnin* by applying it to 'those people of the royal *entourage* in whose houses the *Ratnahavis* . . . was performed in the course of the *Rājasūya*'. The difficulty therefore lies in having (i) to consider *kṣatra* as a mere personification, and (ii) to apply the term to the king, who cannot belong to the 'royal *entourage*'.

Rājasūya (cont.). (vi) *Grāmaṇī*, (vii) *Kṣattṛ*, (viii) *Saṃgrahītṛ*, (ix) *Bhāgadugha*, (x) *Akṣāvāpa* and *Govikartana*, (xi) *Pālāgala*, (xii) *Parivṛktī*.[1]

On the first day, the king goes to the house of the commander of the army and offers a cake to Agni-Anīkavat (Agni being the commander of the gods),[2] thereby consecrating himself for the officer, and expressing the desire that the officer might be faithful to the king.

The remaining offerings are made on successive days at the houses of the respective persons concerned excepting *Kṣatra* [item (iii) in the above list], and *Akṣāvāpa* and *Govikartana* together [forming item (x)], for whom offerings are made at the royal palace. The recipients of the remaining oblations on the several occasions are as follows in the order of the aforesaid persons:—(ii) Bṛhaspati, [(i) Agni has been mentioned already], (iii) Indra, (iv) Aditi, (v) Varuṇa, (vi) Maruts, (vii) Savitṛ, (viii) Aśvins, (ix) Pūṣan, (x) Rudra, (xi) the way personified, (xii) Nirṛti. The intention of the sacrificer in all these rituals is to make the officers and others faithful to himself.[3] The participation of the aforesaid persons in the ceremony and the application of the term 'king-makers' (*rājakartṛ*) to at least some of these are indicative of the deference paid to them by the king. Some of the *Ratnins* were perhaps representatives of the people or certain classes of the subjects, and the reason why their allegiance was an object of special attention with the king shows the political power resting in the hands either of themselves or the classes whom they represented.

…iation. The contact of those[4] 'unworthy of sacrifice' with the sacrifice creates evil which is removed by the next offerings to Soma and Rudra, and Mitra and Bṛhaspati.[5]

…Abhi…nīya. The next rite *Abhiṣecanīya* (consecration) has as its im-

[1] The duties of the officers in this list have been detailed in a previous chapter 'Evolution of the Principal State-officials'.

[2] See Sāyaṇa's commentary on *Ś. Br.*, v. 3. 1. 1.

[3] *Ś. Br.*, v. 3. 1.

[4] 'Sāyaṇa specifies the "commander of the Army and others" as *Śūdras* and the "huntsman and others", as of whatsoever low caste.' *S. B. E.*, xli. 66 n. 1.

[5] *Ś. Br.*, v. 3. 2.

mediate basis the *Ukthya* sacrifice, which is nothing but an *Agniṣṭoma* covering five days with these additional rituals, viz. the slaying of a second victim to Indra and Agni on the last day, the chanting of the *Ukthya-stotra* followed by the recitation of the *Ukthya-śastra*.[1] To develop this *Ukthya* sacrifice into the *Abhiṣecanīya*, certain rites are further added: after the preparation of the *Paśu-puroḍāśa* on the fourth day, offerings are made to the divine Quickeners, namely, Savitṛ Satyaprasava for quickening the king for powers of ruling, Agni Gṛhapati for making him the master of the house, Soma Vanaspati for plants, Bṛhaspati Vāc for speech, Indra Jyeṣṭha for excellence, Rudra Paśupati for cattle, Mitra Satya for the Brahman, Varuṇa Dharmapati for control over the law. The *Aḍhvaryu* utters *mantras* in which the above blessings are invoked upon the sacrificer. There is a passage in these *mantras* worthy of special note: 'This man, O ye people, is your king, Soma is the king of us *Brāhmaṇas*.' A difference is meant to be drawn between the king's ordinary subjects and the people of the *Brāhmaṇa* caste in regard to the king's control over them.[2]

Rājasūya (cont.).

Seventeen kinds of liquid are collected for the king's anointment, to be held at the mid-day *soma*-feast of the *Ukthya* sacrifice forming the basis of the *Abhiṣecanīya*. These are: (1) Water from the river Sarasvatī, (2) water drawn from amidst the ripples before and behind a man plunging into the water, (3) and (4) waters flowing with and against the current of a river, (5) overflowing water, (6) sea-water, (7) water from a whirlpool, (8) water from the stagnant portion of a river in a sunny spot, (9) rain falling during sunshine, (10) water from a pond, (11) well-water, (12) dew-drops, (13) honey, (14) embryonic waters of a calving cow, (15) milk, (16) clarified butter, and (17) water exposed to the sun-motes.[3]

Collection of liquids.

Of these kinds of liquid, the first symbolizes speech, next three vigour, fifth abundance, sixth lordship, tenth allegiance of the people to the king, twelfth food, fourteenth to sixteenth cattle, and the last independence.

[1] *Ibid.*, iv. 2. 5. 14 and *S. B. E.*, xli, p. xiv.
[2] *Ibid.*, v. 3. 3. This is repeated later on.
[3] *Ibid.*, v. 3. 4.

Rājasūya (cont.). The liquids are mixed up and deposited in a vessel of *udumbara* wood representing vigour.

Pārtha oblations. Before the *Māhendra* cup is drawn at the midday *soma*-feast of the aforesaid *Ukthya* sacrifice, the ritual of anointing is inserted preceded by six *Pārtha* oblations, the last of which is given to Bṛhaspati representing priestly vigour. After the anointing, six *Pārtha* oblations to other divinities are again given, the first being offered to Indra identified with *Kṣatriya* vigour. The king, who is anointed between these two sets of *Pārtha* oblations, is thus encompassed by priestly and princely (*Kṣatriya*) vigours.[1]

Dressing and proclamation. The king then bathes dressed in the prescribed manner, and after bath wears another dress, takes from the *Adhvaryu* a bow and three arrows for protection, each act being accompanied with proper *mantras*. The deities and mortals are formally apprised of the anointing to be shortly held, and asked to approve of the same.[2]

Symbolic conquest of the four quarters and the upper region. After the performance of the rite of putting a piece of copper into the mouth of a long-haired man as a charm against injuries specially from the mordacious creatures, the *ascension of the regions*, east, west, north, south, and the sky, takes place for procuring for the king supremacy in all those quarters.[3]

Anointment. The king then stands on a tiger-skin previously spread before one of the *dhiṣṇyas* (hearths) called Maitrāvaruṇa, on the hind part of which a piece of lead is placed for being kicked off by him, thereby symbolically beating off the fiends. A piece of gold is put under the king's foot signifying that he takes thereby his stand on immortal life represented by gold. On his head is placed a plate of gold perforated with nine or one hundred holes, the first number implying the nine vital airs, and the second a hundred years of life. His two arms (standing for Mitra and Varuṇa) are then raised, signifying that the two gods have mounted a chariot—the king's body—and are seeing, as the *mantra* uttered on the occasion shows, Aditi and Diti, i.e. their own property and that of others.

[1] *Ś. Br.*, v. 3. 5. 4–9.
[2] *Ibid.*, v. 3. 5. 20–37.
[3] *Ibid.*, v. 4. 1. 3–8. Cf. Mitra, *Indo-Aryans*, ii. pp. 40, 41.

Standing thus with up-stretched arms and facing the east, the king is besprinkled with water[1] by the *Adhvaryu*, or the royal priest, and also by the king's relations, a friendly *Kṣatriya*, and a *Vaiśya*, the appropriate *mantras* being uttered therewith.[2] The water on the king's body is rubbed by himself with the horn of a black antelope, thus supposed to be imbibing into his system the vigour in the water.[3] The anointment over, the king takes three steps on the tiger-skin corresponding to Viṣṇu's three steps for the symbolic ascension of the three worlds—heaven, earth, and upper regions, thereby placing himself high above everything here. The remnants of the water are then poured by him into the *Brāhmaṇa's* vessel as an emblem of respect due to *Brāhmaṇas*. This vessel is given away to the king's dearest son to have the former's vigour perpetuated through the latter. The linking of vigours of the father and the son is completed by some oblations with *mantras*.[4]

Rājasūya (cont.).

The reason underlying the ritual of mimic cow-raid is that Varuṇa lost his vigour after consecration and recouped it from cows. Though the king does not actually lose his vigour on the present occasion, he suspects it to have vanished, and where can it go unless to his relative foremost of all? Hence, in this ritual he mounts a chariot yoked with four horses, drives to a place among the relative's hundred cows stationed on the north of the *Āhavanīya* fire, and touches one of them with the end of his bow, believing to be taking back thereby to himself his vigour. The stoppage of the chariot amongst the cows transfers the ownership of the cattle to the king. The king in return gives the relative a hundred cows or more, incapable as he is of committing forcible seizure.

The mimic cow-raid.

The chariot is brought back to its place and four oblations are made to the four deities presiding over the different parts

Conclusion of cow-raid.

[1] The seventeen kinds of water mixed in an *udumbara* vessel are divided into four parts in four buckets, the *Brāhmaṇa* sprinkling from the bucket of *palāśa* wood, the kinsmen of *udumbara*, the *Kṣatriya* of *nyagrodha*, and the *Vaiśya* of *aśvattha*. (*Ś. Br.*, v. 3. 5. 11–14.)

[2] Either now, or after the game of dice later on, the *Hotṛ* tells the story of Śunaḥśepa.

[3] *Ś. Br.*, v. 4. 1. 9 to v. 4. 2. 5.

[4] *Ibid.*, v. 4. 2. 6–10.

Rājasūya (cont.). of the vehicles, in order to render kingship favourably circumstanced in regard to prosperity and vigour, the nobility and the peasantry. While yet in the chariot the king puts on a pair of shoes of boar's skin with the object of having abundance of cattle, the principal item of wealth in those days, the legend connected with the boar being the basis of this ritual. Certain *mantras* are uttered to establish a friendly relation between the king and the earth, down upon which he now steps, followed by the charioteer, who jumps down on a place different from that trodden by his master. Two minor rites for conferring on the king long life, glory, and strength, conclude this ritual.[1]

A throne of *khadira* wood is placed on the tiger-skin spread before the *Maitrāvaruṇa* hearth and mantled over with another piece of the same skin betokening increase of *Kṣatriya* power. The duties of the *Hotṛ* in this ceremony as detailed in the *Aitareya-Brāhmaṇa* deserve special mention. The term *Punarabhiṣeka* or second consecration is used in the *Brāhmaṇa* to stand for the ritual of *Abhiṣecanīya*, the first consecration (*Abhiṣeka*) of the king performing the *Rājasūya* having taken place in connexion with his ordinary coronation. The duties and *mantras* of the *Hotṛ* in regard to the *Punarabhiṣeka* are given in a few chapters,[2] while those in regard to Mahābhiṣeka, in imitation of Indra's consecration, are given in certain other chapters.[3] But it appears that they are to operate in unison at this stage of the *Abhiṣecanīya*. The two noteworthy features of the proceedings of the *Mahābhiṣeka* are (1) the oath[4] administered to the king before he sits on the throne, and (2) the various kinds of supremacy that are desired to be attained by him and appear to have been the cherished objects of kingly aspirations.[5] The oath is as follows: 'If I (the king) ever do you (the priest or perhaps the *Brāhmaṇas* generally) any harm, may I be deprived of all pious acts done by me from my birth till death, the spiritual worlds acquired by me, my religious merit, life, and offspring.'

[1] *Ś. Br.*, v. 4. 3.
[2] *Aitareya-Brāhmaṇa*, viii. 5–11.
[3] *Ibid.*, viii. 12–23.
[4] *Ibid.*, viii. 15.
[5] *Ibid.*, viii. 15–19.

The *Adhvaryu* recites a *mantra* in which the king is called 'upholder of the sacred law', upon which the *Śatapatha-Brāhmaṇa* expatiates by saying that he is so indeed 'because he is not capable of all and every speech nor of all and every deed, but that he should speak only what is right and do what is right; of that he as well as the *Śrotriya* (the *Brāhmaṇa* versed in sacred writ) is capable; for these two are the upholders of the sacred law among men.'[1] *Rājasūya (cont.).*

Five dice are handed over the king to be thrown by him, different significations being attached to the results of castings, such as the king's victory in all the quarters or the dominance of the *Kali* age (representing the king) over the three other ages.[2] **Dice-throwing.**

The next rite crystallizes the idea that the king can do no wrong. The *Adhvaryu* and his assistants strike the king on the back with sticks (punishment), thereby putting him beyond the reach of judicial punishment.[3] **The king can do no wrong.**

After the rites of *choosing a boon*, and *colloquy* between the *Brahman* priest and the king, is held the *passing round of the sacrificial sword*. The *Adhvaryu*, or the royal priest, makes over a wooden sword to the king with a *mantra*, thereby rendering the latter weaker than a *Brāhmaṇa* but stronger than his enemies. It is then handed over to the king's brother, who passes it on either to the *Sūta* (charioteer) or to *Sthapati*[4] (governor of a district), who again transfers it to the *Grāmaṇī* (village-headman) to be taken over by a clansman (*sajāta*), each making his successor weaker than himself. This rite gives an insight into the order of precedence of several officials.[5] **The passing round of a sacrificial sword.**

One or two minor rites coming next conclude the *Abhiṣecanīya.*

After the five days of *Abhiṣecanīya* follows *Daśapeya*, in which are included ten *saṃsṛpaḥ* oblations. The whole ritual, *Daśapeya.*

1 *Ś. Br.*, v. 4. 4. 5.

2 *Ibid.*, v. 4. 4. 6.

3 *Ibid.*, v. 4. 4. 7.

4 On the meaning see below.

5 *Ś. Br.* v. 4. 4. 15-19. The discrepancies between the description given here and that in the *Indo-Aryans*, vol. ii, are due to the reason that Dr. Mitra follows the *Taittirīya-Brāhmaṇa* and not the *Śatapatha.*

Rājasūya (cont.). occupying ten days, is intended to impart vigour to the king who takes part in its proceedings.[1]

Pañcabila offerings. The *Pañcabila-caru*, or offerings to several gods in five plates, are meant to remove from the king's mind any feeling of arrogance that might arise from his symbolic ascension of the regions, seasons, hymns, and metres.[2]

Oblations of teams. The object of the *Prayujām* oblations is thus laid down in the *Śatapatha-Brāhmaṇa*:[3]

'The anointed thereby yokes the seasons, and thus yoked those seasons draw him along, and he follows the seasons thus yoked.'

Hair-cutting. After a year is held the *Keśavapanīya*[4] for cutting the hair of the king's head, which is allowed to grow during the interval after the consecration. The belief underlying the ceremony was that it was the hair of his head that imbibed first the vigour of the water sprinkled during the consecration, and if it was shaved the vigour would vanish. The present ritual, by clipping hair at the prescribed time, serves to preserve it.[5]

Vyuṣṭi-dvirātra and *Kṣatra-dhṛti*. The following two rituals, viz. *Vyuṣṭi-dvirātra* and *Kṣatra-dhṛti*[6] are not mentioned in the *Śatapatha* because they involve no features different from the ordinary *soma* sacrifice. The former lasts for two nights and is meant to purge the king of all sins,[7] while the latter, occupying a day, appears from its name to be a rite for the support of the king's power.[8]

The *Sautrāmaṇī*[9] is then performed as an expiation for

[1] *Ś. Br.*, v. 4. 5. The *Daśapeya* is a modification of the *Agniṣṭoma* with the oblations added.

[2] *Ibid.*, v. 5. 1.

[3] *Ibid.*, v. 5. 2.

[4] *Keśavapanīya* is a modification of *Atirātra*, which is again a modification of *Agniṣṭoma*.

[5] *Ś. Br.*, v. 5. 3. The king is henceforth prohibited from shaving his hair and standing on the ground with bare feet.

[6] *Kṣatra-dhṛti* is held a month after the *Vyuṣṭi-dvirātra*, which again comes off a month after *Keśavapanīya*.

[7] See *Pañcaviṃśa-Brāhmaṇa*, xviii. 11. 11, for the object of the ritual.

[8] The object of this ceremony is nowhere, so far as I see, expressly given.

[9] This takes place a month after *Kṣatra-dhṛti* and is a combination of oblations with sacrifice of animals.

excesses in the drinking of *soma*-juice during the whole of the preceding period of the *Rājasūya*, followed by the closing oblation called *Traidhātavī*.[1]

Rājasūya (cont.). Sautrāmaṇī and Traidhātavī.

The description of the *Rājasūya* as given in the *Mahābhārata* does not detail the rituals, but lays down a condition precedent which makes it performable by very powerful kings after they have completed a *digvijaya*[2] (conquest of the quarters). The Vedic *Rājasūya* does not depend on any such condition, and can be celebrated even by petty kings. In the epic as well as later periods, therefore, the sacrifice must have been a source of great unrest, though of course it was, by the above restriction, of infrequent occurrence.

Vājapeya.

(C) (ii). *Vājapeya.* The rituals of the *Vājapeya*, performed, according to the *Śatapatha*, by an emperor for installation to his imperial position, or by a *Brāhmaṇa* for inauguration to his supreme position as such, are identical with those of the *Agniṣṭoma* with certain additions. The legend upon which this sacrifice is based is that, once upon a time, the gods and the *asuras*, both children of Prajāpati (the lord of creatures), tried to be supreme. Each *asura* in his arrogance thought himself supreme, and, as he recognized none superior to him, made offerings into his own mouth as the token of his presumption. Each god, on the other hand, made offerings to his fellows. Prajāpati for this reason sided with the gods, and the universe became theirs. But a rivalry set in among the gods, each of whom wanted to have Prajāpati or the universe all to himself. To set it at rest, they ran a race in which Bṛhaspati impelled by Savitṛ became the winner. This race furnished the nucleus of a sacrifice, namely, the *Vājapeya*, by which Indra sacrificed and became supreme. As Bṛhaspati

The legend.

[1] *Ś. Br.*, v. 5. 4-5.
[2] *MBh.*, ii. 13. 47:

> Yasmin sarvaṃ sambhavati yaś ca *sarvatra pūjyate*,
> yaś ca *sarveśvaro rājā rājasūyaṃ* sa vindati.

See also *Ibid.*, 14. 68, 69, where the independence of Jarāsandha, who had imprisoned a number of princes, was considered as essential to the fulfilment of the condition precedent.

The *Kauṭilīya* makes mere mention of the *Rājasūya* in connexion with the salaries of government servants, but gives no clue to the point under notice. *Kauṭilīya*, v. iii, p. 246.

Vājapeya (cont.). was the *Purohita* of the gods, and Indra a divine *Kṣatriya*, both *Brāhmaṇas* and *Kṣatriyas* are eligible for the performance of the sacrifice.[1]

Grahas. After some preparatory rites for some days, the rituals of the first four days of the *Agniṣṭoma*[1] are celebrated on as many days, followed by the performances of the fifth day, among which are found these additions or differences: With the morning pressing of *soma*-plants are drawn the *aṃśu-graha*, *Agniṣṭoma-grahas* up to the *āgrayaṇa*, three *Pṛṣṭhya-*, *Ṣoḍaśī-*, five *Vājapeya-*, seventeen *soma-*, *surā-*, and *madhu-* and *Ukthya-* and *dhruva-grahas* for various objects such as long life, superiority, winning the worlds, truth, prosperity, and light. With the exception of the *soma-*, *surā-*, and *madhu-grahas*, which are used at the mid-day *soma*-feast, the rest are offered and drunk along with the evening ceremonies.[3]

Victims. The principal animal victims are four, to which are added eighteen subsidiary ones, namely, a spotted sterile cow (the earth piebald with vegetation) offered to the Maruts representing the peasants, for ensuring the supply of food in the kingdom, and seventeen goats of a particular description offered to Prajāpati for the same purpose.[4]

At mid-day, before the *Māhendra* cup is drawn, takes place the chariot-race, the sacrificer competing with sixteen rivals. The sacrificer's chariot is taken from its stand to the north-eastern part of the *Mahāvedi*, four horses to be harnessed to it are sprinkled with water accompanied with *mantras* in order that they might win the race for their master. A rice-pap is prepared for Bṛhaspati, the winner of the first race of this kind, and taken to the horses to be smelled by them for the same purpose. The *Brahman* stands on a cart-wheel fixed to a post and sings a *Sāman* to gain for his client the air-world, the terrestrial world being left to be won by the chariot-race. Seventeen drums put in a row from the Āgnīdhra hearth westwards are beaten for making an auspicious sound favourable to the sacrificer's purpose. A post

[1] *Ś. Br.*, v. 1. 1. 1–11.

[2] For description of the *Agniṣṭoma*, see the first portion of the section on the *Rājasūya*. [3] *Ś. Br.*, v. 1. 2. [4] *Ibid.*, v. 1. 3.

is fixed at the end of seventeen arrows' range to indicate the farthest limit of the racecourse. The sacrificer prays to Savitṛ for impulsion and mounts his chariot, as also do his sixteen rivals. During the race the *Adhvaryu* utters *mantras* addressed to the horses of the sacrificer's chariot. The cars run up to the post round which they turn and come back in such a way that the sacrificer happens to be the first to reach the altar. It is this winning of the chariot-race by the sacrificer as an emperor (or by a *Brāhmaṇa* recognized as supreme by virtue of his qualities inborn and acquired) that formally proclaims and installs him to the high position that has been already his by general consent. The horses are made to smell again the Bārhaspatya rice-pap with the thought that the establishment of the sacrificer's superiority upon the terrestrial world is now an accomplished fact. The *Adhvaryu* and the sacrificer next put the *madhu-graha* previously mentioned in the hand of a *Vaiśya* or *Kṣatriya* competitor in the race, who in turn makes it over to the *Brahman*, while the *Neṣṭṛ* (an assistant of the *Adhvaryu*) a *surā* cup in the hand of the same person. By the former rite, the recipient obtains long life and other benefits, and by the latter the sacrificer is imbued with 'truth, prosperity, and light', leaving with the *Kṣatriya* or *Vaiśya* 'untruth, misery, and darkness, but enjoyment of all benefits'.[1]

Vājapeya (cont.).

It is supposed by some authorities that the *Vājapeya* sacrifice grew very probably out of the 'chariot racing transformed into a ceremony which by sympathetic magic secures the success of the sacrificer'.[2]

After twelve *Āpti* and six *Kḷpti* offerings on the *Āhavanīya* fire for procuring for the sacrificer all that the twelve months of the year and the six seasons can bestow, the sacrificer climbs up a ladder put against the post at the end of the racecourse, followed by his wife, who has been led up to the place by the *Neṣṭṛ*. The company of the wife is intended to make the sacrificer complete by addition to him of one-half of his own self. A lump of wheaten dough fixed on the post as its head-piece is then touched by him with the *mantra*, 'We

[1] *Ś. Br.*, v. 1. 4 and 5.

[2] *V. I.* ii. 281.

Vājapeya (cont.). have gone to the light, O ye gods,' the touching of the dough symbolizing the obtainment of food and drink that give him the strength to reach the supreme goal. He then rises over the post by the measure of his head saying, 'We have become immortal,' whereby he wins the celestial world. Then he adds 'Ours be your power, ours your manhood and intelligence, ours be your energies', for by the *Vājapeya*, the celebrant obtains Prajāpati, who is everything here. Seventeen packets of *Aśvattha* leaves containing salt are thrown up to him by the *Vaiśyas* to indicate that they would never fail as agents for supply of food. Homage is then made by him to Mother Earth in order that she might not shake him off. A goat's skin with a gold coin on it is spread by the *Adhvaryu* for the sacrificer to step upon after descending from the ladder. Gold being the symbol of immortality, the sacrificer is supposed to take his stand on immortal life by this ritual.[1]

Sprinkling. A throne of udumbara wood is placed behind the *Āhavanīya* fire in front of the cart-shed, and a goat's skin is spread on it.[2] The sacrificer is seated on the throne with this *mantra* uttered by the *Adhvaryu*, 'Thou art the ruler, the ruling lord! Thou art firm, and steadfast! (I seat) Thee for the tilling! Thee for peaceful dwelling! Thee for wealth! Thee for thrift!'[3] The Bārhaspatya pap is now given to Bṛhaspati, but its *Sviṣṭakṛt* is left to be offered later on after the *ujjiti* oblations. Several kinds of food are brought to the sacrificer to be tested by him, and those that are not brought are to be eschewed by him through life.[4] Out of these articles are offered with formulas seven *Vājaprasavanīya* oblations to increase his strength. The remnants are sprinkled on the sacrificer with a *mantra* which declares his supremacy and entrusts him to the protection of the deities. This is followed by the *ujjiti* oblations which are supposed to give him control upon life, men, three worlds, cattle, five regions, six seasons, seven kinds of domestic animals, &c., in short *Prajāpati* himself. After one or two other rites, the *Māhendra* cup is drawn, and while the *Pṛṣṭha-stotra* is chanted, to be followed

[1] *Ś. Br.*, v. 2. 1. 1–21.
[2] *Ibid.*, v. 2. 1. 22–4.
[3] *Ibid.*, v. 2. 1. 25.
[4] Authorities differ as to this point.

by the recitation of its *Śastra*, the sacrificer comes down from the throne and attends to the chanting and recitation.[1]

(C) (iii). *Aśvamedha.* It is agreed on all hands in the Vedic texts that the performer of the *Aśvamedha* sacrifice should be a *Kṣatriya* king. The achievement of the political object of assertion of power no doubt required that he should be very powerful, but this requirement is not expressly mentioned in several of the aforesaid texts. The *Śatapatha-Brāhmaṇa* clearly points out 'Let him who holds royal sway perform the horse-sacrifice; for, verily, whosoever performs the horse-sacrifice, without possessing power, is poured (swept) away. . . . Were unfriendly men to get hold of the horse, his sacrifice would be cut in twain ',[2] and the warning thus conveyed is also found in the *Taittirīya-Brāhmaṇa*.[3] The *Sūtra* of this work gives rather a vague definition of the eligibility by laying down that it can be celebrated by a *sārvabhauma* (king ruling the whole land) as well as by an *asārvabhauma* (king not ruling the whole land). The rest of the *Brāhmaṇas* and *Sūtras* named in the following paragraph are silent on any distinctive qualities other than what has been mentioned at the outset. Prof. Eggeling[4] elucidates the point by remarking that the performance of the sacrifice involved assertion of political authority which was possible only for a monarch of undisputed supremacy able to face with confidence the risk of humiliation; for the entrance of the sacrificial horse into a neighbouring territory implied a challenge to its king. The necessity of having a hundred royal princes to guard the horse while ranging about perhaps indicates the wide political influence of the sacrificer.

Aśvamedha. Eligibility.

Over and above the implied object of asserting political supremacy, various other objects were kept in view and believed to be achieved by the sacrifice. Wealth, strength, male progeny, and freedom from sins are prayed for in a hymn of the *Ṛg-Veda*[5] relating thereto. The characteristics of the sacrifice according to the *Taittirīya-Brāhmaṇa*[6] as interpreted by

Objectives.

[1] *Ś. Br.*, v. 2. 2.
[2] *Ibid.*, xiii. 1. 6. 3.
[3] *Taittirīya-Brāhmaṇa*, iii. 8. 9. 4.
[4] *S. B. E.*, xliv, pp. xv, xxviii.
[5] *Ṛg-Veda*, i. 162. 22.
[6] *Taittirīya-Brāhmaṇa*, iii. 9. 19.

Aśva-medha (cont.). Sāyaṇa are (1) the presence of all kinds of riches in the kingdom, (2) the existence of all sorts of welfare, (3) abundant food, (4) abundance of yields from cattle, (5) its continuous flow of benefits, (6) its specially abundant benefits, (7) its steadiness, (8) its glory, (9) its power to produce fame for the *Brāhmaṇas* of the country, (10) its power to remove sins, and the corresponding ability of every *Kṣatriya* in the kingdom to kill the enemy, (11) its power to ensure long life, and (12) to secure acquisition of property by the subjects and preservation thereof; according to the *Śatapatha*,[1] fulfilment of all desires and attainment of all attainments, while its *Sūtra*[2] as well as that[3] of the *Ṛg-Veda* mentions the former alone.

The *Aśva-medha*, a three-days' *Soma*-sacrifice. The *Aśvamedha* occupies in fact one year and a fortnight, but is regarded notwithstanding as a *triduum*,[4] the last three days covering the essential rituals proper and the preceding period the preparations.

Preparations. The preliminaries commence either in summer or in spring, but preferably in the latter season six or seven days before the full moon of *Phālguna*. The four chief priests meet together Mess of rice. and eat a mess of rice prepared by one of them. The king and Night ritual. four of his wives pass the night in the sacrificial hall with self-restraint intending to reach successfully the end of the preparatory year. This is followed by the morning offering and Oblations. *pūrṇāhuti* (full-offering) by the *Adhvaryu* and oblations to Agni (mouth of the sacrifice) and Pūṣan (overlord of roads), the objects of which are the accomplishment of the sacrificer's desires and the safety of the sacrificial horse while roaming for Sprinkling of the sacrificial horse. a year to follow.[5] The horse possessing supreme excellence and other prescribed qualities is tied up with a rope of *darbha* grass twelve or thirteen cubits long with proper *mantras* and sprinkled with water to make it acceptable to the gods; while the water is dripping from its body, a rite is performed for

[1] *Ś. Br.*, xiii. 4. 1. 1.
[2] *Kātyāyana-Śrauta-Sūtra*, xx. 1.
[3] *Śāṅkhāyana-Śrauta-Sūtra*, xvi. 1. 1.
[4] *Ś. Br.*, xiii. 4. 1. 1; *Pañcaviṁśa-Brāhmaṇa*, xxi. 4; *Śāṅkhāyana-Śrauta-Sūtra*, xvi. 1. 1. Cf. *Rām.*, i. 14. 40, and *MBh.*, xiv. 88. 13, in which the sacrifice is mentioned as an *ahīna*, i.e. belonging to a class of sacrifices that last for two to twelve days.
[5] *Ś. Br.*, xiii. 4. 1.

averting seizure of the horse by enemies during its year's journey. In this rite a dog is put under the horse and killed.[1] *Aśva-medha (cont.).*

Three offerings are made the next morning to Savitṛ Prasavitṛ, Savitṛ Āsavitṛ, and Savitṛ Satyaprasava for speeding the sacrifice, the fore-offerings attached thereto being succeeded by songs sung by a *Brāhmaṇa* to the accompaniment of a lute played by himself. These songs, like the bardic recitations, related the past liberalities of the king now celebrating the *Aśvamedha*, and the sacrifices performed by him. Savitṛ offerings.

The horse is then brought to the grounds in front of the sacrificial hall and let loose among a hundred worn-out horses to be guarded by four hundred armed men, namely, a hundred princes clad in armour, a hundred warriors with swords, a hundred sons of heralds and headmen with quivers and arrows, and a hundred sons of attendants and charioteers. The *Adhvaryu* with the sacrificer, just before letting it loose, whispers into its right ear certain *mantras*, in which the horse is lauded and entrusted to the care of the guardian deities of the quarters and the four classes of human guardians of the four regions just enumerated. The duties of these human guards are not only to protect the horse, but also to keep it away from waters suitable for bathing, and mares. It was believed that the successful accomplishment of these duties by the hundred princes for the prescribed period of a year made them kings, while their failure in this respect deprived them of this high position and made them mere nobles and peasants instead.[2] A number of *Stokīya* and forty-nine *Prakrama* oblations (addressed to the different qualities of the horse) are then made in order to make up for the wear and tear that it, as an object of offering to the gods, will undergo before it is sacrificed.[3] Horse let loose; whispering; and oblations.

The horse set at large is to roam about in whichever direction it likes, without the slightest restraint being put upon its will. It is supposed that the oblations offered daily for a year at the sacrificial hall operate as the chain that brings it back to the sacrificial grounds at the end of its journey. These oblations are offered to the same as those already described, namely, to Savitṛ Prasavitṛ, Savitṛ Āsavitṛ, and Savitṛ Satyaprasava, Roaming of the horse.

[1] *Ś. Br.*, xiii. 1. 2. [2] *Ibid.*, xiii. 4. 2. [3] *Ibid.*, xiii. 1. 3.

Aśva-medha (cont.).

Savitṛ being here regarded as the earth, the bounds of which the horse cannot cross. These rituals are accompanied as formerly with the songs of the lute-player.[1]

The revolving legends.

The *Hotṛ*, after the oblations, takes his seat upon a cushion wrought of gold threads, surrounded by the sacrificer, the *Brahman*, the *Udgātṛ*, seated on similar cushions, and the *Adhvaryu* on a gold stool or slab. Addressed by the *Adhvaryu*, the *Hotṛ* tells the above listeners as well as some householders unlearned in the scriptures the first *Pariplava* (revolving) legend about King Manu Vaivasvata, whose subjects were Men and during whose rule the *Ṛk* formulas were the *Veda*. Thus saying the *Hotṛ* goes over a hymn of the *Ṛk*. On nine successive days the *Hotṛ* relates nine legends about (1) King Yama Vaivasvata whose subjects were the Fathers, and the *Yajus* formulas the *Veda*; (2) King Varuṇa Āditya, whose people were *Gandharvas*, and the *Atharvans* the *Veda*; (3) King Soma Vaiṣṇava, whose people were *Apsaras*, and the *Aṅgiras* the *Veda*; (4) King Arbuda Kādraveya, who ruled over *Snakes*, *Sarpa-vidyā* (science of snakes) being the *Veda*; (5) King Kubera Vaiśravaṇa, ruling over the *Rakṣas*, the *Devajana-vidyā* (demonology) being the *Veda*; (6) King Asita Dhānva, lord of the *Asuras*, magic being the *Veda*; (7) King Matsya Sāmmada, having *Water-dwellers* as his subjects, the *Itihāsa* being the *Veda*; (8) King Tārkṣya Vaipaśyata; whose people are the *Birds*, the *Purāṇa* being the *Veda*; (9) King Dharma Indra, ruling over the gods, the *Sāman* (chant-texts) being the *Veda*.

On each of these days the additional listeners are similar to or belong to the same class as the subjects of the various kings, namely, (1) householders unlearned in the scriptures as already pointed out, (2) old men, (3) handsome youths, (4) handsome maidens, (5) snake-charmers with snakes, (6) evil-doers such as robbers, (7) usurers, (8) fishermen with fish, (9) bird-catchers (or knowers of the science of birds) with birds, and (10) learned *śrotriyas* (theologians) accepting no gifts. Likewise the *Hotṛ* reads a hymn of the *Ṛg-Veda* on the first day, a chapter (*anuvāka*) of the *Yajur-Veda* on the second, a section (*parvan*) of the

[1] *Ś. Br.*, xiii. 4. 2. 6–17.

Atharvan, the *Aṅgiras*, the *Sarpa-vidyā*, the *Devajana-vidyā* on the third, fourth, fifth, and sixth respectively, performs some magic trick on the seventh, tells some *Itihāsa*, and some *Purāṇa* on the eighth and ninth respectively, and repeats a decade of the *Sāman* on the tenth.[1] *Aśva-medha (cont.).*

Lute-players sing of the sacrificer every day, associated with the righteous kings of yore, just after these rites. The ten days on which the ten legends are related form a cycle which is repeated thirty-six times during the year the horse is abroad. Each of the different gods or mythic personages is regarded as king on each successive day, with the special class of beings as his subjects and the particular texts[2] as the *Veda*.

The telling of these legends, says the *Śatapatha*, covers 'all royalties, all regions, all *Vedas*, all gods, all beings; and, verily, for whomsoever the *Hotṛ*, knowing this, tells this revolving legend, or whosoever ever knows this, attains to fellowship and communion with these royalties, gains the sovereign rule and lordship over all people, secures for himself all the *Vedas*, and, by gratifying the gods, finally establishes himself on all beings.'[3]

Dhṛti oblations.

The *Dhṛti* oblations made, like those to *Savitṛ*, at the sacrificial hall every evening for a year, are believed to give the sacrificial horse safe-dwellings at night.[4]

Having noticed the rituals connected with the roaming of the horse and the belief in their control and benign influence upon the animal as well as the benefits accruing to the sacrificer and others, let us turn to the practical complement of these rituals. The horse is let loose in the company of a hundred other horses, and though there is a *formal prohibition to put restraint upon the will of the former* as regards the course of its roaming, *the latter can be freely managed.* This may have been a good expedient for keeping the sacrificial horse within

[1] *Ś. Br.*, xiii. 4. 3. 1–14.

[2] 'Regarding the form and nature of some of the specified texts such as the *Sarpavidyā*, *Devajanavidyā*, *Asuravidyā*, we really know next to nothing. . . . Even regarding *Itihāsas* and *Purāṇas* . . . additional knowledge would by no means be unwelcome. . . . The legends related would seem to have been, as a rule, of the simplest possible description.' Eggeling, *S. B. E.*, xliv, pp. xxxi, xxxii.

[3] *Ś. Br.*, xiii. 4. 3. 15.

[4] *Ibid.*, xiii. 1. 4. 3.

Aśva-medha (cont.). desirable bounds and giving the intended turns to its course.[1] The guards watching it have to spend every night at the dwelling of a carpenter all along their journey. This injunction may be easily practised so long as they do not cross the limits of the sacrificer's domain, but may present difficulties in foreign territories.[2]

The challenge. Not merely the entrance of the horse upon a foreign territory is a challenge to its sovereign, but also the mere release of the horse is a challenge to any one that ventures to capture it and frustrate the object of the sacrificer by defeating him and his people in the fights that ensue. But, as it is not practicable, as a rule, for any of the sacrificer's subjects to take upon himself the risk and its fatal results, or for a rival king to use his forces successfully within the sacrificer's territory, the horse is practically secure so long as it does not go beyond its limits; nevertheless the mere release[3] of the horse is as much a challenge as its setting foot upon a foreign soil. In view of the restraint put in practice upon the roamings of the steed, its course was perhaps made to suit the particular purposes with which the horse-sacrifice was performed on particular occasions. If the obtainment of children were the object, it was not necessary to allow it to enter a foreign territory, where needless carnage might be the consequence. Daśaratha's horse-sacrifice[4] for the above purpose is described in the *Rāmāyaṇa* with so little emphasis upon the wanderings of the horse that it might well be taken as lending colour to the above inference. When the assertion of sovereign authority was in view, the wanderings were made to assume a different character. The sacred animal had to pass through those States upon which the sacrificer's suzerainty was intended to be asserted, for its roamings within a limited area round the sacrificial grounds could not have achieved the desired ends. Should the

[1] In the description of Yudhiṣṭhira's *Aśvamedha*, the horse is called kāmacara (i.e. roamer at will—*MBh.*, xiv. 83. 2) but the previous *śloka* uses the causative verb *cārayāmāsa* (caused it to proceed), which may show that the injunction of non-restraint was not literally followed.

[2] *Ś. Br.*, xiii. 4. 2. 17, and Eggeling, *S. B. E.*, xliv, p. xxx.

[3] The details of the *Aśvamedha* in the late Sanskrit work the *Jaimini Bhārata* speak of a written challenge put upon the head of the horse.

[4] *Rām.*, i. 14.

practical direction of the rangings of the steed be admitted, as it should be, though from the orthodox point of view it was either ignored or not believed and attributed to the influence of the ritual, we get a clue to the solution of the question as to how the horse could be managed while 'wandering at will', and made to return to the sacrificial hall neither a day sooner nor a day later than the prescribed period. Had the steed set free by Yudhiṣṭhira for his *Aśvamedha* been permitted to stray within a few miles of Indraprastha, the intention of having the formal submission of the numbers of princes upon whom the imperial sway was sought to be yoked would have been rendered nugatory. It was looked upon as a cowardice and a sign of submission on the part of a king not to take up the challenge implied in the progress of the horse through his State, and those kings that captured the horse to keep off the stain upon their bravery paid for it dearly. The king of Maṇipura, the capital of Kaliṅga, was put to shame by Arjuna for not opposing him like a true *Kṣatriya*.[1] Thus the horse-sacrifices, when performed for assertion of political power, evoked bloody opposition, and proved to be a prolific source of unrest to the many kingdoms that had to draw the sword in order to preserve their independence. *Aśvamedha (cont.).*

Dīkṣā. Just after a year from the release of the horse is held the initiation (*Dīkṣā*) of the sacrificer. The object of this ritual is the same as that of the *Agniṣṭoma* already dealt with. The ceremony lasts for seven days, of which the first six are spent in the daily offering of four *Audagrabhaṇas* (elevatory) and three *Vaiśvadeva* oblations for the upholding of the *Aśvamedha*. The *Dīkṣaṇīyeṣṭi* of the *Agniṣṭoma* is performed on the seventh day with an increase in the number of the aforesaid daily offerings, which are followed by one or two rites of the *Agniṣṭoma*. After this, some *mantras* are uttered praying for the birth of *Brāhmaṇas* with spiritual lustre; for *Kṣatriyas*, heroic, skilled in archery, mighty, car-fighters, and good shots; for well-favoured women, victorious warriors, blitheful youths; for milch cows, draught oxen, swift racers, and rain whenever wanted; and for an heroic son to be born to the sacrificer.[2] In

[1] *MBh.*, xiv. 79-81. [2] *Ś. Br.*, xiii. 1. 7-9.

Aśvamedha (cont.). the evening the lute-players, whose work continued for a whole year and ceased just before the commencement of the *Dīkṣā* ceremony, are again called upon to sing of the sacrificer along with the gods in order that he might share the same world with the gods. These songs are repeated on the three *upasad* days of the *Agniṣṭoma* of which this *Dīkṣā* is the beginning and also on the succeeding days up to the end of the sacrifice. On each of the three *upasad* days, forming, as it does, a part of the *Aśvamedha*, animal victims are offered, the third day having a larger number of victims than is usual in the *Agniṣṭoma.*[1]

First *Soma*-day. The *upasad* days are succeeded by the three days that make the *Aśvamedha* a triduum. The rituals of the first are identical with those of the last day of the *Agniṣṭoma* except for the manner of chanting hymns, number of victims quieted, and food-oblations (*Anna-homas*).

Second *Soma*-day. The second *Soma*-day is the most important in view of the ceremonies it involves. Like the preceding *Soma*-day modelled on the last day of the ordinary *Agniṣṭoma*, this *Soma*-day is a modification of the last day of the ordinary *Ukthya*, to which the following are the additions:—When the *Bahiṣpavamāna Stotra* is chanted, the sacrificial horse is taken to the place of chanting. Its sniffing or turning on the occasion is interpreted as a token that the sacrifice has been successful.[2] The *Hotṛ* then sings the merits of the horse, which is yoked to a chariot along with three other horses. The sacrificial horse is identified with the Sun—a conception to which the roaming of the horse for a year was but a corollary corresponding to the annual course of the Sun. The present harnessing of the animal to the chariot is meant to put the sacrificer in the leading of the Sun, i.e. the horse for the gaining of the heavenly world. The animal is anointed and decorated by the wives of the sacrificer, after which the horses are driven to an adjacent pond where certain *mantras* are uttered by the sacrificer. After their return to the sacrificial ground, a theological colloquy is held between the

[1] *Ś. Br.*, xiii. 4. 4. 2–4, and *S.B.E.*, xliv. 372, n. 1.
[2] *Ibid.*, xiii. 2. 3 and xiii. 5. 1. 16.

Brahman and the *Hotṛ* sitting face to face with the central sacrificial stake in the middle to imbue the sacrificer with fiery spirit and spiritual lustre.[1] *Aśvamedha (cont.).*

The number of animal victims in this sacrifice is very large. Two classes of these should be distinguished, namely, those that are killed and those that are symbolically sacrificed by fire being taken round them, the former numbering 349 and the latter 260.[2] The sacrificial horse with sixteen other animals is tied to the central stake while to the different parts of the body of the horse are leashed *twelve* similar victims called *Paryaṅgas* (circum-corporal). In each of the twenty interspaces between the stakes is placed a set of thirteen wild victims. The sacrificial horse is compared to a chieftain, the *Paryaṅgas* to heralds and headmen, and the other victims to the peasantry. The tying of the *Paryaṅgas* to the different parts of the body of the horse serves to make the heralds and headmen subservient to the chieftain or the sacrificer. The killing[3] of the staked animals was believed to exert beneficent influences on the means of communication, demarcation of villages, and the attempt to ward off bears, tigers, thieves, murderers, and robbers, even in the forest, but the slaughter of the wild victims would have produced the opposite results. But as the sacrifice could not be complete without the slaughter, symbolic slaying was resorted to as the *via media.* Victims.

The staked victims included domestic animals of various descriptions, viz. horse, goat, sheep, antelope, cow, and suchlike, while those in the interspaces might well be said to have ranged from the biggest born of earth to the tiniest worm that crept the ground, from the tawny lion, scaly crocodile, and treacherous serpent of sinuous trace to the soft-cooing dove and liveried peacock, from the dwellers of the deep or burrows to the rangers of the densest forests or the highest hill-tops. The sacrificial ground assumed at this time the appearance of

[1] *Ibid.*, xiii. 2. 6 and xiii. 5. 1. 16–17.

[2] The *Vājasaneyi-Saṃhitā*, xxiv, names the various gods to whom these 609 victims are dedicated.

[3] Slaughtering-knives of three different metals—gold, copper, and iron—were used to kill the horse, the *paryaṅgas*, and the other staked victims respectively.

Aśva-medha (cont.).

a well-stocked menagerie that could have regaled the eyes of a zoologist or an ornithologist. As all these creatures, some of which were rare or difficult to entrap, had to be preserved alive, a good deal of care and money must have been spent for the purpose.[1] The sacrificial horse and other animals are sprinkled with water with the utterance of appropriate formulas. The *Adhrigu* litany addressed to the slaughterers is recited by the *Hotṛ* and a cloth and a big upper cloth with a piece of gold on them are spread on the ground under the horse for slaying it thereon. Three oblations are made at the time of quieting,[2] after which the wives of the sacrificer turn round the horse nine times and fan it, the object being to make amends for the slaughter and put nine vital airs into themselves. Next follows a ceremony in which the four wives of the sacrificer, a damsel, and the principal priests take part.

Post-quieting ceremony with its colloquy.

The sacrificial horse is looked upon as Prajāpati, the lord of creatures, and the place where it is lying as heaven. The object of the ceremony is to bestow fertility on the sacrificer's principal wife, who takes the chief part on the occasion.[3] Prof. Eggeling[4] says that this was evidently a primitive custom that had nothing to do with Vedic religion and was distasteful to the author of the *Brāhmana*, as evinced both by the brief way in which it has been referred to, and by the symbolic explanations attached to the formulas and colloquies; but it was too firmly established in popular practice to be excluded from the sacrifice. Decorum does not permit me to give here its details, which may be gathered from the references noted below.[5]

Knife-paths.

Knife-paths (*asi-patha*) are then prepared by the wives of the sacrificer by means of needles of gold, silver, and copper. They are intended to serve the sacrificer as bridges to the heavenly world and secure for him people and royal power, the needles standing for the people and the *Aśvamedha* sacrifice itself the royal power.[6]

[1] See *Vājasaneyi-Saṃhitā*, xxiv. 20–40.

[2] The slaughtering of the other animals bound to the sacrificial stakes takes place next.

[3] *Ś. Br.*, xiii. 2. 7 and 8. 1–4.

[4] *S. B. E.* xliv. 322 n.

[5] *Vājasaneyi-Saṃhitā*, xxiii. 18–32; *Ś. Br.*, xiii. 2. 8 and xiii. 2. 9.

[6] *Ś. Br.*, xiii. 2. 10.

The priests repair to the *Sadas*, where they take their seats and enter into a theological colloquy of which only four questions are asked and answered at this place. It is resumed in front of the *Havirdhāna* shed, where the priests remove and adds the sacrificer to their company. Here the rest of the questions, five in number, are asked and answered.[1]

Aśvamedha (cont.). Theological colloquy.

After the drawing and offering of the first *Mahiman* (greatness) cup to *Prajāpati* by the *Adhvaryu* in the *Havirdhāna* shed for conferring greatness upon the sacrificer, the cooked omentum and gravy oblations are made to the deities in an order about which there are differences of opinion. They are favoured by the offering of the second *Mahiman* cup to Prajāpati.[2]

Mahiman cups and omentum and gravy offerings.

Among the additions to the rituals of the *Ukthya* sacrifice performed on this most important day of the *Aśvamedha*, none other worthy of note are left to be mentioned than the large numbers of oblations such as the three sets of *Araṇye-'nūcya*, two to Death, six called *Dvipadā* and the *Sviṣṭakṛt*.[3]

Other oblations.

The rituals of the last day of the *Aśvamedha* are the same as those of the last day of an *Atirātra* sacrifice except the larger number (about twenty-four) of bovine victims,[4] and a few additions to the concluding rituals such as the oblation offered on the head of a deformed person during the purificatory bath of the sacrificer, preparation of the twelve messes of rice for the priests, gifts to the *ṛtviks*, and seizure of twenty-one barren cows.[5]

Last day of the *Aśvamedha*.

The sacrifice practically comes to a close with the performance of the rituals of this day, but as a supplement six animal victims are offered by the sacrificer to each of the six seasons during the next year.[6]

[1] *Ibid.*, xiii. 5. 2. 11–22. To give an idea of the dialogues, I put below two questions and answers: *Question.* 'Who is it that walketh singly?' *Answer.* 'Sūrya (the sun) walketh singly.' *Question.* 'Whose light is there equal to the sun?' *Answer.* 'The Brahman is the light equal to the sun.' See *Ś. Br.*, xiii. 5. 2. 12, 13.

[2] *Ibid.*, xiii. 5. 2. 23 and 5. 3. 1–7.

[3] *Ibid.*, xiii. 3. 4–5 and 6. 1–4.

[4] *Ibid.*, xiii. 3. 2. 3 and 5. 3. 11. I have left out of account in my descriptions as a rule the many *śastras* and *stotras* with their varied tunes and arrangements.

[5] *Ibid.*, xiii. 3. 6. 5 and 7, and xiii. 5. 4. 24–7.

[6] *Ibid.*, xiii. 5. 4. 28.

Bṛhaspatisava. Objectives and eligibility.

(C) (iv) (*a*). *Bṛhaspatisava.* The objectives for the performance of the sacrifice are:—(1) The installation of a qualified *Brāhmaṇa* to the office of the royal priest.[1] (2) The formal declaration of the supremacy of a *Brāhmaṇa* who is regarded as fit for such a position by the kings and *Brāhmaṇas.*[2] (3) The acquisition of strength and spiritual lustre by a *Brāhmaṇa.*[3] (4) The attainment of prosperity by a *Vaiśya* according to one of the *Śrauta-Sūtras.*[4] (5) The installation of a *Sthapati* (Governor of a district)[5] to his office.[6]

In some of the texts, as already pointed out, the *Vājapeya* is mentioned as an adjunct to the *Bṛhaspatisava,*[7] the *Śatapatha*[8] merging the latter in the former. The *Sūtra*[9] of the *Śatapatha* does not follow the *Brāhmaṇa* in this respect, prescribing that the *Bṛhaspatisava* is performed a fortnight before and after the *Vājapeya.*

Principal ritual.

The *Bṛhaspatisava,* as usual, lasts only for a day, its principal ritual being the sprinkling of the performer with *ghee* (a symbol of strength) while seated on the skin of a black antelope.[10]

Pṛthisava.

(*b*) The *Pṛthisava* takes its name from its first performer, Pṛthi, son of Vena. The object achieved by this *sava* is the attainment of supremacy upon all beings, including men. A few rites of the *Rājasūya* compose this sacrifice.[11]

Rāḍ-yajña.

(*c*) The celebration of the *Rāḍ-yajña*[12] was intended to

[1] *Taittirīya-Brāhmaṇa*, ii. 7. 1. 2; *Pañcaviṃśa-Brāhmaṇa*, xvii. 11. 4 and 5.

[2] *Lāṭyāyana-Śrauta-Sūtra*, viii. 7. 4.

[3] *Śāṅkhāyana-Śrauta-Sūtra*, xv. 4. 1 and 2.

[4] *Āpastamba-Śrauta-Sūtra*, xxii. 25. 1.

[5] According to Monier Williams' *Sanskrit-English Dictionary*; cf. *V.I.*, ii. 486.

[6] *Pañcaviṃśa-Brāhmaṇa*, xvii. 11. 6; *Āpastamba-Śrauta-Sūtra*, xxii. 7. 6. The *Brāhmaṇa* calls it *Sthapatisava*, in view of its particular purpose on the occasion.

[7] *Śāṅkhāyana-Śrauta-Sūtra*, xv. 4. 1; *Āśvalāyana-Śrauta-Sūtra*, ix. 9. 1.

[8] *Śatapatha-Brāhmaṇa*, v. 2. 1. 19.

[9] *Kātyāyana-Śrauta-Sūtra*, xiv. 2.

[10] *Taittirīya-Brāhmaṇa*, ii. 7. 1. 4.

[11] *Ibid.*, ii. 7. 5, with Sāyaṇa's commentary.

[12] *Pañcaviṃśa-Brāhmaṇa*, xix. 7. 1–4.

restore[1] a deposed king to his kingdom, or procure the allegiance of the refractory subjects to a reigning king. The noteworthy ritual of this ceremony is the *Abhiṣeka*, in which the celebrant is surrounded by the eight *Vīras* and sprinkled, the *Vīras* being (1) king's brother, (2) king's son, (3) royal priest, (4) queen, (5) *Sūta* (charioteer), (6) *Grāmaṇī* (village headman), (7) *Kṣattṛ* (gate-keeper according to Sāyaṇa), and (8) *Saṃgrahītṛ* (collector-general). *Rāḍ-yajña (cont.).*

(C) (v). *Rājyābhiṣeka* (coronation). The *Nītimayūkha*,[2] a late Sanskrit work, gives details of the ceremony, according to the *Gopatha-Brāhmaṇa* of the *Atharva-Veda*, as also particulars not dependent on its authority. The existence of the coronation can be traced much earlier than the *Gopatha-Brāhmaṇa*. The *Taittirīya-Brāhmaṇa*[3] gives its details as an independent performance in three sections which are separate from those devoted to the *Rājasūya*. Wilson and Goldstücker observe that 'the rites of the *Abhiṣeka*, which is not part of a *Rājaṣūya* sacrifice, but a ceremony performed at a king's accession to the throne, are similar to, but not identical with, those of the *Punarabhiṣeka*; they are founded on the proceedings which took place when Indra was consecrated by the gods as their supreme ruler, and which forms the subject of the thirty-eighth chapter of the *Aitareya-Brāhmaṇa*'.[4] If the *Taittirīya-Brāhmaṇa* be older than the *Aitareya*, as Prof. Macdonell[5] suggests, then the similarity between the Corona-tion.

[1] Hymn 3 of the *Atharva-Veda*, iii, which is used with the one next following, has also for its object the restoration of a king. Hymns 87 and 88 of book vi of the same *Veda* are directed towards establishing a king in sovereignty.

[2] *Nītimayūkha*, by Nīlakaṇṭha Bhaṭṭa (MS. in *A. S. B.*), p. 3. The discourse on coronation in the *Bhārata-rahasya* (in Bengali) by Rāmadāsa Sena cites a short passage from the *Gopatha-Brāhmaṇa* without any reference to its location in the *Brāhmaṇa*. I could not trace it either in the *Bibliotheca Indica*, or the Bombay edition of the work. I do not understand why, unless the passage has eluded my search, it should be omitted in the editions.

[3] *Taittirīya-Brāhmaṇa*, ii. 7. 15–17. *Ṛg-Veda*, x. 173 and 174 refer to rites for securing the king in his office by the propitiation of certain deities. It is not clear whether they have any connexion with the coronation, if any, prevailing at that time.

[4] Goldstücker's *Sanskrit-English Dictionary*, p. 277, under *Abhiṣeka*. Sāyaṇa styles the *Taittirīya* ceremony 'sacrificial and not mundane'.

[5] Prof. A. Macdonell's *History of Sanskrit Literature*, p. 203; the

Coronation (cont.). *Abhiṣeka* and the *Punarabhiṣeka* cannot be taken as indicative of the derivation of the one from the other. The *Abhiṣeka* appears therefore to have been an independent ceremony existing side by side with the *Rājasūya*. The *Abhiṣeka* as detailed in the *Taittirīya-Brāhmaṇa* begins with seven *Homa.* *mantras* to be uttered by the priest for performing a *Homa* before the ritual of sprinkling takes place. The first *mantra* speaks of the prince's re-birth as the son of the *ṛtviks* (sacrificial priests), with his vigour immensely increased by his symbolic entrance into the *Homa* fire and exit therefrom, and wishes him capability to keep his subjects from sinful ways. The second wishes him an extended kingdom, a stout physique for its efficient administration, and a good supply of cattle for the performance of the sacrifices. The third wishes him to be the guide of men, and wants him to solemnly say that he would protect the good and punish the wicked. The fourth and fifth invoke blessing on him for prosperity, while the sixth and seventh for the glorification of the castes by his power, the prosperity of his subjects, and the extension of Prajāpati's protection to him.

In these *mantras*, two points are noteworthy: (i) The belief of the prince's *re-birth as the son of the sacrificial priests*; which appears akin to the re-birth of the twice-born by the *upanayana* sacrament for their initiation into the study of the Vedas. The prince as it were becomes a totally different being, with his faculties and physical vigour renewed and increased for the discharge of the new duties that the assumption of kingly office will devolve upon him. Such a belief perhaps made the performance of the coronation ceremony an imperative necessity to every prince; for, otherwise, in the estimation of the people, the prince will stand bare of the 'kingly fitness' which he omits to formally bestow upon himself by the ceremonial, and for which no natural capabilities of the prince, however great, could perhaps be an adequate substitute. After the death of a king or after his retirement, some time must have elapsed before the coronation

opposite view is taken by Prof. Berriedale Keith, *Taittirīya Saṃhitā*, pp. xcvii ff.; *Ṛgveda Brāhmaṇas*, pp. 45 ff.

rituals could be performed by his successor; and hence, the question naturally suggests itself whether the latter could exercise the rights and duties of a full-fledged king immediately after the end of the previous régime without formally going through the ceremony. In the case of the initiation sacrament, the uninitiated boy had no right to the acquisition of sacred lore before he went through the necessary rite; but not so, perhaps, in the case of the coronation ceremony, as will appear from evidence later on. (ii) The solemn assertion by the prince, which looks very much like the *coronation oath*, to protect the good and punish the wicked, that is to say, the paramount duties of the protection of life and property of his subjects and an impartial administration of justice. *Coronation (cont.).*

After the performance of the *Homa*, a tiger-skin is spread, with the *mantra* 'Thou art the sky, thou art the earth', and the prince is seated thereon. The priests bless him saying, 'May you be unconquerable, may the various quarters protect you, may your subjects be loyal, and may the kingdom never slip away from your rule', and sprinkle him with water in which barley and *dūrvā* grass have been steeped—the ritual being accompanied with blessings. **Sprinkling.**

The prince is then asked to repair to and ascend a chariot standing before the *Āhavanīya* fire of the sacrificial ground where the ceremony is taking place, appropriate benedictory formulas (some of which are repetitions of those used in the sprinkling ceremony) being uttered during the time. The object of this ascension of the car appears from the last formula addressed to the chariot to be a symbolic expression of the desire that the prince might achieve success in his rule. The king next prays the royal priest to help him by a faithful discharge of his duties that serve to keep the realm free from danger, and contribute to its well-being. He then asks the charioteer to sit on the car and hold the reins. The king then recites to the effect, 'May I never hear within my dominion the sound of bows of my enemies coveting my kingdom, may that harsh sound change into a sweet one by making the hostile army friendly'. **Ascending a car.**

The *Brāhmaṇas* as well as the king's friends and relations **Smearing**

Coronation (cont.). embrace him, after which his body is smeared with unguents. At this time, the king has to look towards the sun and the royal priest addresses him thus: 'May this king be lustrous like the noonday sun; may my blessings be likewise powerful in their effects; may you (king),—glorious sun, attain prosperity by my blessings; may my words be in a special degree discriminatory of right and wrong; may my blessings be firm in their efficacy; may the rivers (in the kingdom) be full, clouds rain in time, and crops fructify; may the king be the lord of a rich country veritably flowing with milk and honey.'

Hair-cutting. After oblations to the fire intended for the *keśins*, i.e. Agni, Vāyu, and Sūrya, the king is asked to sit on a throne of *udumbara* wood, when the *Purohita* says, 'O king, subdue your enemies completely. Now that I have finished the consecration bearing the two names of *Vaśinī*[1] and *Ugrā*,[2] pay fees to the *Purohita*. May you attain long life and be freed from Varuṇa's snares'. Then the priest shaves the king's head with a *mantra*, which indicates that it is an imitation of what Prajāpati had done for Soma and Varuṇa. The hair is collected on a tuft of *kuśa* grass, serving thereby to preserve the king's strength.[3] The king is then anointed with a mixture of milk and *ghee* with the same object in view, with a formula which asks the Aśvins to have the king's beauty devoted entirely to the queens.

References to coronation in the Epics. The *Rāmāyaṇa* and the *Mahābhārata* speak of a few coronations of princes: the former mentions those of (1) Sugrīva,[4] (2) Vibhīṣaṇa,[5] (3) Rāma,[6] (4) Kuśa and Lava,[7] (5) Aṅgada and Candraketu,[8] (6) Śatrughna's sons Subāhu and Śatrughātin,[9] and the latter those of (1) Janamejaya,[10] (2) Vicitravīrya,[11] (3) Puru,[12] (4) Yudhiṣṭhira,[13] (5) Śarabha, son of Śiśupāla,[14] and

[1] & [2] Called *Vaśinī* because the ceremony is believed to bring the subjects under the king's control, and *Ugrā* because it effects the subjugation of enemies.

[3] A similar belief is noticed in connexion with the *keśavapanīya* ritual of the *Rājasūya*.

[4] *Rām.*, iv. 26. [5] *Ibid.*, vi. 112.

[6] *Ibid.*, vi. 128, and vii. 63. [7] & [8] *Ibid.*, vi. 107.

[9] *Ibid.*, 108. [10] *MBh.*, i. 44. [11] *Ibid.*, 101.

[12] *Ibid.*, 85. [13] *Ibid.*, xii. 40. [14] *Ibid.*, ii. 45.

(6) Parīkṣit.[1] Full ritual details are given nowhere in the epics. The common features of the rituals, so far as we can gather them from their fragmentary descriptions in the first-named epic, are the collection of waters from seas and rivers in gold pitchers, the sprinkling of them on the prince seated on a throne, the crowning, and the prince's gifts to Brāhmaṇas, while their distinguishing features are (1) the performance of a *Homa* (in Sugrīva's coronation), (2) presents offered by the subjects to the prince (e.g. in Vibhīṣaṇa's coronation), (3) presents offered by the prince (as in Rāma's coronation), (4) a difference as to persons who sprinkle water, and (5) a difference as to those who put the crown on his head.

Coronation (cont.).

Yudhishthira's coronation.

The *Mahābhārata* furnishes some details of the ceremony of only one prince, Yudhiṣṭhira, who sat on a throne made of gold surrounded by others seated likewise. To begin with, he touched white flowers, auspicious symbols (*svastikas*), unhusked barley-corns, earth, gold, silver, and jewels. Auspicious articles, such as earth, gold, gems, and other things necessary for the coronation were brought by the subjects, who came there headed by the priest. Jars made of gold, *udumbara* wood, silver, and earth, and full of water, as well as flowers, fried rice, *kuśa* grass, cow's milk, *śamī*, *pippala* and *palāśa* wood, honey, *ghee*, ladles of *udumbara* wood, and conches decked with gold were there for the ceremony. The royal priest, Dhaumya, made an altar sloping north and east and marked with the necessary signs. The prince with his consort Draupadī was then seated upon a firm and effulgent stool called *sarvatobhadra*[2] covered with tiger-skin, and Dhaumya poured libations of *ghee* upon fire with appropriate *mantras*. Kṛṣṇa poured water from a sanctified conch upon the prince's head, as also Dhṛtarāṣṭra and the subjects. The presents brought by the people were formally accepted by Yudhiṣṭhira, who in turn honoured them with presents in profusion and gave a thousand *niṣkas* to the *Brāhmaṇas* who uttered benedictions for his welfare.

Most of the features of the coronation as found in the epics

[1] *Ibid.*, xvii. 1.
[2] Cf. *Yukti-kalpa-taru* (edited by Paṇḍit Īśvar Candra Śāstrī), śāmānyāsanoddeśa, p. 56, ślk. 402.

Coronation (cont.). Coronation in the *Agni-Purāṇa.* Main divisions.

have been reproduced in the *Agni-Purāṇa*[1] which, as usual with the *Purāṇas*, adds to them new rituals making the whole ceremony much more elaborate. The main divisions of the ceremony may be marked out into (1) *Aindrī Śānti* on a day previous to that of *Abhiṣeka*. (2) (On the *Abhiṣeka* day) (*a*) Performance of *Homa*; (*b*) symbolic bathing (i. e. touching the prince's body with earth brought from various places—*mṛttikā-snāna*); (*c*) sprinkling of liquids on the prince by ministers; (*d*) sprinkling of liquids by Ṛg-Vedic and Sāma-Vedic *Brāhmaṇas*, and the royal priest; (*e*) sprinkling of water through a pitcher (perforated with a hundred holes) by the royal priest; (*f*) rites by the Yajur-Vedic and Atharva-Vedic *Brāhmaṇas*; (*g*) seeing auspicious things; (*h*) crowning; (*i*) presentation of officials to the prince; (*j*) payment of fees to *Brāhmaṇas* and coronation feast; (*k*) royal procession through the metropolis; (*l*) return of the procession to the royal palace and gifts to the people.

If the reigning king instals his successor on the throne just before his retirement, he may have the *Abhiṣeka* performed under his auspices on a day prescribed as appropriate for the purpose. If, however, he dies without performing this ceremony for his successor, the *Agni-Purāṇa*[2] allows for the latter a provisional *Abhiṣeka* which can be celebrated irrespective of the auspicious or inauspicious nature of the day on which it is held. The reason for such a provision is obvious: the formal vesting of regal powers in the prince in order to enable him to discharge kingly duties cannot be long postponed; for such postponement may lead to difficulties. The rituals of the ceremony are succinctly mentioned as symbolic bathing of the prince with sesamum and white mustard at which the royal priest and the astrologer officiate; the hailing of the prince with the cry of victory, after which he sits on a *bhadrāsana*, proclaims safety for his subjects, and issues order to his officers for releasing prisoners. The coronation, whether performed under the

[1] *Agni-Purāṇa*, ccxviii, ccxix.

[2] The *Agni-Purāṇa*, ccxviii, devotes vv. 5 and 6 to this provisional *Abhiṣeka*, and the real meaning of the passage can easily elude the reader unless light be focussed on it from other works, such as the *Viṣṇudharmottara*, ii. 18.

supervision of the retiring king or, in the case of his death, after the provisional coronation, has to be held on an auspicious day which is fixed in accordance with recommendations of the texts [1] on the subject. *Coronation (cont.).*

Aindrī Śānti. The details of the aforesaid main divisions are:—The *Agni-Purāṇa* does not furnish the ritual of the *Aindrī Śānti* which, however, are given in later works like the *Nītimayūkha*,[2] which may be summarized thus: After the formal declaration of the king's intention to perform the *Śānti*, the officiating priests are formally entrusted with these duties:—A *Vedi* (altar) is constructed and upon it a *Mahāvedi* (great altar) on which three lines are drawn on sand, a cavity is made and refilled with sand, earth is bowed to, and fire is ignited. A gold, silver, or copper pitcher full of water is covered with a piece of cloth, and an image of Indra made of gold is placed on two eight-leaved lotuses drawn on the cloth. This is followed by offerings to Indra, five oblations to fire, and the seating of the *Brahman* priest who with the *Hotṛ* next engages in the offering of the following oblations, viz. eight to the four cardinal points, and seventeen to Agni and other deities, followed by *samṛddhi*, *sannati*, *upastīrya*, *sviṣṭakṛt*, *prāyaścittātmaka*, *saṃsthiti*, *samāna*, and *saṃśrāva-bhāga Homas*. Then follow offerings to the ten presiding deities of the ten quarters of heavens, and to demons of various descriptions. The *pūrṇāhuti* comes next, and then the throwing of the remnants of *Homa-fire* into holy water. In the concluding rite of *Śānti* for averting evil, the king with his consort, relatives, and ministers is sprinkled by the *Hotṛ* with water from the *Śānti* pitcher. Then both the king and the queen take a bath in water mixed with herbs, wear white dresses and garlands, and smear their bodies with the paste of white sandal. Gifts are made to the priests, and the gold image of Indra after symbolic relinquishment is given to *Ācārya*. The whole ceremony is then brought to a close by the feasting of *Brāhmaṇas*.

[1] See, for instance, *Viṣṇu-dharmottara*, ii. 18. 5–14; Goldstücker's *Sanskrit-English Dictionary* refers to *Jyotiṣaratnamālā* and *Muhūrtacintāmaṇi* on this point.

[2] *Nīti-mayūkha* (MS. in *A. S. B.*), pp. 4–10. Minor details and *mantras* have been omitted in the above summary.

Coronation (cont.). The object of this ritual is no doubt the welfare of the king, implying that of his relatives, officials, and subjects, but the central idea in it is the coronation of Indra, the king of the gods. We have seen in connexion with the *Rājasūya* that the *mantras* for the *Punarabhiṣeka* are uttered in unison with those of the *Aindra-mahābhiṣeka*, which goes upon the supposition that the king of the gods was installed on his throne in remote antiquity with the selfsame *mantras* which appear in the *Aitareya-Brāhmaṇa* in connexion with the *Aindra-mahābhiṣeka*, and which, when uttered at the *Punarabhiṣeka*, ensure the special well-being of the subject of the *Punarabhiṣeka*. In the coronation ceremony with which we are now dealing, much more prominence is given to the idea by devoting a special day with its special rituals to Indra, who is worshipped to make the coronation of the mortal king as much fraught with potentialities for good as his own coronation was in the remote past.

The *Abhiṣeka* Day. Preliminaries. On an auspicious day fixed for the *Abhiṣeka*, the king has formally to declare his intention (*saṃkalpa*) to perform the *Abhiṣeka*.

Homa. (*a*) After the ignition of fire[1] and the offering of seventeen oblations as previously mentioned in connexion with *Aindrī Śānti*, the *Purohita* has to perform *Homas* with five sets of *Atharva-Veda mantras*, viz. *śarma-varma*, *svastyayana*, *āyuṣya*, *abhayā*, and *aparājitā*, which are intended to secure for the king welfare for himself personally and his kingdom. On the southern side of the *Homa* fire is kept a gold pitcher (*sampātavān kalasa*) in which are deposited the residues of offerings. *Brāhmaṇas* learned in the Vedas as well as *Brāhmaṇa*, *Kṣatriya*, *Vaiśya*, and *Śūdra* ministers are honoured with presents and seated at the place where the ceremony is to take place. The royal priest, who has to fast on that day, puts on a garland and a turban, and enters into the bathing-house, where he has to put nine gold pitchers with waters from various places of pilgrimage as well as an

[1] Certain characteristics of the flame of this fire, such as brightness like melted gold, resemblance to *svastika* mark, &c., were regarded as portents for good or evil.

earthen pitcher with water, a gold pitcher with *ghee*, a silver pitcher with milk, a copper pitcher with curds, and an earthen pitcher with water in which *kuśa* grass has been soaked. A gold pitcher with a hundred perforations as also an earthen pitcher filled with water from a well and the four seas are also to be there. *Coronation (cont*

(*b*) The prince is then bathed symbolically with various descriptions of soil. This bathing consists in touching his head with soil from the top of a hill, ears with that from the top of an ant-hill, face with that from a temple of Viṣṇu, neck with that from a temple of Indra, chest with that from a royal palace, right arm with that dug up by an elephant by its tusks, left arm with that dug up by a bull by its horns, back with that from a lake, belly with that from a confluence of rivers, sides with that from the banks of a river, waist with that from the door of a brothel, thighs with that from a sacrificial ground, knees with that from a cowshed, shanks with that from a horse-stable, and feet with that from the wheel of a chariot. This ceremony is concluded by the final ablution of his head with *pañcagavya* (a mixture of milk, curds, clarified butter, and cow's urine and dung). **Symbolic bathing.**

(*c*) Four vessels made of gold, silver, copper, and earth are filled respectively with clarified butter, milk, curd, and water. The *Brāhmaṇa*, *Kṣatriya*, *Vaiśya*, and *Śūdra* ministers take the gold, silver, copper, and earthen vessels in succession and sprinkle their contents on the prince's head from the east, south, west, and north respectively. **Sprinkli by ministers.**

(*d*) After the ministers, a Ṛg-Vedic *Brāhmaṇa* sprinkles honey and a Sāma-Vedic *Brāhmaṇa* water (in which *kuśa* grass has been immersed) upon the prince's head. The royal priest commits the sacrificial fire to the care of the *Sadasyas* (assistants), and sprinkles from the aforesaid *sampātavān* pitcher, with the *mantras*[1] that were uttered in connexion with Anointment forming part of the *abhiṣecanīya* of the *Rājasūya*. **Sprinkli by two *Brāhmaṇas* and the royal priest.**

[1] The *Agni-Purāṇa* (ccxviii. 22) speaks of these *mantras*. That they are borrowed from the *Rājasūya* ceremony is not clear from this *śloka*, but appears to be so from works like the *Nītimayūkha*. Had the first verse of the couplet commenced with the words *rā asūyābhiṣeke ca* instead of with *rājaśr.yābhiṣeke cha*, the meaning would have been clearer.

Coronation (cont.). Rite with the perforated pitcher.

(*e*) The prince is then taken to the base of the altar and seated upon a *bhadrāsana*. The royal priest sprinkles water on his head through a gold jar perforated with a hundred holes, uttering 'yā oṣadhīḥ, &c.',[1] as also perfumed liquids, and water in which flowers, seeds, gems, and *kuśa* grass have been dipped, with the recitation of other formulas.[2]

Rites by the Yajur-Vedic and Atharva-Vedic *Brāhmaṇas.*

(*f*) The Yajur- and Atharva-Vedic *Brāhmaṇas* touch with *rocana* (yellow pigment) the prince's head and throat with the *mantra*, 'Gandhadvārā, &c.'.[3] This rite is brought to a close by the assembled *Brāhmaṇas* sprinkling on the prince's head water brought from various sacred places.[4]

Seeing auspicious things.

(*g*) Auspicious things such as a jar filled with water, chowry, fan, mirror, clarified butter, and herbs are brought before the prince, music is played (eulogistic songs being sung by the bards, and Vedic psalms chanted by the *Brāhmaṇas*).[5]

Crowning.

(*h*) The royal priest, in the meantime, makes offerings of milk and honey to the divinities and sits on a chair covered with a tiger's skin. So seated he binds the prince's head with a fillet and puts on it the crown, with the formulas 'Dhruvā dyauḥ, &c.', an English rendering of which is given below:

'Firm is the heaven, firm is the earth, firm are these mountains, firm is this entire world, so may this king of men be firm.'[1]

[1] See *RV.*, x. 97.

[2] Some explanatory details have been taken from the *Nītimayūkha*. The formulae referred to have been borrowed as follows:
(i) 'Oṣadhayaḥ pratigṛbhṇīta puṣpavatīḥ &c.' *VS.*, xi. 48.
(ii) 'Āśuḥ śiśāno &c.' *RV.*, x. 103. 1.

[3] *RV.* Khila, v. 87. 9.

[4] According to the *Nītimayūkha* (MS. pp. 2 and 11) not only the *Brāhmaṇas* but also the assembled *Kṣatriyas, Vaiśyas, Śūdras*, and persons of mixed castes sprinkle water as above.

[5] *Nītimayūkha* (MS.), pp. 2 and 11. The work puts after the above rite the sprinkling of propitiatory water (*śāntijala*) from the *sampātavān* pitcher by the astrologer. This rite is accompanied by the utterance of a long *mantra*, '*surās tvām abhiṣiñcantu*' etc., of about 180 ślokas addressed to the gods, heavenly bodies, clouds, continents, hills and mountains, places of pilgrimage, sacred rivers, birds, horses, elephants, universal monarchs of yore, ascetics, *Vedas*, fourteen branches of learning, weapons, supernatural beings, in short to quite a string of divine, natural, or supernatural forces with powers for good or evil, in order that they might all be propitiated to the prince about to be coronated. The location of the *mantra* in the ceremony is not manifest in the *Agni-Purāṇa*, but has been indicated by works like the *Nītimayūkha*.

'May the royal Varuṇa, the divine Bṛhaspati, may Indra and Agni ever give stability to thy kingdom.' *Coronation (cont.)*

'With a constant oblation we handle the constant *Soma*; therefore may Indra render thy subject people payers of (their) taxes.'[1]

The throne-seat,[2] on which the prince is next seated, is covered with the skins of five animals, bull, cat, wolf, lion, and tiger. A symbolic meaning, not given in the texts, was no doubt attached to the spreading of these skins one over another. The tiger-skin, as has been seen in connexion with a previous ritual, indicated kingly power.

Presentation of officials.

(*i*) The *Agni-Purāṇa* next speaks of the *Pratīhāra* presenting officials to the king. It is added by the *Nītimayūkha* that distinguished townsmen, merchants, and other subjects are also admitted to this honour.

Payment of fees to the *Brāhmaṇas*, procession and feasts.

(*j*, *k*, and *l*). The king now presents the royal priest and the astrologer with cows, goats, sheep, houses, &c., and honours the other *Brāhmaṇas* with similar gifts and a sumptuous feast. After going round the sacrificial fire and saluting the *Guru* and one or two minor rituals, he sits on a sanctified horse, but gets down the next moment to sit on the state-elephant similarly sanctified, and rides through the principal thoroughfares of the metropolis amid a gorgeous procession. After return to his palace, he accepts the presents made by his subjects, whom he receives with honour and entertains to a feast. Presents in return are also made by the king to his subjects.

European coronation.

It will not be out of place to recount succinctly the principal features of the English coronation of the past in order to show the degree of parallelism between it and that of the Hindus. The early English coronation had many features found in those of other European countries in the past, and may, for this reason, be taken for our purposes as a type of the early European coronations generally:[3]

[1] *RV.*, x. 173. 4-6 (translation by Prof. H. H. Wilson).

[2] The *Mānasāra*, as quoted in Goldstücker's *Sanskrit-English Dictionary* (p. 284, under *Abhiṣeka*), names two officers *sthapati* and *sthāpaka* taking part in a function not detailed in the texts used above. The queen is also mentioned as sitting on a throne along with the king.

[3] For the following information on the European coronation, see

Corona-tion (cont.). (1) The prince, attended by a large number of nobles and government officers, made a stately progress to the Tower of London, where he resided a day or two to dub as Knights of the Bath a number of candidates who had to perform vigil and other rites preparatory to this honour.

(2) Amid a solemn and gorgeous procession in which the new Knights of the Bath, nobles, government officers, and clergymen occupied the particular positions allotted to them, the prince under various marks of honour displayed by the citizens rode to Westminster Hall on the day previous to the day of coronation.

(3) Next morning, the nobles and others, marshalled according to their respective ranks, accompanied the prince to the adjacent Westminster Abbey, some of the regalia[1] being carried by certain persons having title to this honour.

Recognition. (4) The first rite performed within the Hall was Recognition, in which the Archbishop declared to the people assembled there the prince's rightful claim to the throne and asked them whether they were ready to give their assent thereto. In this rite were laid the traces of development of coronation from an earlier form of election.

First oblation. (5) Next came the First Oblation, the essence of which was the rite in which a 'pall of cloth of gold, and an ingot of gold of a pound weight', received by the prince from the Lord High Chamberlain, were made over to the Archbishop of Canterbury, who placed them on the altar.

Service of the day. (6) In the Proper Service of the Day, prayers were said for blessings upon the prince.

Oath. (7) At the conclusion of the sermon forming part of the previous rite, the Coronation Oath was administered by the Archbishop. The prince swore to govern the kingdom according to the established laws and usages, administer justice tempered with mercy, and uphold the religion of the

Chapters on Coronations, author not mentioned; *Glory of Regality*, by Arthur Taylor; and *Encyclopædia Britannica*, 11th edition, under 'coronation'.

[1] The principal regalia are: St. Edward's Chair, St. Edward's Crown, Crowns and Circlets, Orb with the Cross, Sceptre with the Cross, St. Edward's Staff, Ampulla, Ivory Rod, Chalice, Paten, Swords, Rings, Spurs, Curtana (or pointless sword of mercy), and the Bible.

land, and the rights and privileges of the members of the church. *Coronation (cont.).*

(8) The Dean of Westminster anointed, with oil from the Ampulla, the palms of the prince's hands, his chest, shoulders, arms, and the crown of his head. **Anointing.**

(9) The next rite consists in investing the prince with vestments, girdle, buskins, sandals, spurs, sword, &c., which were made over to him on this occasion. Two noteworthy features of this function are that the Archbishop (*a*) while passing the sword to the prince requested him to protect the church, people, widows, orphans, restore things gone to decay and maintain those that were restored; and (*b*) while delivering to him the Orb with the Cross, he uttered the formula, 'Receive this . . . Orb, and remember that the whole world is subject to the power and empire of God, and that no one can happily reign upon earth, who hath not received his authority from heaven'. At the time of Augustus, the Roman emperor, the Orb was regarded as the symbol of universal dominion. The Cross was affixed to it by Constantine the Great, signifying that universal dominion was but possible by faith.[1] **Investing.**

(10) The Archbishop assisted by other clergymen put the Crown on the head of the prince seated on St. Edward's Chair, saying, 'God crown thee with a crown of glory and righteousness, with the honour and virtue of fortitude, that (thou) by (our ministry having) a right faith and manifold fruits of good works, thou mayest obtain the crown of an everlasting kingdom, by the gift of Him whose kingdom endureth for ever. Amen'. **Crowning.**

(11) The sovereign was invested with the Ring of faith, held the Sceptre of kingly power, the Rod of virtue and equity, and the Bible. He then received the Archbishop's Benediction in appropriate words. **Delivery of the Ring, Sceptre, Rod, and the Bible. Benediction.**

(12) The sovereign was conducted to the throne by the Archbishop, who was followed by the bishops and great officers of state. After he was seated on the throne, the Archbishop delivered an exhortation and took the Oath of Fealty. This Oath was also taken by the bishops and the premier Duke, **Enthroning and Homage.**

[1] *Chapters on Coronations*, pp. 27, 118.

Coronation (cont.). Marquess, Earl, Viscount, and Baron, each of them representing himself and the rest of his rank. During the performance of the Homage, medals of gold and silver struck for the occasion were thrown among the people, and if there were any general pardon, it was read publicly by the Lord Chancellor.[1]

Holy Communion and Second Oblation. (13) In the Holy Communion, the sovereign advanced towards the altar after the commencement of the Communion Service and made an offering of bread and wine. Then a wedge of gold, called a mark, weighing eight ounces was received by the Archbishop from the sovereign and laid upon the altar. This constituted the second oblation.

The sovereign then returned to Westminster Hall attended by the clergy and others marshalled as before.

Coronation Feast. (14) A noticeable feature of the Coronation Feast held in the Westminster Hall was the proclamation of a challenge to the effect that if any one dared deny the rightful claim of the present sovereign to the throne, he was a liar and false traitor, and the Champion was there to fight a duel with him to prove the falsity of his assertion. The Champion threw down his gauntlet, which after a short time was taken up by the herald. Until the completion of the arrangements for the feast, the sovereign reposed in the Court of Wards. Several tables were placed in the Hall, the royal table being set on a raised platform. Special duties in connexion with this feast were allotted to special officers or noblemen: the royal table, for instance, was covered by the sergeant and gentleman of the ewery; the first course of hot meat was served up with the combined assistance of the sergeant of the silver scullery, and two gentlemen-at-arms or two Knights of the Bath, and other dishes were brought with a procession composed of several officers. A full delineation of this coronation being outside the scope of this Section, details of this as well as other functions, which may have value for other purposes, have been omitted.

In the evening were held a general illumination, a display

[1] The rites in which the Queen Consort took part have been omitted.

of fireworks in Hyde Park, the principal theatres being opened free to the public. *Coronation (cont.).*

The features common to the two systems of coronation of India and Europe may now be summed up. The commonness is due in some instances to the very nature of the ceremony, and in others, to other causes. **Common features.**

Both the systems are endued with a religious character, difference lying only in the degree. In the one, God, His Son, and the Holy Ghost were solicited by prayers and offerings to bless the sovereign and secure the welfare of his kingdom, while in the other, the divinities, together with various natural and supernatural forces credited with powers for good or evil, were for the same purpose entreated or propitiated through a multiplicity of prayers, offerings, and other religious rites.

The coronation of the Hindus, in its later form, lost all traces of its connexion with the elective principle pointed out in a previous chapter[1] to have been operative in the epic period, in which it could be traced in the *recognition* forming part of the installation ceremony. In the European form of coronation, it was traceable in the formulary of election, expunged in later times, as also in particular functions incorporated in the coronations of various European countries pointing to some form of election as their origin, e. g. the practice of elevating a sovereign on a shield among the later Romans, and the custom of having stone circles to serve as seats for electors and a large stone in the centre for the sovereign.[2]

The practice of taking an Oath to protect the people and perform other regal duties existed in the Hindu coronation, as evidenced by the *Taittirīya-Brāhmaṇa*, but it disappeared later on. Therefore, the similarity of the European and the Indian systems in this respect is not found all along their respective lines of development.

Smearing with unguents in the Indian type may be taken to correspond with anointing in the Western, sprinkling of liquids obtaining greater prominence in the former.

[1] See the chapter, 'Forms and Types of States'.
[2] See *Chapters on Coronation*, chap. i, and chap. ix, p. 99.

Coronation (cont.). Crowning, blessing for universal dominion, presentation of nobles and officials, jail-delivery, stately progress through the metropolis, feast and the devotion of a day or two to a ceremony preliminary to the coronation proper may also be regarded as points of similarity between the two types.

Degree of antiquity of the ceremony. (C) (v). (b). *Yauvarājyābhiṣeka.* It is in the epic period that we find the first mention of the ceremony for the inauguration of the crown-prince. Prof. Goldstücker is doubtful as to whether this ceremony is hinted at in the passage of the *Aitareya-Brāhmaṇa*[1] relating to the 'king-makers' (*rājakartāraḥ*) in the chapter on the *Mahābhiṣeka.* These 'king-makers' refer, in the *Atharva-Veda*[2] and the *Śatapatha-Brāhmaṇa*,[3] to 'those who, not themselves kings, aided in the consecration of the king'. According to Sāyaṇa's commentary on the aforesaid passage of the *Aitareya-Brāhmaṇa*, the king's father is one of the king-makers, and this was a ground for Prof. Goldstücker's doubt whether the ceremony in which the father took part might be that for the installation of a crown-prince.[4] A closer examination would, however, make it clear that such a doubt is baseless, for the following reasons:

(1) The *Mahābhiṣeka* is not an independent ceremony, and the chapter devoted to it is meant to bring out that, in days of yore, the *Abhiṣeka* of Indra (called *Mahābhiṣeka*) took place on certain lines with certain *mantras* followed later on by several emperors of antiquity on the occasion of the celebration of the *Rājasūya*, and if these rituals and *mantras* are woven into the *Punarabhiṣeka* (i. e. the second *Abhiṣeka*, the first having been performed at the time of installation to a simple kingship) of the celebrant of a *Rājasūya* of later times, they will be of great efficacy.

(2) The inclusion of the king's father in the list of king-makers by Sāyaṇa is not borne out by the Vedic texts themselves.

[1] *Aitareya-Brāhmaṇa*, viii. 17. 5. [2] *AV.*, iii. 5. 7.
[3] *Ś. Br.*, iii. 4. 1. 7 and xiii. 2. 2. 18. See *V. I.*, ii. 210.
[4] See Goldstücker's *Sanskrit-English Dictionary*, under '*Abhiṣeka*', p. 282.

(3) The presence of the father in any installation ceremony cannot of itself raise the presumption that the son performing the ceremony must needs be a crown-prince, for, first, the father might not at all have been a king, and possessing therefore no kingdom to which he could choose his son as successor; and secondly, he might be retiring from his regal position, making his son a full-fledged king by the ceremony.

Yauvarājyābhiṣeka (cont.).

(4) The question of installation to crown-princeship cannot rise at all in view of the setting, in which the king-makers are mentioned, namely, the delineation of the rites and formulas of Indra's *Mahābhiṣeka* intended to be woven into the *Punar-abhiṣeka* of the *Rājasūya*.

Hence, there is at present no evidence by which the ceremony of the installation of the crown-prince can be traced to the Vedic period.

References to the ceremony.

References are found in the Epics to the *Yauvarājyābhiṣeka* of Rāma,[1] Aṅgada,[2] Bharata,[3] Yudhiṣṭhira,[4] Bhīṣma,[5] Bhīma,[6] and Satyavat.[7]

Details of the ceremony are not forthcoming from any of the works consulted by me. The *Rāmāyaṇa* furnishes a short account of the preparations made for Rāma's *Yauvarājyābhiṣeka*, but as they are not perhaps exhaustive, we cannot draw from them any correct inference as to either the things needed for the ceremony or the rituals and functions in which they were used. The short account is, however, striking in that it does not include water or soil brought from various places, which form a prominent feature of the coronation ceremony and as such receive the first attention in the preparations for Rāma's coronation.[8]

No age-limit.

There was no restriction as to the age at which a successor to a sovereign was installed as the crown-prince. Rāma was twenty-five [9] years old at the time of his proposed installation to crown-princeship, and Bharata about forty [10] when he was so installed; both Yudhiṣṭhira and Satyavat were young [11]

[1] *Rām.*, ii. 3. 1 ff. [2] *Ibid.*, iv. 26. 13. [3] *Ibid.*, vi. 128. 93.
[4] *MBh.*, i. 139. 1. [5] *Ibid.*, i. 100. 43. [6] *Ibid.*, xii. 41. 9.
[7] *Ibid.*, iii. 298. 11. [8] *Rām.*, vi. 128. 48–57.
[9] *Ibid.*, iii. 47. 10. [10] *Ibid.*, i. 18.
[11] *MBh.*, i. 141. 27; iii. 293. 25.

Yauvarājyābhiṣeka (cont.).

when they went through the ceremony, but Bhīma was far more advanced in years when he became a crown-prince. There was, therefore, no hard and fast age-limit for this ceremony, though it seems to have been the usual practice for the king to choose his successor as soon as the latter completed the prescribed period of studies and was ready to share as crown-prince the responsibilities of a ruler.

Yauvarājyābhiṣeka whether a bar to *Rājyābhiṣeka*; restoration to lost kingdom an occasion for a fresh coronation.

No instances are forthcoming to show whether *Yauvarājyābhiṣeka* was a bar to the subsequent celebration of the coronation ceremony when the crown-prince became the king. Yudhiṣṭhira's coronation after the recovery of his kingdom and subsequent to his *Yauvarājyābhiṣeka* cannot be taken as a case in point, in view of its merger in that of restoration to a lost kingdom.[1] That the recovery of a lost kingdom was an occasion for a fresh coronation stands clear from the case of Dyumutsena.[2] Prof. Goldstücker inclines to the view that the performance of the *Yauvarājyābhiṣeka* 'held good for the inauguration of the prince at his accession to the throne, after the father's death, since no mention is made, in the epic poems, of a repetition of the ceremony. The object of the inauguration of a prince as *Yuvarāja* is to secure to him the right of succession, and, besides the advantages supposed to arise from the religious ceremony, as mentioned before, a share in the government, or perhaps all the privileges of a reigning king. For when Daśaratha intends to make his son Rāma a *Yuvarāja*, he addresses him with these words (in the Ayodhyākāṇḍa[3]): 'Rāma, I am old; . . . To-day, all my subjects want thee for their king; therefore, my son, I shall inaugurate thee as junior king'.[4] In the above argument, stress is laid on the words spoken by Daśaratha to the effect that the subjects wanted Rāma as their king (*narādhipa*), but the force of the very next words uttered by him, viz. 'therefore, my son, I shall inaugurate thee as junior king', is ignored. Whatever Daśaratha might have said on the occasion, the ceremony was nothing else than *Yauvarājyābhiṣeka* and should be viewed as such.

[1] *MBh.*, xii. 40. [2] *Ibid.* iii. 298. 11. [3] *Rām.*, ii. 4.
[4] Goldstücker's *Sanskrit-English Dictionary*, under *Abhiṣeka*, p. 282.

(C) (V). (c). *Inauguration of the Commander-in-Chief.* References to this ceremony are found in the *Mahābhārata* in connexion with the inaugurations of Bhīṣma,[1] Droṇa,[2] Karṇa,[3] Śalya,[4] and Aśvatthāman,[5] as the military heads of the Kaurava army. This inauguration ceremony is modelled on that of Kārttikeya,[6] the Commander-in-Chief of the gods, whose inauguration again followed in some respects the still earlier *Rājyābhiṣeka* of Varuṇa,[7] the water-god. Details of the ceremony aggregated from the several descriptions are scanty. Those that are expressly mentioned are oblation to the *Homa*-fire, seating of the Commander on an appropriate seat, sprinkling of water[8] on his head from a vessel, the utterance of the big formula '*surās tvām abhiṣiñcantu*, &c.',[9] which happens to be the same as that used in the coronation ceremony just before crowning and gifts of coins, bullion, cows, cloths, &c., to *Brāhmaṇas*. It is superfluous to mention that the rituals were accompanied with music, eulogies sung by bards, and joyous and benedictory ejaculations. The inauguration of the several commanders-in-chief mentioned above was performed on the battle-field. In times of peace the same ceremony is likely to have been celebrated on the occasion of the assumption of his office by the commander-in-chief. It is probable that in the former case the exigencies of the situation compelled a curtailment or abridgement of the rituals which could be allowed to be in their full form in times of peace.

Inauguration of the Commander-in Chief.

RÉSUME

If the mental constitution of the Hindus contained in its composition a preponderance of religious or other beliefs which left their impress upon their polity, vague surmises as to their quantity ought to be replaced by an exact estimate.

[1] *MBh.*, v. 155. 26–32.
[2] *Ibid.*, vii. 5. 39–43.
[3] *Ibid.*, viii. 1. 11, 12.
[4] *Ibid.*, ix. 1. 6, 7.
[5] *Ibid.*, 65. 36–43.
[6] *Ibid.*, 45. 1 ff.
[7] *Ibid.*, 45. 22.
[8] In the legend, the water of the Sarasvatī was sprinkled on Kārttikeya from a golden jar.
[9] In the legend of Kārttikeya's inauguration to generalship, the above formula was not recited at all; the deities named in the formula personally appeared before him to take part in the sprinkling.

Résumé (cont.). Surmises on this subject, difficult as it is, can hit the truth but rarely, and are very often made the ground either for wholesale condemnation or indiscriminate eulogy of the whole system of ancient Hindu polity. The only means to avoid this pitfall is to take a comprehensive survey of the various ways in which the beliefs of the Hindus influenced their political system. Such a survey has been attempted in the several sections of this chapter with a view to focussing light on the various branches of the subject and facilitating reasoning relating thereto by supplying the facts which might be used as a basis for drawing correct inferences. It has been seen that the fourfold division of caste which emerged so early among the Hindus, perhaps through religious exigencies, and which branched out into quite a number of ramifications later on, has through the whole history of their polity stood out as a rock, determining more than any other factor the entire structure of their public administration. The general eligibility of the members of the second caste to kingship, the placing of the *Brāhmaṇa* in the highest rank of the social, and by reason of that, in many respects, of the political hierachy, the gradation of rights and privileges according to the particular positions of the people in their caste framework, resulting in a differential treatment even in the administration of justice to them, the gradual deification of the king and the *Brāhmaṇa* by magnifying step by step the respect due to them socially and politically, the mutual public relations between the king and the castes or among the castes themselves, are the principal results issuing from the caste-system supplying the framework of the polity. It is difficult to strike a balance between the net advantages and disadvantages of such a system of polity, especially in view of the fact that the period of which we are speaking is a long one, during which the beliefs themselves as well as the numbers of their adherents underwent changes which introduced factors varying the actual net results of its working, or its subjective estimate by particular classes of citizens. If an implicit faith was placed in the beliefs by the majority of the people—and it is not unreasonable to suppose that there was such a period at least in pre-

Buddhistic times—many of the aforesaid points in the ancient Hindu body-politic which might appear as unjust, productive of evil, and subversive of political peace and happiness in the present dry light of reason, cannot have appeared as such to the people immediately affected by the system. But even after making allowance for a difference in the angles of vision of the present and the past, it would be erroneous to put nothing but advantages on its credit side and no disadvantages on its debit. Beliefs served no doubt, to a great extent, to dull the edges of those features that otherwise would have been keenly felt; but it should be borne in mind that, while on the one hand the degree of this belief was not uniformly deep in all classes and sects of the people, the working out of the letter and spirit of the customs and regulations of the system in actual practice must have, as in all times, their own drawbacks which also varied the effects of their operation in different times and localities. If we leave out of account these complications, confine ourselves only to the already recorded features and provisions as they appear from the Sanskrit works, including the law-codes and works on polity, and judge them by the state in which the majority of the people must have been under an administration faithfully reflecting in practice the features and provisions as they stand, assuming this majority to be partisans of the politico-religious beliefs and conceptions enumerated already—looking, for instance, upon the king and the *Brāhmaṇas* as deities but with responsibilities, for breaches of which there were both secular and religious sanctions, and considering their own caste positions and the relative treatment meted out to them at the hands of the State (e.g. in the levying of taxes, infliction of punishments, acquisition of learning, appointment to state offices, collection of wealth, &c.) as inevitably issuing from their own actions in their present and previous births—we can safely draw the inference that the working of the system could, so far as its religious aspect is concerned, bring contentment to the majority of the citizens. But if they had only partial or no faith in the beliefs, they would no doubt have resented government by laws that required in them

Resume (cont.).

Résume (cont.). a frame of mind without which they could not live contented. In the history of India there were periods when people with shaken or no faith in these beliefs were in the majority, and in such circumstances we have perhaps no reason to think that the discredited provisions of the Hindu law-codes of Manu and others were forcefully imposed upon the unwilling majority without modifications or, if necessary, radical changes. If, however, such a forcible imposition took place at any time, the case of the majority thus yoked against their will and faith must have been hard indeed. Changes in early Indian laws to adapt them to altered circumstances were not a new phenomenon in early times in spite of the conservative character of the Indians. Faith in the creeds forming the fundamentals of the laws was a *sine qua non* for their cheerful reception by the subjects on the one hand, and also for serving, on the other, as a safeguard against abuse of power by those placed in positions of authority. Given this faith, the whole machinery of administration might have worked well—perhaps, in many respects, much more smoothly than those governments in which reason and not faith supplies its wheels; but take away the faith, and the whole apparatus would be out of gear. Many of the numberless points of friction that crop up frequently between the different groups of interests or between the government and the people of the present day could not in those days arise at all, and the few that did arise met with ready solvents in appeals to faith and its composites, or to readjustments of interests seen in a light not uncoloured by faith in its various shapes. The Hindu religion, it should be remembered, was not a collection of creeds with certain fundamental rules of conduct superadded. It supplied not merely articles of creed but complete codes of conduct, moral, physical, social, and so forth, intended to regulate not merely the faith but also the details of conduct of every individual within its fold. The rules of conduct laid down were either suggested by, or at least were in general harmony with, the creeds, and hence the elements of faith permeated more or less the whole life and conduct of the individual units composing the society upon which they operated. The political actions were not outside their purview, and the ways they were influenced by religion, as already shown, were very various and far-reaching. The main distinguishing feature of the Hindu polity was the caste-system, which, with its later ramifications, was assimilated into the body-politic and became the principal cause of the diffusion of the politico-religious ideas with which the duties and the mutual relations of the members of the castes were intimately associated. It was this caste-system that made the members of the second caste, as a rule, eligible to kingship and segregated them for devotion, life-long and hereditary, to their onerous military duties. The members of the two other higher castes could generally participate in the higher administrative duties, though rare instances of *Śūdras* filling up government posts are met with in Sanskrit literature. There was hardly a country in which the people did not come to be classed into more or less sharply divided groups, ranking one above another by intelligence, riches, faith, profession, power, and so forth. The features that distinguished, in this respect, the ancient Hindus from other peoples were that the most important groups, by being reduced into castes, became, as evidenced in the law-codes, much more rigid than those in any other country with a more or less rigid location of each in the caste scale and with defined political and other rights and privileges of each. Points of advantage arguing judicious choice may be adduced for the primary divisions of the society for social, political, and other purposes into four castes; but the multiplication of these divisions into numerous subdivisions, each more or less rigid and stereotyped—though it may receive favour with many Hindus even of the present day—proved, as it has done at present, a source of weakness to the whole body-politic, each sub-caste being a fresh centre with its own particular interests of various kinds, with its strong likes and dislikes, and with its surrounding rigid wall of partition that hinders a real and practical identification of its own self with that of the other castes and sub-castes, and with the broader self of the whole body-politic. The early caste divisions, so long as they were small in number, might have

Résumé (cont.).

Résumé (cont.). proved a source of strength to the whole society. It may be argued in opposition that the numerous functional castes, by ministering to particular branches of skilled labour or artizanship, did much good to the country from the economic standpoint, but what was an economic benefit for a time contained within itself the seeds of political bane.

The Atharva-Vedic rituals are an index to the frame of mind of the people who performed them for political purposes. There was hardly, in ancient times, a country in which the people were completely free from the mental proclivities betokened by the ritual practices, which in themselves are harmless so long as they do not prove an obstacle to the performance of political duties or are not carried out for baneful and mischievous objects. Astrology, as we have also seen, played an important part not only in fixing the auspicious times for political actions, but also in giving rise to the idea of the dependence of the affairs of human life upon the heavenly luminaries, which in its extreme form stops the spring of actions by deepening fatalism. The Hindu lawgivers and statesmen saw this danger and tried to counteract it by preaching the doctrine that human effort was superior to fate, and that exertion could make benign a malignant fate. But the mental current, set aflow in ancient times, could not be completely stemmed, judging from its efforts in the political and other fields of action of the Hindus in later times. This defect was perhaps shared by the Hindus in common with their brother nations of the East, and it was this that made Burke refer to it in his own brilliant way: 'The Eastern politicians never do anything without the opinion of the astrologers on the fortunate moment. They are in the right if they can do no better; for the opinion of fortune is something towards commanding it. Statesmen of a more judicious prescience look for the fortunate moment too; but they seek it, not in the conjunctions and oppositions of planets, but in the conjunctions and oppositions of men and things. They form their almanack.'[1] The striking *ślokas* in which Kauṭilya tried to check the said mental tendencies of

[1] Burke's Letter to a Member of the National Assembly, 1791.

his fellow countrymen are well worthy of being memorized by their present descendants: *Resume (cont.).*

'Nakṣatram atipṛcchantaṃ bālam artho 'tivartate,
Artho hy arthasya nakṣatraṃ kiṃ kariṣyanti tārakāḥ.
Sādhanāḥ prāpnuvanty arthān narā yatnaśatair api,
Arthair arthāḥ prabadhyante gajāḥ pratigajair iva.'[1]

(Wealth passes away from the simpletons who consult the stars too much. For wealth is the star of wealth; what can the constellations do? People by energy can secure wealth even after a hundred attempts. It is wealth that captures wealth, as hostile elephants elephants.) In early times, no fixed boundaries were recognized as marking out the respective provinces of law, politics, religion, &c., and in spite of their mutual connexion in certain respects, there were chances, unless they were carefully avoided, of attribution of occurrences in one of them to wrongly supposed causes in another. As illustrations of this mis-attribution, we may refer to the two legends, one in the *Rāmāyaṇa* and the other in the *Bhāgavata-Purāṇa*. In the former, a *Brāhmaṇa* accused Rāmacandra of remissness in his regal duties for the reason that his son died a premature death. Rāmacandra consulted his councillors, who attributed the occurrence of the premature death of the *Brāhmaṇa* boy to the making of penance by a *Śūdra* within Rāma's kingdom—a practice not allowed by the *śāstra*; for *Śūdras* were not eligible to perform penances for the attainment of their objects.[2] The instance in the *Bhāgavata-Purāṇa* is similar: a *Brāhmaṇa* accused the king of Dwārakā of breaches of regal duties for the death of his infant son.[3]

Trials by ordeals in courts of justice may be cited as another instance of how an incident belonging to the province of law or morals was supposed to be capable of causing a physical phenomenon to be used as a conclusive evidence of guilt.

The practising of the magical rituals of the *Atharva-Veda*, as well as other such rituals, is as much an evidence of the

[1] *Kauṭilīya*, IX. iv, p. 349.
[2] *Rām.*, vii. 73-6.
[3] *Bhāgavata-Purāṇa*, x. 89. 21-3.

[R]ésumé [(c]ont.). mental cast of the people as it was at the same time an agency that helped the above mis-attribution of an effect to a wrong cause. The illustrations serve also to show that the duties of a sovereign of the times were much more onerous than now in view of the fact that he was held responsible for many things besides what may be called purely political questions.

Regarding the more or less elaborate ceremonials, two only engage our attention as sources of political disturbances. I mean the *Rājasūya* and the *Aśvamedha.* They were, however, of infrequent occurrence, for, of those that were performed, only a few were intended for the acquisition of political suzerainty.

The end of the State, in its later full-fledged form, as already pointed out, stood influenced by religious ideas.

There are the aspects of polity in which it was influenced by the beliefs of the people. The criticisms of this polity in connexion with this *résumé* have been made in view of these aspects alone, and not in view of the whole polity, though remarks of a general nature have sometimes been necessitated in the course of the criticisms. It must not be supposed that, as beliefs influenced the polity in so many ways, there was no scope left for the Hindus for actions free from the above influences. On the other hand, there were wide and various fields of political actions in which the Hindus showed considerable judgement and acumen, undeflected by the force of beliefs. There were, again, many political deeds which they performed much more smoothly and efficiently under the influences of religious beliefs than perhaps could have been done otherwise. In spite of the political errors and aberrations, therefore, the Hindus could claim to their credit many political actions that were far in advance of their age or can well bear comparison with their similars in modern times. These actions, which should be detailed in their appropriate places, need not be enumerated at present. Suffice it to say, that the religious aspects of polity summed up in this chapter had both advantages and disadvantages, and, mere aspects as they are, they should not be mistaken for the whole of polity.

INDEX